D0175317

LOST PRINCE

Also by Jeffrey Moussaieff Masson

When Elephants Weep: The Emotional Lives of Animals
(with Susan McCarthy)

My Father's Guru: A Journey Through
Spirituality and Disillusion

Final Analysis: The Making and Unmaking
of a Psychoanalyst

Against Therapy: Emotional Tyranny and the
Myth of Psychological Healing

A Dark Science: Women, Sexuality and Psychiatry in the
Nineteenth Century

The Assault on Truth: Freud's Suppression of the
Seduction Theory

The Oceanic Feeling: The Origins of Religious
Sentiment in Ancient India

The Complete Letters of Sigmund Freud to
Wilhelm Fliess 1887–1904 (Editor)

The Peacock's Egg: Love Poems from Ancient India
(Editor, translations by W. S. Merwin)

The Dhvanyaloka of Anandavardhana with the
Locana of Abhinavagupta
(Translator, with D. H. H. Ingalls and M. V. Patwardhan)

The Rasadhyaya of the Natyasastra (Translator and editor,
with M. V. Patwardhan. Two volumes)

Santarasa and Abhinavagupta's Philosophy of Aesthetics

THE FREE PRESS

New York   London   Toronto   Sydney   Tokyo   Singapore

LOST PRINCE

The Unsolved Mystery of Kaspar Hauser

Translated and Introduced by

Jeffrey Moussaieff Masson

THE FREE PRESS
A Division of Simon & Schuster Inc.
1230 Avenue of the Americas
New York, NY 10020

THE FREE PRESS and colophon are trademarks
of Simon & Schuster Inc.

Designed by Carla Bolte

Manufactured in the United States of America

10 9 8 7 6 5 4 3 2 1

Library of Congress Cataloging-in-Publication Data
is available.

ISBN 0-684-82296-2

For

LEILA

my found Princess

CONTENTS

ACKNOWLEDGMENTS

I would like to thank first and foremost Marianne Loring, my long-term associate in all my projects involving German. We have worked together since 1978, and without her help I could not have written most of the books I have written since then. In this case she read with me Feuerbach's entire German text, and spent many hours going over sections of the translation with me. She has a wonderful command of both English and German, and was, as ever, a delight to work with. Catharine MacKinnon gave up much of her own very valuable time to read over the English translation and suggested many changes. I also appreciate the many long conversations I had with her about this fascinating text. I am deeply grateful for the many ways in which she has been a strong support to me over the many years of our friendship. My old friend Alan Keiler, a master linguist, read through the translation along with the German text, and made numerous helpful suggestions, all of which I invariably accepted. Alan is never wrong. For orienting me in Kaspar Hauser research when I knew virtually nothing, I am grateful to Ulrich Struve of Princeton University. He saved me many hours by ordering my reading priorities and sent me many hard to obtain articles and books. He also put me in touch with a number of scholars in Germany. I am especially grateful to him for suggesting that I meet with Dr. Oskar Adolf Bayer, now more than ninety years old, who turned out to be a fountain of knowledge and put his Kaspar Hauser files at my disposal. Our discussions during the two days I spent with him in Ansbach were fruitful. I was privileged to spend a year (1993–1994) at the Institute for Advanced Study in Berlin and received invaluable assistance from many people there. Even though I was not a fellow, the library staff, under the direction of Gesine Bottomley, good-naturedly allowed me to use their facilities and helped me track down and order many obscure books and articles relating to Kaspar Hauser. In fact, the staff of the institute was unfailingly courteous, and one cannot pass up the opportunity to thank the amazing Barbara Sanders, who did so much to make everyone's stay there a pleasure. Katrina and Hans Magnus Enzensberger were particularly gracious, and I owe them much for their help and friendship. I went over the entire German text with Tanja Determann, whose wonderful command of nineteenth-century German was of enormous help. But above all I wish to thank the Kaspar Hauser scholar Johannes Mayer of Stuttgart. Not only is he the author of two of the most useful contemporary books on the subject, he also has an incomparable library, with thousands of original letters and documents, the finest resource in the world for Kaspar Hauser research. He allowed me complete access and was always ready to discuss research questions with me. It was in his precious library that I found the Daumer manuscript, which had gone unnoticed for 160 years, and it was thanks to his generosity that I was able to use passages from it for my introduction. As this book goes to press, the volume has just been published in German as part of the series *Die andere Bibliothek* (The other library) (series ed., Hans Magnus Enzensberger): Georg Friedrich Daumer, *Anselm von Feuerbach: Kaspar Hauser,* mit einem Bericht von Johannes Mayer und einem Essay von Jeffrey M. Masson (Frankfurt am Main: Eichborn Verlag, 1995).

Susan Arellano of The Free Press has been a fine editor, and I am thankful for her light touch and patience. Susan Llewellyn saved me from a number of errors and added a great deal to the accuracy and readability of the entire book. I am very grateful to her.

Kaspar Hauser said that he was lost in wonder when he saw the night sky for the first time in his life in 1828. I dedicate this book to Princess Leila, for I am lost in wonder at the love that radiates from her, as the foundling was at the stars he saw in Nuremberg.

INTRODUCTION

Kaspar Hauser, Europe's most famous wild child, was a sixteen-year-old boy who turned up in the streets of Nuremberg, Germany, in 1828. He immediately drew local interest because he seemed to be unable to speak and barely able to walk, and was apparently not able to understand what was said to him. Rumors, at first dismissed as nonsensical, began to circulate that he was the heir to the throne of Baden, the son of Napoleon's adopted daughter, Stéphanie de Beauharnais, Grand Duchess of the House of Baden. He drew international interest when it became apparent that somebody wanted him dead: A year after he first appeared, an unknown person tried to murder him. Soon all the newspapers of Europe and even the United States (the latter, no doubt, the source of Herman Melville's abiding interest in Kaspar Hauser) were discussing him, his life, and the rumors. Was he a prince? Was he a wild man? Did his "goodness" represent the original nature of man? How easily did he learn language, and what did he talk about in that language? In 1833, less than five years after he first appeared in Nuremberg, Kaspar Hauser was lured to a deserted park on the pretext that his true origins would be revealed to him. He was stabbed in the heart, and died of his wounds three days later. The murderer was never found, despite a large reward offered by the king of Bavaria. The mystery of who he was, where he came from, and why he was killed has not been solved to this day.

Called the "child of Europe," this "foundling" is known in the United States as the name of a psychiatric syndrome[1] and through a lovely song by Suzanne Vega called "Wood Horse (Caspar Hauser's Song)."[2]

For the last 165 years there has been unceasing interest in this mysterious story. Every year in Germany at least one new book comes out, most of them on the side of Kaspar Hauser, but a few aiming to prove he was a fraud. The literature is immense: More than three thousand books have been written about Kaspar Hauser, and at least fourteen thousand articles.[3] The 1899 edition of the German *Brockhaus*, in its long article about Kaspar Hauser, avers that he was probably a fraud. The 1954 edition of the same encyclopedia says the opposite. The major historical and scholarly work, however, is clearly on the side of the pro-Hauser forces.

There are many reasons for this interest: Writers and poets found something haunting and compelling in this melancholy and solitary boy who had been kept for all or most of his childhood in a lonely dungeon. Educators and intellectuals were fascinated by the light his imprisonment shed on the so-called "natural man." The general public was convinced, not without reason, that Kaspar Hauser was really the legitimate heir to the throne of Baden, a prince who had been robbed of his birthright. For me the story resonates with my interest in child abuse.

The Brief Life of Kaspar Hauser

Kaspar Hauser was a young boy who was first seen wandering the streets of Nuremberg in May 1828 (the very year in which the Wild Boy of Aveyron died). The police put him in a tower, where he immediately became the focus of attention: The citizens of Nuremberg thought he was a *Tiermensch* (a feral child) since he could barely walk, evidently could speak but a few bizarre sentences, and could hear but not understand what was said to him. The English poet Spenser relates of his wild man that ". . . other language had he none, nor speech, / But a soft murmur and confused sound / Of senseless words, which nature did him teach."[4]

He showed an aversion to every kind of food—especially meat—except bread, and he would drink nothing but water. He carried a letter for the captain of the garrison of the light cavalry. He appeared to be between fifteen and eighteen years old, though in most respects he seemed more like a boy of eleven. The one sentence he repeated continually, and used as an all-purpose means of communication, was: *"Ich möcht' ein solcher Reiter werden wie mein Vater einer war."* That is the High German version of what he actually said, which was: *"Reutä wähn, wie mei Vottä wähn is,"* or *"Ä sechtene möcht ih wähn, wie mei Vottä wähn is,"* something like: "I would like to be a rider the way my father was."

Mayor Binder's Proclamation

Kaspar Hauser remained solitary and withdrawn. The mayor of the city, Jakob Friedrich Binder (1787–1856), was forty-one years old when he first met him. The day after Kaspar arrived in the city, Binder invited the city doctor, Preu, to examine him in his presence, since he had not been able to extract anything from him. Over the next few days Binder continued to meet with Kaspar, had friends speak with him, and finally issued a public proclamation, which he wrote on July 7, 1828, and published on July 14.[5]

It was the first published document in the history of the Kaspar Hauser case and quickly achieved almost canonical status as the *Keimzelle* (germ cell) of all future versions. Since the actual text has never been translated into English, and because it contains no doubt the earliest comments of Kaspar Hauser himself (although not in direct quotations), I reproduce the entire document (see appendix 1), which is written in stilted nineteenth-century official German (most sentences in the original are a page long), but I omit its appendices since they are almost identical to information that will be supplied from elsewhere.[6]

In spite of the many problems raised by the text (for example, could Kaspar Hauser really have provided all this information within less than two weeks of his arrival?), it is a

5

document that must be read and reread. I urge the reader at this point to turn to it in the appendices and read it through before continuing with this introduction.

Newspapers all over Europe and as far away as New York, Boston, and Philadelphia immediately reported on the strange boy.[7] A day after the proclamation was issued, however, a sharply critical letter was sent to the local authorities complaining that the publication may well have compromised the investigation—which should, in any event, be under the jurisdiction of the superior court, and demanding that all the documents assembled be sent immediately to it. A government official replied immediately, agreeing with the criticisms and letting the author know that the proclamation had already been published in two newspapers (though only in small numbers), but that all remaining copies had been seized and would no longer be published. The letter was signed by the legal counsel to the court of appeals in Ansbach, a small town not far from Nuremberg. It was also signed by the president of this court, the great German jurist Paul Johann Anselm Ritter von Feuerbach (1775–1833), the man responsible for the abolition of torture in Bavaria.[8] As presiding chief judge in the court of appeals for Ansbach, he headed the court that had jurisdiction over the Kaspar Hauser case. Feuerbach was not happy with this proclamation:

> This official story, if one wants to call it that, contains some unbelievable and contradictory things. There were also many details that were given with such completeness and assurance that it is hard to ascertain what came from the questioner and what from Kaspar Hauser; how much really flows from his dim memories and how much he was unwittingly talked into, or how much was adapted from the many questions; what was added to or created through suppositions; what was grounded in simply misunderstood comments he made, since he was an animal-like man barely capable of speech, still unacquainted with the most commonplace

natural phenomena, and impoverished in everyday concepts. Nevertheless, the story told in the declaration agrees by and large—that is, with respect to the *essential major circumstances*—with what Hauser himself, duly sworn, was to write later in an essay, incorporated into official court depositions that were taken in the year 1829, as well as with what he has told me and many other people on different occasions, all of them in essential agreement.[9]

This may well be true; nonetheless the document is unique in that it represents the fruit of the earliest discussions (if that is what they were) with Kaspar Hauser. Although it is difficult to know what Binder "guessed" or "invented," as Feuerbach says, it is the only document that testifies to the fact that Kaspar Hauser claims, at least, to have spoken with toy horses he played with in the prison, which means that he was capable of speech (though what he said to them is unknown). If Binder is correct, contrary to the generally accepted notion that Kaspar had no idea what any words meant, he knew approximately fifty. What is not certain is whether he knew them before he arrived, or acquired some or many of them in the first few days.

The document is also important in giving us a sense of what was already, from the very beginning, expected of Kaspar Hauser. He was, for reasons that Binder passionately conveys, considered to have come from a noble family. The expectations were obviously high, which may have had something to do with his later depression. The reason that Binder thought Kaspar was of high birth had to do with what he calls his *Anlage*, a word with high visibility in German nineteenth-century psychiatry,[10] and refers to a person's inherited capacities. Because Kaspar Hauser seemed in the beginning to learn very quickly—words, phrases, manners, music, drawing—it was assumed that he was born with certain talents that he could only have had through noble birth!

Before the proclamation was actually published on July 14, on July 11, Feuerbach himself paid a visit to Kaspar Hauser. It was a fateful day, for Feuerbach evidently was as touched by the meeting as the mayor, and soon took it upon himself to begin an elaborate investigation of both Kaspar Hauser and the circumstances that brought him to Nuremberg. From that day on, probably no child living in Europe at the time was observed in such close detail as was Kaspar Hauser. The book that Feuerbach would write just four years later, *Kaspar Hauser: Beispiel eines Verbrechens am Seelenleben des Menschen* (Kaspar Hauser: A case of a crime against the soul of a human being) would make the boy famous in Europe and beyond from that day to the present. Considered one of the masterpieces of German judicial literature, Feuerbach's book has remained popular. It has also been enormously influential, and is the source of most of the films, as well as the poems and other literary works, about Kaspar Hauser from 1832 down to our own time.[11]

Kaspar immediately became a sensation, even a tourist draw. People would visit the tower where he was kept to watch him play with wooden toy animals.[12] He was often sick, however, and subject to profound melancholy.

Kaspar Hauser Finds a Teacher

When Feuerbach visited Kaspar Hauser on July 11, 1828, he said that unless his situation was quickly changed, he would "die of fever of the nerves or fall into idiocy or insanity." To the public at large, he may have been a freak (a point made in the various films about him) or the subject of rumors that he was of royal blood, but to one man, Georg Friedrich Daumer (1800–75), only twelve years older than Kaspar himself, he was a boy in need of care and a family. This is the man Feuerbach and Binder selected to take Kaspar Hauser out of the tower and into his own home, which he did on July 18, 1828. Daumer had been a student of the philosophers Friedrich Wilhelm Schelling (1775–1884) and Georg Wilhelm Hegel (1770–1831), and was now the tutor to Hegel's children.[13]

Daumer had taught at the Saint Egidius Gymnasium in Nuremberg, but his poor eyesight forced him into retirement at the young age of twenty-eight. He was a strange man, progressive in many ways: the founder, in 1840, of the German Society for the Prevention of Cruelty to Animals, an early follower of homeopathy (more on this in the section about Daumer's interests in Kaspar Hauser), and a poet.[14]

Even though more is known about the daily events in the life of Kaspar Hauser than possibly any other child of the time, we are still able to piece together his life only with great difficulty. Thus any authentic new information is an important addition to our meager knowledge. For the year and a half, between 1828 and 1830, that Kaspar Hauser lived with him and his family, Daumer kept a diary in which he recorded Kaspar's progress and quoted his words. This diary was long presumed lost. As mentioned earlier, I had the good fortune to find it in Germany. My edition of it (in collaboration with the Kaspar Hauser scholar, Johannes Mayer), has just been published in German. I describe the discovery in greater detail in appendix 2. Although the amount of previously unknown material it contains is limited, Daumer's diary is an essential document. Perhaps one of the most important sentences in that diary helps considerably in understanding more about Kaspar Hauser's first days in Nuremberg. On page 124 of the recently published German text, we read the following previously unpublished note by Daumer, dated 1828: "Initially he was treated harshly, because it was assumed he was dissimulating. At that time he cried incessantly for eight days and eight nights." These two short sentences tell us a great deal that was previously unknown about Kaspar Hauser's earliest moments in Nuremberg. The "legend" has it that he was an overnight sensation. But the first sentence hints at something much likelier and darker, namely that he was neither believed nor accepted.[15]

At first Daumer seemed to have amazing success with Kaspar Hauser, whose vocabulary grew by leaps and bounds. He gave evidence of possessing strange faculties: He could read in pitch darkness, he could "feel" somebody pointing at him from behind, and his sensorium was inordinately sensitive. Loud noises could occasion convulsions in him, bright light caused him exquisite pain. He was often sick and subject to profound melancholy.

Daumer taught Kaspar Hauser to speak, to draw, to play the piano, and to wonder about his own past. Everybody who met Kaspar was impressed with his gentle nature and his extraordinary ability to say profound things in simple words.

Daumer made seemingly rapid progress with his pupil. We learn from the unpublished diary some important details about the chronology of Kaspar Hauser's education. Kaspar first appeared in Nuremberg on May 26, 1828. In the diary Daumer tells us:

> At the end of August 1828 . . . he began to express himself fairly fluently and in a manner that could be understood. He distinguished without further confusion between living and lifeless things, organic and inorganic objects. He began to differentiate between jokes and serious topics and enjoyed jokes with other people. Humor became part of his statements and responses, and his activities were not merely comprehending and imitative but partially productive. He drafted letters and essays himself, even though they were filled with mistakes. At the beginning of September he began to write the story of his life. (page 149)[16]

The Autobiography

It is not entirely clear if the idea of writing down the story of his life was Daumer's, Kaspar's, or Mayor Binder's. In fact Binder and other authorities wanted Kaspar to provide a coherent narrative account of his life, no doubt the better to be able to pursue their criminal investigations. This is not something that had ever occurred to Kaspar. To whom would he have told it? Evidently he never told it to himself, and he had nothing prepared, nothing ready. It obviously took some time for him to understand the concept, even, of the story of his life. But when he did, it is clear that he became obsessed with it. Yet the three different versions (at least—these are the only ones to have come down to us) give evidence that he found the task confusing. For whom was he writing?

Kaspar did begin, however, and the result has fortunately been preserved. Since it has never, oddly enough, been translated into English, let me translate the beginning of the fragment:[17]

It is dated, by Kaspar himself, the beginning of November 1828, five months after he first appeared:

> I will write the story of Kaspar Hauser myself! I will tell how I lived in the prison, and describe what it looked like, and everything that was there. The length of the prison was 6 to 7 feet, and 4 feet in width. There were two small windows which were 8 to 9 inches in height and were [the same] width; they were in the ceiling as in a cellar. But there was nothing in it but the straw where I lay and sat, and the two horses, a dog, and a woolen blanket. And in the ground next to me was a round hole where I could relieve myself, and a pitcher of water; other than that there was nothing, not even a stove. I will tell you what I always did, and what I always had to eat, and how I spent the long period, and what I did. I had two toy horses, and a [toy] dog, and such red ribbons with which I decorated the horses. And the clothes that I wore it was short pants, and black suspenders, and a shirt, but the pants and suspenders were on my bare body, and the shirt was worn on top, and the pants were torn open in back, so I

could relieve myself. I could not take off the pants, because nobody showed me how. I will give a picture of how I spent the day, and how my day went.

When I woke up I found water and bread[18] next to me. The first thing I did, I drank the water, then ate a little bread until I was no longer hungry, then I gave bread and water to the horses, and the dog, then I drank it all up. Now I start to play, I remove the ribbons. It took me a long time until I had decorated a horse, and when one was decorated, then I again ate a little bread, and then there was still a little water left; this I finished, then I decorated the second one, which also took a long time, as did the first, then I felt hungry again, then I ate a little bread, and would have liked to drink water: but I no longer had any with which I could quench my thirst. So I picked up the pitcher probably ten times, wanting to drink, but never found any water in it because I assumed the water came by itself. Then I spent time decorating the dog. When the thirst was too terrible, I always went to sleep because I was too thirsty to play. I can imagine I must have slept a long time, because whenever I awakened, there was water, and bread. But I always ate the bread from one sleep to another. I always had enough bread but not enough water, because the pitcher was not large, it did not hold enough water, perhaps the man could not give me more water; because I [*sic;* mistake for "he"?] could not obtain a bigger pitcher. And how long I had been playing I cannot describe because I did not know what was an hour, or a day, or a week. I was always in a good mood and content, because nothing ever hurt me. And this is how I spent the entire period of my life until the man came and taught me to draw. But I did not know what I was writing.

Here is the same description written by Kaspar Hauser in February 1829, some four months later:[19]

The prison in which I was forced to live until my release was about six to seven feet long, four wide, and five high. The ground seemed to me made of hard earth, on one side were two small windows with wooden shutters, which looked black. Straw was put on the floor, upon which I sat and slept. My legs were covered from the knees up with a blanket. Next to my bed of straw, on the left side, was a hole in the earth, in which a bucket was placed; there was also a lid over it, which I had to move and then

12

put back again. The clothes that I wore in the prison were a shirt, short pants, in which however the back part was missing, so that I could relieve myself, since I could not take off my pants. The suspenders were on my naked body. The shirt was over that. My nourishment consisted of nothing but water and bread; sometimes I did not have enough water; there was always enough bread, I ate little bread, since I could not move; I could not after all walk and did not know that I could stand up, since nobody had taught me to walk; the idea never occurred to me to want to stand up. I had two wooden horses and a dog with which I always entertained myself; I had red and blue ribbons and with them I decorated the horses and the dog, but sometimes the ribbons fell off because I did not know how to tie them.

As this passage demonstrates, Kaspar Hauser was learning the skills of writing and expression much more quickly than could possibly have been anticipated. It is as if he was recapturing skills he once possessed, rather than learning them afresh. The astonishing progress that Kaspar Hauser made in understanding the world around him—in remembering his own past, in being able to talk about it, describe it, and even to some extent be philosophical about it—was both a marvel to those of his friends and well-wishers who heard it, and also ammunition for his critics. How, they exclaimed, could Kaspar Hauser possibly have been as ignorant as he seemed to be, only to acquire the knowledge expected of an adult in a matter of mere months? Once again Daumer's unpublished manuscript gives us more information than was previously available on Kaspar's philosophical reflections: On one page of the manuscript we read:

1828: In September and October he often said that he was completely unable to imagine himself in his former mental state. He would love to be able to see himself as he had been earlier when he spent all his time playing. When he was alone he was often preoccupied with attempting to understand the state he had been in. He said that it was completely incomprehensible to him that during his imprisonment he had no self-awareness at all and never wondered whether there were any other living beings beside himself, or whether anything existed outside his cage, nor did he ever wonder where the bread and water came from that he found and consumed daily. The entire time[20] prior to the period when he began to learn to read was only vaguely and dimly remembered.[21]

This passage invites speculation. Is the language actually that used by Kaspar Hauser, or is Daumer altering it in some way? The evidence seems to suggest that Daumer was taking notes on the same day Kaspar Hauser said something. My impression, then, is that this is actually what Kaspar said. But are these reflections spontaneous, or were they suggested or otherwise imposed by Daumer, Feuerbach, or other well-meaning adults?

Kaspar Hauser Is Stabbed

A year and a half after he came to Nuremberg, two things happened that were to have grave consequences for the later life of Kaspar Hauser. During the week of October 17, 1829, there rode into town in great splendor a rich English lord — Philip Henry, fourth earl of Stanhope, son of Charles (who invented the steam-driven battleship); nephew of William Pitt the Younger, and half-brother of Hester Stanhope, "queen of Thadmore." Although we now[22] know that Stanhope was indeed very interested in Kaspar Hauser at the time, and asked his banker to collect *all* information and publications about him, he said nothing at the time about Kaspar Hauser and in public displayed no interest or awareness. What, exactly, he was doing in Nuremberg that week was not clear.[23]

A few days later Kaspar Hauser's life took a dark and unexpected turn. Two strangers had an inordinate interest in Kaspar's autobiography, as we learn from an important document, previously untranslated, written in Feuerbach's house by Kaspar Hauser himself, on June 15, 1831, which reads:[24]

> About six weeks after the attempt on my life two unknown gentlemen came to visit me. One had a very evil-looking face, with a black half beard and a mustache and asked me what I was writing then. I answered: My story, how I was treated in the cage, and how this man brought me to Nuremberg. Then one of them took it and read about two pages while the other one with the black mustache asked me about all kinds of things, especially whether I frequently go for walks. No was my answer, since my feet start to hurt me right away. Do I go to classes and what do I learn . . . I told them everything. Afterward he took the story and read it from the first lines to the last. Then they left, and I accompanied them, which I do with other people as well, to the door. But when we went downstairs, they asked me what it was, and I said, it is an outhouse, and opened it for them to see. After I had shown them everything, I asked them where they came from. They answered me that they were from far away and I would not know the place, even if they were to tell me, and so they left.

On October 17, 1829, when Kaspar was alone in Daumer's household, a man dressed in black approached a small outhouse where Kaspar was sitting, and with what looked like a butcher's knife (Kaspar was able to draw it later), tried to cut his throat. Kaspar was wounded but did not die. In a delirium he addressed broken sentences to his unknown assailant: "Why you kill me? I never did you anything. Not kill me! I beg not be locked up. Never let me out of my prison—not kill me. You kill me before I understand what life is. You must tell me why you locked me up!"[25] Feuerbach described his visit to Kaspar Hauser in a handwritten report found among his papers after his death. In that report Feuerbach quotes Kaspar as telling him:

> If I survive this time, I will still be murdered by the man—my intuition always told me so; he himself told me as well, that he would kill me eventually. After all, he has to do it—he surely

learned that I have described my captivity, that I was able to give an exact description of the route by which he brought me to Nuremberg. He will think that I have already said things of which he must be afraid. He must murder me, because he must fear that I will eventually remember what happened to me, and where I was kept prisoner, and why he did that to me, that man, who took everything, everything, from me.[26]

Once again this sounds like an authentic quotation, something that Feuerbach wrote down as he heard it directly from Kaspar Hauser. (It is also an extremely intelligent analysis of his situation; one wonders whether anyone else at the time shared this view.) The language is not dissimilar from that of those passages reported by Daumer. Kaspar clearly feared that he would die: The man had told him so, in so many words. Kaspar was deposed by the police eleven days after the stabbing[27] and said that the man told him: "You must die before you leave the city of Nuremberg."

Kaspar was deeply upset by the fact that he was called a *Hasenfuss* (sissy) by the townspeople. People made much of his "cowardice," for example of the fact that he was terrified to cross a gangplank. However, Gottlieb Freiherr von Tucher (1798–1877), his guardian, told the police when he was deposed:[28] "Who could hold this fear of death against him, he who had just recently begun to live, and saw his precious life already threatened in so terrifying a way?" Who wanted Kaspar Hauser dead, and why? What interests was he threatening? This was a question on many people's minds, especially Feuerbach's.

The mayor appointed two policemen to accompany Kaspar Hauser wherever he went. For safety reasons, and because Daumer became ill, which made it harder for him to continue to work with Kaspar Hauser, he was moved to the house of a wealthy businessman, Johann Christian Biberbach, in January 1830. This was not a happy period for him, and he did not thrive. Six months later he was moved again, this time to the house of his legal guardian, Freiherr von Tucher, the brother-in-law of the philosopher Hegel, where he stayed from May 1830 until November 1831. Tucher had first met Kaspar Hauser during the initial weeks of his stay in the tower. He met with him almost daily when he was living with Daumer.

A year later the earl of Stanhope rode back into Nuremberg. This time he was interested in only one thing, and very publicly so: Kaspar Hauser, by now christened the child of Europe. He befriended the boy in an ostentatious way, dividing him from Tucher and other well-wishers. Kaspar Hauser responded, especially to Stanhope's encouragement of his belief in his "noble" status. For example, in January 1831, Stanhope ends a letter to Kaspar: "The most pleasant trip I could take would be one with you to your own country estate of which you were so unjustly and cruelly robbed."[29]

Kaspar began to speak of how he would treat his "underlings" when his wealth was returned to him. Daumer was suspicious of Stanhope, as were von Tucher[30] and other people who had Kaspar's best interests at heart (though evidently not Feuerbach since he dedicated his book to him). Daumer even noticed an underlying homosexual current, though he attributes the observation to somebody else: "I knew somebody who observed with astonishment the caresses the earl gave Kaspar Hauser, even in public."[31] Stanhope publicly announced that he wished nothing less than to adopt Kaspar Hauser and take him (as his heir?) to Chevening Castle, in Kent. He provided money (five hundred Gulden) to the city for the boy's upkeep, and demanded (and received) legal guardianship over him. Surprisingly, though, in his large correspondence with his wife, children, and other relatives in 1831 and 1832, he never once mentions Kaspar Hauser, let alone bringing him to live in Chevening.[32]

The Murder of Kaspar Hauser

While waiting to take Kaspar Hauser to England, Lord Stanhope claimed that he wished to safeguard his life by sending him to the small town of Ansbach, some fifty miles from Nuremberg. There he would live with a schoolteacher and organist especially selected by Stanhope, by the name of Johann Georg Meyer (1800–68), who though only thirty-two at the time, seemed and behaved like an old man. For a bit less than two years, while he was living with Daumer, Kaspar had been happy. But almost deliberately, it would seem, Stanhope moved him, on December 10, 1831, into the dark, somber house of this typical, narrow-minded German schoolteacher—into what Feuerbach called "a second prison."

Meyer tortured him on a daily basis by insisting that he was telling minor lies. This treatment was, even by Meyer's own account, extremely intrusive and hostile. For example, when Kaspar told his teacher that he had felt bad all night and had vomited, Meyer demanded to know where. When Kaspar told him that he had gone to the bathroom, Meyer told him that this could not be true; since he had such a highly developed sense of smell, he would never have gone there unless absolutely necessary, he would have used the sink in his room. "I told him: Either it is not true that you have a sensitive sense of smell, or it is not true that you vomited in the bathroom or anywhere else for that matter." Meyer was determined that Kaspar become a devout Christian, and expended a great deal of energy in telling him about the dire fate that awaited him if he did not.

"Do you pray?" asked Meyer.

"Every night," responded Kaspar.

"Then tell me the prayers."

"I don't know them by heart."

"You are lying."[33]

Kaspar was never allowed out of the house unaccompanied, and it was Meyer's greatest complaint that he found every reason to flee on his own. The sadism clearly had an effect on Kaspar, and he began a gradual spiritual decline, ending in his taking religion seriously, something that had never occurred to him before.[34] Before his religious instruction, before he was force-fed Latin and mathematics and all the other topics of which he previously knew nothing, he seemed completely devoid of any religious sense yet was noted for his extreme kindness toward all living creatures, even his own original jailer.[35]

Stanhope left Ansbach on January 19, 1832, promising to adopt Kaspar Hauser and bring him to England. Kaspar was never to see him again. Stanhope went directly to the palace at Mannheim, where Grand Duchess of Baden Stéphanie de Beauharnais (married to Karl of Baden) was then residing. He gave the duchess a copy of Feuerbach's book, which had just been published. She read the book, wept, and begged to meet Kaspar Hauser. Stanhope promised to arrange a meeting but did not. He had other plans for Kaspar Hauser.

Meyer was a petty tyrant but a major sadist. Kaspar spoke of longing to return to his first prison, but a worse fate awaited him. On December 14, 1832, barely five years after he appeared, he was lured to the deserted Court Garden in the Orangerie in Ansbach by a man who said he had news of his mother. There he was stabbed in the chest. Meyer himself[36] admits that he threatened the dying Kaspar:

> I explicitly advised him against making any more fuss, *that in fact he deserved a good thrashing* [italics in original]. Later I was inclined to blame myself for being so strict. But when I take into account that it could not hurt him if he was really in a delirium, and that if he was only faking, then he richly deserved it, I am able to comfort myself. Moreover, from the moment of my serious reprimand until the last evening of his life, his delirium did not recur. Then, too, his behavior on his sickbed greatly astonished me. Kaspar

Hauser was normally such a sissy, I could not bear the fuss he made over the slightest hurt. He always noticed every little twitch, real or imagined. But this time he did not complain about his pain with a single word, unless asked, and even then he was monosyllabic. [Meyer is hinting that since Kaspar killed himself, he knew he could not blame anyone else].

An extraordinary picture emerges from these words alone of the horror it must have been for Kaspar Hauser to live with this tyrant.[37] Meyer also said: "I have to add that on the way back from the bridle path [where Kaspar was stabbed], I said to Hauser: 'This time you have played the most stupid prank, this time it won't go well for you' [as opposed to the last time, in Nuremberg—Meyer is definitely telling him: That was as phony as this is]. When I said this he looked up at the sky and said: 'In the name of God, God knows [that I am telling the truth.].'"[38]

A letter from Privy Council Andreas Hofmann to Klüber,[39] of February 3, 1834, refers to a meeting with Meyer that provides a sad and astonishing picture of these last days of Kaspar Hauser's life:

Meyer said in a tone of great outrage that Hauser was making a play for the compassion of the century; the whole event was nothing but a repetition of the earlier fabricated attempt on his life in Nuremberg. He would not lose any sleep over it today (December 14) the way Professor Daumer had then in Nuremberg. In fact he had told Hauser to his face as he was leaving him in order to tell me about the incident, that *he deserved a good thrashing*. [Here there is a footnote by Daumer which expresses what anybody would feel upon hearing these words: "One could cry bloody tears when one thinks about the fate of poor Kaspar, who had just received a mortal wound to his heart and then was threatened, in the meanest way, with a beating!"] Meyer even insisted that, since Hickel was gone, I should have him (Kaspar Hauser) removed from [Meyer's] house, since he did not want to keep him any longer. . . . I told him that Dr. Albert, with whom I had spoken the previous evening, did not believe that Hauser was out of danger, and declared that moving him to another dwelling was not possible.

Meyer was so proud of this threat to the dying boy that he repeated it.

Meyer was the source of the rumors about Kaspar Hauser's death being a suicide. Evidently he did not have a difficult time convincing the men of the town. There is a report, dated December 16, 1833—part of an official inquiry into Kaspar Hauser's death—which reads: "On December 14, in the first moments that Kaspar Hauser's accident became known, perhaps nine-tenths of the people living in Ansbach (I am referring here only to the male population) said to themselves: 'This is the second edition of the Nuremberg attempt on his life.'"[40] [that is, it is unreal]. One of the nastiest examples of this point of view was written by Karl Heinrich Ritter von Lang (1764–1835), and published in *Blätter für literarische Unterhaltung* on January 4, 1834. Here is a partial translation of this mean-spirited, ugly text, since it was to prove so influential and because it was not atypical:

> On December 14, in the evening, the well-known Kaspar Hauser who was being taken care of by a schoolteacher here in Ansbach, returned home with a wound in his chest from which he died on December 17. His claims, that an unknown man invited him to go for a walk in the palace garden (in this horrible storm and nasty weather), that in front of the statue to the poet Uz he handed him a silk purse with a note in it and, as Hauser started to open it, stabbed him with a dagger in the chest—all of these statements were found, upon examination, to be false and invented. . . . What can we conclude from this? This Kaspar Hauser has shown himself to be a vicious, lying, and additionally a lazy and unteachable youth. There has been no lack of ridiculous attempts . . . to claim him as the child of the Grand Duchess Stefanie.[41]

Lang concludes by saying that Kaspar Hauser had originally belonged to a tribe of beggars that went on a pilgrimage on which he "pretended to be a cripple or a ridiculous simpleton," but left them to carry on his deceptions and lies on his own account in Nuremberg.

The poets knew better. In 1834, two years after Kaspar Hauser's death, there appeared an anonymous poem, "The Unsolved Riddle of Nuremberg," which ends with these two stanzas:

> Has no prince shed a tear
> Which will perhaps make clear to humanity
> Why his blood had to flow
> And who the poor boy really was?

> Twenty-five silver coins
> Would I gladly pay to he who names the name
> But I know that others will pay gold
> So that nobody learns who Kaspar Hauser really was.[42]

Meyer was slow to call a doctor. When it became apparent that the wound was serious, Meyer told people Kaspar Hauser had done it to himself, to revive flagging interest in him. This did not persuade everybody. Two doctors (Albert and Koppen) who attended Kaspar, told the police that "credible people claim to have heard out of his own mouth that he would like to become an officer, but only if there were no war; he had only begun to live five years ago, and wanted to live longer."[43] Kaspar was not spared a police inquiry—a skeptical one, as if influenced by Meyer or others—even as he lay dying. One of the official questions put to him over three days of questioning was the following:[44] "Given that you had already had an accident in Nuremberg, how could you dare to accept an invitation to visit a deserted area with somebody completely unknown to you?"[45] Kaspar Hauser had to undergo one final indignity, when he learned that Meyer was telling people he had inflicted the wound on his own body. Asked on his deathbed if he had anything to add to what he had told the police (who insisted on deposing

22

him) he replied:[46] "People are saying that nobody stabbed me. I already heard this from Mr. Meyer; they have spoken of it in hushed tones among themselves." Kaspar also said: "Many cats are the death of the mouse,"[47] and his last words were: "Tired, very tired, still have to take a long trip."[48] He then lay down on his right side and died.

The perpetrator was never found, in spite of a large reward offered by the king of Bavaria.

Stanhope, it turned out, had written a final letter to Kaspar Hauser.[49] The letter was addressed as follows: *Herrn Hauser, abzugeben bei Herrn Schullehrer Meyer in Ansbach. Franco.* (To Mr. Hauser, to be delivered to Meyer, the schoolteacher, in Ansbach. Prepaid.) It was postmarked Munich, December 25, 1833. The letter, dated in Stanhope's hand, "Vienna, December 16 and 17," ends with these words: "A letter I have received from my wife makes it imperative to leave immediately for Munich. Therefore we will have the pleasure of seeing each other much earlier than would otherwise be the case, and hopefully before the end of next month. I think I will finish this letter when I am in Bavaria, so that you will have the pleasure of knowing that you are in the same country as your godfather, who loves you with all his heart, Earl Stanhope."

The perspicacious German writer Georg Friedrich Kolb (1808–84)[50] commented early on: "Why the comedy of this touching letter after the death of Hauser?" He is right. Hauser's death was in all the local newspapers on December 17, the very day he died. It was announced in all the Munich newspapers from December 20 on.[51] We know Stanhope was in Munich on the twenty-fifth. Aware, as he had to be,[52] that Kaspar Hauser was dead, why send him a letter? Undoubtedly to attempt to show, at some later date, that he was not in the least involved in the murder. But that is not all: The next day, December 26, Stanhope visited the prince of Öttingen-Wallerstein, Bavarian minister of the interior, in an attempt (vain, as it turned out) to persuade him that Kaspar Hauser was a fraud. If he really sent the letter on the twenty-fifth, as he claims, could he—a single day later—so have changed his mind that he was convinced he was dealing with a complete fraud, merely because Kaspar Hauser had died? And if the letter's content was fraudulent, what does that say about Stanhope himself? Becoming feverish in his obsession, he goes so far as to conduct his own depositions in Nuremberg of all the people who witnessed Kaspar Hauser's first days, in an attempt to get them to recant or alter their stories so as to show that Kaspar had invented everything. He was even willing to falsify his *own* written evidence—to lie, fabricate, and do anything at all to persuade people that Kaspar Hauser was a charlatan.

In his quest to persuade the world that Kaspar Hauser was a fraud who had committed suicide, Lord Stanhope within days was visiting other dignitaries throughout Europe. In fact the most recent research, by Johannes Mayer, shows that it was *Stanhope* who was a fraud, at least complicit in the murder of Kaspar Hauser. In a fascinating passage published in 1859, Daumer himself prefigured Mayer:

> After Kaspar's death Stanhope came to see me and tried to persuade me to bear witness against Hauser. As the educator and closest observer of the foundling I was a not insignificant expert. If my testimony could be used against him (Hauser) he would be completely discredited. The object was to see whether I could be drawn into this nefarious plot. To this end the count visited me several times, and gradually it became clearer what his intention was. Stanhope's behavior amazed me greatly, and since, in my innocence, I trusted him implicitly, I did not know what to think. Women can usually see more clearly in these matters. Not I but my mother became deeply suspicious, and when I expressed my amazement over Stanhope's behavior she used a word that I shall refrain from repeating. ("Can you not see that he is the _ _ _ _ _ _?" she exclaimed.) That was the end of my trusting relationship with

this frightening man. The last time he came he could not fail to notice my deep ill-feeling. The conversation became uncomfortable for him, and all of a sudden he jumped up and ran down the stairs and out of the house as if pursued by the Furies and was not seen again.[53]

The six blank spaces are clearly intended to represent the German word *Mörder*, "murderer." Daumer was to soften this judgment in his later book,[54] in which he recounts the same episode:

My mother became aware of what [Stanhope] had in mind. She begged and beseeched him with deep emotion not to besmirch the memory of this unfortunate creature who had given him his childish trust as his fatherly friend and benefactor. She was absolutely certain that he, Kaspar, had not been an imposter or a villain. "He's beyond any pain now," replied Stanhope, turned red, broke off his visit, ran down the stairs and was never seen here again. I will not repeat what my mother had in mind and said at the time [Daumer gives here the following footnote: "The count was to hear a similar statement from the mouth of no less than a royal personage."] Appearances can deceive, she may have made a mistake. I am only recounting facts that I personally witnessed and can swear to, facts that appear to me to be part of this obscure and ghastly episode without accusing the count of a crime or participation in a crime.

Nevertheless it is clear that Daumer thought—correctly, it turns out—that Stanhope was implicated in the murder of his ward. A few years after Kaspar Hauser was killed, a book was published by a woman who knew both him and Stanhope—Caroline, countess of Albersdorf (born Caroline Graham)—which hints that Stanhope was up to no good, and points out, too, that he was using letters of credit issued by the Baden court.[55]

To a considerable extent, national pride played a role in the more popular accounts known to the general public. Many people in Germany had suspected that Lord Stanhope played some role in the murder of Kaspar Hauser before the recent work of Johannes Mayer provided the missing documents that clinch the case. But the English were always defensive of Stanhope and derisive of Kaspar Hauser. Thus the famous 1911 version of the *Encyclopaedia Britannica* concludes the entry on Kaspar Hauser by saying that

> he affirmed that the wound was inflicted by a stranger, but many[56] believed it to be the work of his own hand, and that he did not intend it to be fatal, but only so severe as to give a sufficient coloring of truth to his story. The affair created a great sensation and produced a long literary agitation. But the whole story remains somewhat mysterious. Lord Stanhope eventually became decidedly skeptical as to Kaspar's stories, and ended by being accused of contriving his death![57] The evidence has been subtly analyzed by Andrew Lang in his *Historical Mysteries* (1904) with results unfavorable to the "romantic" version of the story. Lang's view is that possibly Kaspar was a sort of "ambulatory automatist," an instance of a phenomenon known by other cases to students of psychical abnormalities, of which the characteristics are a mania for straying away and the persistence of delusions as to identity; but he inclines to regard Kaspar as simply a "humbug." The "authentic records" purporting to confirm the kidnapping story Lang stigmatizes as "worthless and impudent rubbish."

There is, in fact, nothing subtle about Lang's[58] analysis. It is biased, and even for the time it was written, based on questionable sources. For Lang, Kaspar was "a useless, false, convulsionary, and hysterical patient" whom "no one was likely to want to keep" (p. 125). He was one of the few converts to Stanhope's desperate attempt to convince the populace that Kaspar Hauser had killed himself in a vain attempt to gain attention: "Lord Stanhope suggested that Kaspar himself had inflicted the wound by pressure, and that, after he had squeezed the point of the knife through his wadded coat, it had penetrated much deeper than he had intended, a very probable hypothesis" (p. 138).

The Prince Theory

Sigmund Freud, at the beginning of his career, when he still believed that abuse lay at the core of human unhappiness, thought that repetitive dreams pointed to an actual historical event that could not be consciously remembered and could only be worked through in the privacy and safety of a disguised dream. I believe there is some real truth to this theory, and that dreams often do serve to recover latent memories. Whoever imprisoned Kaspar Hauser did not count on his beginning to dream precisely those parts of his early life that were supposed to have been long lost to memory. In appendix 4, I give all the passages in the literature connected with Kaspar Hauser's dreams that have a bearing on memories of his early childhood. It is a fascinating but somewhat complex topic that might disrupt the flow of this introduction, but I urge readers to look at this appendix once they have finished reading the introduction.

It is not clear whether anybody except Daumer ever saw the autobiographical writings at the time Kaspar Hauser was producing them. There had been rumors from the beginning, of course,[59] about Kaspar Hauser's provenance, according to which he was no less than the prince of Baden—the son of Stéphanie de Beauharnais (1789–1860), Napoleon's adopted daughter, and Karl, grand duke of Baden (1786–1818)— who had been born healthy in 1812 and died under mysterious circumstances a few weeks later. We know from the notebooks of K. A. Varnhagen von Ense (the Prussian commercial attaché in Karlsruhe) that there were rumors of poison.[60] Had the prince lived, he would have been just about Kaspar's age. The rumors spoke of a sick, dying child who had been substituted for Kaspar Hauser by the countess of Hochberg (Luise Geyer von Geyersberg, 1768–1820), the second wife of the founder of the dynasty, Karl Friedrich von Baden (1728–1811), who wanted her own eldest son, Leopold (1790–1852), to inherit the throne (which he did in 1830). Kaspar, they said, had been kept hidden in a dungeon, probably for twelve years, and now he was here in Nuremberg. Even Ludwig I, king of Bavaria (1786–1868), wrote a letter to Stanhope on December 8, 1831, in which he spoke of Kaspar Hauser, who, he said, *"gewiss nicht in jener Finsternis geboren wurde, in der er durch seine Feinde gehalten wurde"* (was certainly not born in that darkness in which he was held prisoner by his enemies).[61]

As president of the court of appeals of Bavaria, Feuerbach was given official charge of the investigation into the first attempt to murder Kaspar Hauser. He was of course privy to all the rumors, but initially he paid no attention to them.[62] This is clear from a letter he wrote on April 8, 1830, to King Ludwig I of Bavaria:

> Among the many rumors and charges spread about Kaspar's origins, some of them silly, some proven to be untrue, some beyond the bounds of any possible judicial investigation, there is one which goes as follows: our mysterious foundling is the Prince of the Grand Duke Carl of Baden and Stéphanie, who was exchanged, put in somebody else's place and then caused to disappear. He is, therefore, no less a person than the actual genuine Grand Duke of Baden himself![63]

We know, though, that by the time he came to write his book, in 1832, he was himself the main researcher into the veracity of this very same rumor. In his book Feuerbach writes:

> If the reader's curiosity, his desire for knowledge, wants more from me, should he ask me the results of the usual judicial inquiry, should he like to know in which direction those clues have led, in what places the divining rod really began to vibrate, and what happened next: I must answer that according to law and in the nature of the subject, I cannot, in my capacity as a writer,

speak publicly of matters of which for the present I am allowed to know, or rather to suspect, only in my capacity as a state official. Moreover, may I assure the reader that the authorities in charge of this investigation, using all means at their disposal, even the most unusual ones, have made a tremendous effort to fulfill their duty without rest and without mercy—and, may I add, not entirely without success.

However, not all far, deep, and high places are accessible to the reach of civil justice. With respect to certain places in which we have reason to search for the giant responsible for this crime, we would have to have the power of Joshua's trumpets, or Oberon's magic horn, in order to get to him, in order to do battle, tooth and nail, with the high and mighty Colossuses armed with ball and chain who stand guard in front of certain golden castle gates.

This is beyond question a reference to Kaspar Hauser as the son of Karl von Baden and Stéphanie.[64] The proof is found in the actual manuscript page of this passage, which contains a genealogical table in which Feuerbach explicitly connects Kaspar Hauser to the royal house of Baden.[65]

Feuerbach put the results of his own research into Kaspar Hauser's origins in a strictly secret letter to the queen mother of Bavaria[66] (published after his death by his son, and subject to a restraining order from the Baden court[67]), hand-delivered to Karoline in Munich on February 19, 1832. We know that King Ludwig and the queen discussed the death of Kaspar Hauser on December 18. We have an important letter from the king in which he writes:

Mother told me there in Biederstein (since we knew then that he had been wounded but not that he was dead) that Kaspar Hauser was considered to be the son of her brother, and that another child was substituted for him. The late President Feuerbach had written to her about this, and asked her to protect him [Kaspar Hauser], but she did not do so, in order not to expose him to danger.[68]

This implies that the queen believed Feuerbach (as did the king[69]). We know too that the queen wrote two of her daughters, Sophie[70] and Elise,[71] about receiving the manuscript, and Elise wrote her sister, Amalie, in March after she read Feuerbach's book that "the author believes, without saying so explicitly, that Kaspar Hauser is the son of our uncle Karl. *I know that you already indicated this to me [Ich weiss, Du hast mir schon einmal in diesem Sinne gesprochen].*"[72] The daughter asked Karoline explicitly whom she took Kaspar Hauser to be. Her answer, written on March 12, 1832, was: "In the unanimous opinion of many people, Hauser was one of the sons of my poor brother." Elise then asked her mother whether Stéphanie knew the rumors. She replied that "August Leuchtenberg [one of her courtiers], who had seen him [Kaspar Hauser] in Ansbach, told me she [Stéphanie] had asked many questions about the story."[73] The *Mémoire* was brought to the queen by Lieutenant Hickel,[74] for whom an audience was arranged by Friedrich Ludwig von Schmidt (1764–1857), the priest and confidant of the queen, and somebody whom Feuerbach knew and trusted. He was also present at the birth of the prince (Kaspar Hauser) in 1812. Recently a letter was found from Feuerbach to Stanhope, dated May 12, 1832, which throws important light on how the *Mémoire* was received. After all, Feuerbach addressed it to Kaspar Hauser's presumed aunt, now a queen, accusing her stepmother of a heinous crime. Prince Adalbert said she merely shook her head over the *Mémoire,* implying that she did not take it seriously.[75] The letter, which proves this was not the case, is important enough to deserve a full translation:

> What follows is going to seem to you extremely strange. I heard it from Munich, out of the mouth of the queen mother, through H[ickel]. Before H[ickel] set out on his trip,[76] which took him through Munich, I prepared a memorandum for the queen, in

which I developed the facts and the reasons why I was able to deduce that K[aspar] can be none other than S[téphanie's] oldest son, who had been declared dead. Through her priest[77] I secured an audience with her royal highness. Over a period of two days H[ickel] had an audience lasting several hours with her, during which facts came to light that, when I think about them, cause shivers to run down my spine. They also explain the tears and sleepless nights of S[téphanie], about which you told me in your letter from Frankfurt.[78] H[ickel], just before he left for Hungary, conveyed to me an eight-page-long report about that conversation. I expected, as I was writing the previous pages of this letter, to be able to make a copy of that report and include it in this letter. But when I took it out of my file on K[aspar] and read it over again in order to copy it down for you, I found that it would not be possible to entrust something like this to my letter without great danger. I am therefore forced to remain silent here about the most interesting thing to come out of the whole Hauser affair, and to keep it from you until I have the pleasure of seeing you again in person, or find a secure opportunity to send you the document in question. You will be amazed and you will shudder. *Of all the horrors that I, as an experienced criminalist have witnessed, this one, which I heard about in this manner, is the most horrible.* [italics in original]. K[lüber] in Frankfurt is, as I now also know, and as I could have known earlier were I not, since my illness, so forgetful, contrary to my expectations, a very weak source. K[lüber] has always acted in the interests of that family,[79] which stood to benefit, and indeed has benefited, from the death or removal of Kaspar. He was and is still prejudiced on their behalf — but I fear that in saying even this little, I have already said too much.[80]

That there was such a report at all is new information. The tragedy is that it has not come down to us, and there is no way of knowing what it contained. Clearly it was something sensational, and something having to do with proof of the identity of Kaspar Hauser, involving the royal house of Baden. Queen Karoline, as Stéphanie's sister-in-law, was privy to much that is now lost or obscure. That the information was dangerous can only mean that the original perpetrators of the deed were still active and watchful. The puzzle, as Johannes Mayer points out, is that the document, which must have been among Feuerbach's papers, was not found there after his death. He asks whether it was removed by some interested party, and wonders whether Feuerbach had it with him during his final conversation about Kaspar Hauser with Klüber in Frankfurt just before he died. The tragedy is that Feuerbach is unsuspectingly conveying his most secret information to the one person he should be wariest of—the man who may well have been responsible for the death of Kaspar Hauser and even, perhaps, that of Feuerbach himself just a few months later. It is not impossible that he was killed precisely in order to keep this report from seeing the light of day. Lieutenant Hickel may even have been part of the plot.[81] Perhaps an even greater irony lay in the fact that the Grand Duchess Stéphanie never suspected Stanhope of playing any role in the death of her son. When she visited Queen Victoria in London in 1851, she went to Chevening, some thirty-five miles away, and spent two days with Stanhope. What must have been going through her mind, knowing, as she did, that Stanhope was the greatest enemy of Kaspar Hauser? She gave him a picture of herself (inscribed *"Souvenir de Stéphanie"*), which hangs in his castle, alongside two original watercolors by Kaspar Hauser.

Before his book, *Beispiel eines Verbrechen am Seelenleben des Menschen* Feuerbach had clearly become convinced that Kaspar Hauser was the legitimate heir to the throne of Baden, the son of Stéphanie de Beauharnais and the Grand Duke Karl of Baden. The book caused a great stir, both for its beauty and for the story it had to tell. The hints it contained about Kaspar Hauser's royal provenance were not lost on his audience. Newspapers throughout Europe carried accounts of Kaspar Hauser's life and speculation on his origins. The subject became one of the most talked-about puzzles of the time.

Feuerbach died suddenly at the age of fifty-eight. Before dying, he suspected, and his son Ludwig was certain, that he had been poisoned at the orders of members of the royal house of Baden who did not like his discoveries about Kaspar Hauser's origins. He is reported to have written a note that contained the words: *"Man hat mir etwas gegeben"* (I have been given something [that is, poison]). The note was lost, but his grandson, the physician Johann Anselm von Feuerbach (1842–1916), son of Eduard August von Feuerbach, a professor of law in Erlangen, claims to have read it.[82] We know that he died on his way to Frankfurt, where he went to meet Klüber (coincidentally the lover of Countess Hochberg, a fact of which Feuerbach, of course, was unaware)[83] in order to discuss with him his discoveries about Kaspar Hauser's royal parentage.[84] He died on May 29, 1832.[85] Strangely enough, Stanhope was in Andernach that day, not far away. As Johannes Mayer perceptively notes, "Whenever something tragic happened with reference to Kaspar Hauser, Stanhope was to be found close to the event."[86] In an important letter Johannes Mayer found in England from Feuerbach to Stanhope dated February 4, 1832, less than five months before he died, Feuerbach makes it clear how close he was to solving the mystery of Kaspar Hauser's birth: *"Seltsam!—im Oktober 1812 starb (angeblich) der bewusste schwächliche Erstgeborene und, laut des von Kaspar mitgebrachten Briefes, wurde Kaspar ebenfalls im Oktober 1812 dem Manne, bei dem er immer gewesen, gelegt!"* (Strange! *In October 1812*, the weakling firstborn son [allegedly] died, and, according to the letter Kaspar brought with him, Kaspar was handed over, also in October 1812, to the man with whom he had always been!)[87] The letter goes on to say: "My friend Kaspar is now my guest every Sunday and is the source of great pleasure to me and my family. After dinner he accompanies me into my office, where I take pains to influence his education and studies through conversations. He is somebody in whom my interest will never turn cold and from whom I will one day part only with the deepest sorrow. Only a monster could not love this pure innocent soul," thereby giving the lie to Stanhope's oft-repeated claim that Feuerbach told him he had changed his opinion about Kaspar Hauser and now considered him a charlatan. Feuerbach even says explicitly, in this same letter, that one reason he wrote his book was to protect Kaspar Hauser *"gegen den Verdacht der Betrügerei für immer gerechtfertig"* (against the suspicion of being a fraud once and for all).

Another close relative of Kaspar Hauser seems to have believed that he was the legitimate heir to the throne. His sister Marie von Hamilton[88] who lived in Baden-Baden, was in touch with Tucher in 1874, long after the death of Kaspar Hauser. According to a recently published account, she

> told [Tucher] further that the oldest son of Grand Duke Leopold and Duchess Sophie, the successor to Grand Duke Ludwig, became mentally ill . . . and that she visited him. When she entered his room he fell onto his knees in front of her, put his arms around her, and in a state of tremendous emotional agitation asked that the story of Kaspar Hauser be taken out of his head, then he would be cured. She further told [Tucher] that his father, Grand Duke Leopold, was also much preoccupied with Kaspar Hauser and that upon his deathbed (he died in 1852) he did not want to let go of Kaspar Hauser's portrait.[89]

If this account is accurate (we have only Tucher's word for it, no other document) it indicates that at least Kaspar Hauser's sister believed in his identity as her brother the prince, and that those who later occupied the throne (both father and son, from the other side of the family) as a result of Kaspar's death could not rid themselves of a guilty conscience, even though the son, at least, had had nothing to do with the crime. This is such perfect poetic justice that one cannot help but question the veracity of the account. I would like to believe it is true.

Kaspar Hauser's life before he was put in the dungeon, probably at three or four years old,[90] has been the subject of much research. We now know at least one of the places in which he was held, and also the identity of the castle in whose dungeon he lived for twelve years. On April 22, 1829, Kaspar Hauser made a watercolor drawing of a plant. In 1924 the German novelist Klara Hofer bought a large house, Schloss Pilsach (near Nuremberg), and, as she was having some renovations done, found a secret dungeon. It corresponds in almost every detail to the description given by Kaspar Hauser of the dungeon in which he had been kept. In the dungeon was a large iron window frame shaped like a plant, almost identical to the one that Kaspar Hauser drew. On March 13, 1982, while the new owners of the house were doing further renovations, they found a small white wooden horse, exactly the size, shape, and color of the one Kaspar Hauser described having had in his dungeon.[91] It seems likely, therefore, that this is the place where Kaspar Hauser was kept.

In 1829 Kaspar Hauser drew for his teacher Daumer a crest he had seen in a dream. This crest — almost exactly like those on the doors of the castle Beuggen bei Laufenburg, on the banks of the Rhine (a few miles east of Basel) — allowed researchers to establish that Beuggen was probably one of the three castles in which Kaspar Hauser lived for his first three to four years.

New research has also thrown some light on the people from the court of Baden involved in Kaspar Hauser's imprisonment and their motivation. Grand Duke Karl of Baden was married to Napoleon's adopted daughter, Stéphanie de Beauharnais.[92] In 1812 she gave birth to a prince, presumably Kaspar Hauser, who would have inherited the throne had he not "died." Another son, born in 1816, also "died," whereas three daughters lived. The person who benefited from these sudden deaths was none other than the second wife of Karl's father, Luise von Hochberg. Only Karl himself remained between Luise's son and the throne. When he lay dying, banished to Bad Griesbach, a small, depressing mountain village he hated, he maintained that his two sons had been poisoned, and now he was poisoned as well.[93] He died under mysterious circumstances in 1818, at the age of thirty-three. When the entire line on the side of her husband's first wife died out, Luise's son became grand duke.[94]

What Fritz Klee[95] and other researchers think happened to Kaspar originally was that he was taken out of his crib, and the dying child of Johann Ernst Jakob Blochmann, a gardener (suddenly promoted in 1812), who worked for Countess Luise von Hochberg and had ten children of his own, was substituted for him. It appears from the doctors' reports that Kaspar Hauser was not incarcerated until he was three or four.[96] Little is known about his life until he reached the dungeon, but there is some evidence of a reason for a sudden change of plans. It is a complicated story that need not be gone into here; what seems to have happened is that a bottle was found in the Rhine in November 1816 (when Kaspar Hauser was four), which contained this note in Latin: "To whoever finds this note: I am being kept in a prison, near Laufenburg, on the Rhine. My prison is underground and even the person who seized my throne does not know where it is. I cannot write any more, because I am carefully and cruelly guarded. Signed: S. Hanés Sprancio." Published in 1816 in the Parisian *Le Moniteur Universel*, it did not create a stir. The theory is that somebody wrote this to frighten the countess, and the chief of the secret police, Maj. Johann von Hennenhofer (1793–1850), was deputed to take Kaspar Hauser to a safer place. The article was reprinted in

1834 in the *Hamburgische Abendzeitung,* and a connection with Kaspar Hauser was considered possible. It was suggested that the signature was an anagram of "his son Kaspar."

It is odd that so many people involved in Kaspar Hauser's story died early and suddenly. An unpublished manuscript by Anselm von Feuerbach (a medical doctor, son of Eduard Feuerbach, hence the grandson of the judge), entitled *The Kaspar Hauser Question,* notes that Binder, Biberbach, Dr. Preu, Dr. Osterhausen, and Dr. Albert (who performed the autopsy), all of whom were intimately involved in Kaspar Hauser's life, died between 1833 and 1835.[97] He believed that their deaths were not entirely accidental, and that at least three members of the Feuerbach family were believed to have been poisoned because of their connections to Kaspar Hauser.

Among the reasons that the Kaspar Hauser story has elicited such passionate responses over the last 165 years has been the failure of the powerful myth of the crazed, single perpetrator—that is, that our lives are safe and only threatened by some failure of social order. Why is it that many Americans of singular intelligence refuse to believe that John F. Kennedy was killed by a single person, acting on his own "delusions?" The existence of a conspiracy seems to be an emotional necessity. How could we continue to exist if we believed that completely fortuitous circumstances could end our lives, with no larger meaning to be extracted from such a tragic event? I think the reason we balk at this is that at some deep, unconscious level, we know that the single perpetrator *is* a myth—it is false—and that in fact our greatest danger comes not from a single wild individual but from the powers that be when they feel threatened in any way. While this may not be literally true in Kennedy's case, it probably is very true in the case of Kaspar Hauser.[98] When Kaspar Hauser rose to become a celebrity in Germany, he grew nostalgic for his old life. He complained bitterly that he had been happier when he was alone in his cell than when he was the object of everybody's unbridled curiosity. What, exactly, he got in exchange is something he wondered about, and the same question inevitably tugs at the modern reader. It is a paradox that he was safer in his dungeon than he was in the external world. A murderous attempt was made on his life, and finally he was killed by an unknown assailant. No doubt the people who were responsible for his imprisonment in the first place also saw to it that he was murdered, and probably for the same reason—namely that he represented a threat to their political legitimacy. But it is odd that with all of Germany aroused by his fate, not a single clue (during his lifetime at least) could be found with respect to his jailer, his parents, or anything at all about his past, even after King Ludwig I of Bavaria offered a ten-thousand-gulden reward (a fortune at the time).

Why the Fascination with Kaspar Hauser?

Why were Kaspar Hauser's contemporaries so fascinated by him? There had always been, in Europe, a fascination with the theme of the "wild child," and Western philosophers have long been intrigued by the question: Would a child who had never been subject to parents or to society be different, in fundamental ways, from other children? Wild children, about whom Rousseau had already written in 1775,[99] were ambivalently regarded: On the one hand they were "pure," unsullied by the distorting influence of social prejudice, on the other there were many who claimed they were simply "retarded or idiot" children who had been abandoned by their parents. The Indian myths of children being raised by a wild animal were somehow reassuring: No matter how badly the parents behave, "nature" will not abandon a child, and friendly animals will come forward to act as surrogate, and kindlier, parents. This is, as Harlan Lane[100] has pointed out, behind the tales of Romulus and Remus, and of the wild children in the Renaissance, about whom Shakespeare wrote in *The Winter's Tale:*

> . . . a present death
> Had been more merciful. Come on, poor babe!
> Some powerful spirit instruct the kites and ravens
> To be thy nurses! Wolves and bears, they say,
> Casting their savageness aside, have done
> Like offices of pity.   (2.3.183–88)

In 1970 François Truffaut's haunting film *The Wild Child* had just appeared in cinemas. It was a moving account of the strange relationship between Jean-Marc-Gaspard Itard and the so-called Wild Boy of Aveyron, who met on a summer day in 1800 in the Luxembourg Gardens in Paris. The twenty-six-year-old Itard, recently appointed resident physician at the National Institute for Deaf-Mutes, had been a student of Philippe Pinel, who had recently unchained the city's "lunatics" (but, like so many psychiatrists after him, insisted in maintaining his authority through violence, in this case, the use of straitjackets "when necessary"). Napoleon Bonaparte's brother Lucien had ordered that the small twelve- or thirteen-year-old boy be brought to Paris from the forest region of Aveyron, in the south of France, so that scholars could see Rousseau's "noble savage." Itard was to educate the boy. Pinel observed him, and in a report to the Société des Observateurs de l'Homme, on December 29, 1800, began by saying:

> For some time public attention has been fixed on a child that was found running wild in the woods of one of our departments in the Midi, and who was reduced to the most rustic state possible. The natural interest that children of this age always inspire, combined with the idea of complete abandonment and the extreme dangers that were the consequence, has renewed interest in the history of other children who, in various epochs, were reduced to the same

degree of isolation. We congratulated ourselves on witnessing one of these phenomena which normally can be examined only at some distance and concerning which we still have only vague and inaccurate reports. Certain scholars, those who are concerned particularly with the history of human understanding, were delighted at the possibility of studying the rudimentary character of man and of finding out the nexus of ideas and moral sentiments which are independent of socialization. But soon this brilliant perspective disappeared, confronted with the highly circumscribed mental faculties of the child and with his complete inability to speak.

Pinel decided, in the felicitous words of Harlan Lane, "that the boy was not an idiot because he was abandoned in the woods; he was abandoned in the woods because he was an idiot."[101] Pinel reached this conclusion by comparing his behavior with that of other "insane" children. As an example he told of a child incarcerated in La Salpêtrière (where Charcot was to hold court some years later):

> One of these girls, seven years old, gives a first impression of all the attributes of health and intelligence, ruddy complexion, black hair and eyebrows, an animated and a lively look; she looks at objects with an air of assurance and with a kind of attention . . . but . . . she never laughs and, if she is pinched or injured, she cries out and weeps, but without trying to remove the offending object."[102]

It would be obvious today, however, that this behavior is not a sign of insanity. There could be any number of reasons why a child in a mental hospital does not laugh, starting with the fact that she is imprisoned. It is of course merely speculation, but it is at least possible that these same so-called symptoms could derive from the fact that this girl was sexually abused, and learned early on that there was no point in resisting, that she could do nothing except signal her sorrow by crying. Would not those tears be eloquent language enough? Pinel concluded that Victor (the name Itard was to give him later) "ought to be categorized among the children suffering from idiocy and insanity, and that there is no hope whatever of obtaining some measure of success through systematic and continued instruction." Itard, in any event, thought his teacher was wrong, and dedicated the next years to working with Victor. Victor never learned to speak, and his progress was described as at best limited. Abandoned by the intellectual elite of Paris (including Itard), who had earlier exhibited such interest in him, Victor went to live with his beloved Madame Guérin (Itard's housekeeper), in whose home he died, in his forties, in 1828. The first account of the "wild boy" by Itard had already been published in 1801. It began a discussion that was to last the whole of the century.[103]

The year 1828 was the very one in which Kaspar Hauser appeared for the first time in Nuremberg. As soon as it was learned that he had been kept for all or most of his life in a dungeon, the general public took notice. Why? Why are we so fascinated by those who have been imprisoned for long periods? It seems we yearn to know the answers to certain questions: Are there "natural" thoughts and "natural" emotions? In Kaspar Hauser's case, all who came into contact with him were struck by his unusual gentleness and compassion. Perhaps, some people—notably his teacher Georg Daumer—thought, this is the natural state of man. At least part of the charm of observing Kaspar Hauser was the recognition that he was seeing the world for the first time. Everything was unfamiliar to him.[104] Especially noticeable was his attitude toward other living creatures. He could not believe that they were not like him—that is, able to understand simple sentences spoken slowly. He was admonished early on about speaking to them by everybody, including his enlightened teacher. Shamed, he stopped. But the new manuscript provides some evidence that Kaspar Hauser did not cease altogether. Daumer writes:

> 1828. Even early in October, after he had stopped wanting to treat animals as though they were people, he told the cat that he had seen another one, much resembling her: "Today I have seen a cousin of yours." He thought the cat should understand him and be pleased. (p. 130)

This is no doubt from direct observation. The last sentence, however, is an interpretation made by Daumer, and we cannot be certain on what it is based. Clearly Daumer did not think that Kaspar Hauser was simply joking or engaging in cute animal talk. He meant what he said, namely that since he had seen one cat who resembled (in color) the one he knew from Daumer's house, he assumed they were related. Similarly, on the preceding page of the manuscript, Daumer writes:

> After watching a very obedient dog, upon his return to the house, he decided to tell the cat what an obedient dog he had seen and admonish her to act in the same way. That is what he did. (p. 130)

The first time he saw the night sky filled with stars, he fell into a kind of rapture. His gentleness puzzled and delighted people. He would not return insults or even blows. He showed great solicitude for even the smallest insect. Daumer, in an unpublished diary entry, notes that

> When he saw a bird or some other animal caged, he became sad, and said that this animal would gladly be free, why was it locked up? . . . when somebody started to kill an insect, he stopped him and said: this animal would also prefer to live . . . I once had to allow him to free a bird that was supposed to be roasted, to avoid his becoming enraged at me. (pp. 171–72)

A similar passage is:

> 1828. Once he related, with an indescribably sorrowful expression, [how] so and so had today hunted and shot a hare and two

birds, and he saw them still bleeding. He could not understand that the man showed no compassion for these animals, who after all had never harmed anyone. When he was told, among other things, that these animals were killed in order to be eaten, he said that people could eat something else, bread, for example, the way he does. (p. 172)

In Daumer's first book, published in 1832, we read: "When he saw somebody, as he did a few times when he was in the tower, punish a child, he began to cry and was in a terrible state."[105] His compassion went so far as to encompass his own jailer. Daumer's unpublished diary gives the following passage as an example:

1828. A lovely remark he made at the end of October is the following: He said that one reason for not wanting to think back to the time he was a prisoner was that he could imagine the anxiety that his unknown jailer, who kept him prisoner, must have experienced. The jailer probably always hoped he would die. Since he did not, he believed that the unknown jailer must have been tortured by constant anxiety until he actually got rid of him. This thought hurt him, when he imagined it. (p. 173)

Why was Feuerbach so intrigued—indeed, obsessed—with Kaspar Hauser? We know from an important letter he wrote to Elise von der Recke, a distinguished older friend, on September 20, 1828, how involved he had become in the case, "officially and unofficially."[106] Of course he was the highest authority in the land for criminal activity, and therefore he first of all wanted to know what had happened. There was a crime to be solved, and an injustice to be righted. But so far he had gotten nowhere, despite all the efforts of the police and court officials. Kaspar Hauser was a puzzle and might perhaps "remain one forever." He writes:

the deed is done, and in Kaspar Hauser we see a seventeen- to eighteen-year-old marvel [*Wundermensch*[107]] such as the world has never seen, a person who from earliest childhood was buried, who about six [actually four] months ago saw the sun for the first time and discovered that apart from himself and the monster who fed him bread and water there were other people on this earth.

For Feuerbach there was also a human consideration. He met Kaspar Hauser on July 11, 1828, barely more than a month after he appeared in Nuremberg. He was struck by the innocence, the childlike quality, the purity of the boy. "He is a living refutation of the doctrine of original sin," wrote Feuerbach, "with his pure innocence and the goodness of his heart." He could not believe that Kaspar Hauser learned "in days what others took months or even years to learn." Nor did he ever tire of asking questions, of catching up on everything he had never learned about or known in his prison. "His sole passion," wrote Feuerbach in the letter, "is the process of learning itself." Clearly Feuerbach felt that Kaspar was hungry to learn about all he had missed during his years of imprisonment. And indeed, perhaps initially he was. Feuerbach was intrigued by the gentle demeanor of this boy who had been so terribly abused. Daumer had seen evidence of his kindness to his own jailer, and so did Feuerbach. Early on he was aware of this gentleness, for he wrote in the letter that

> when among other things I told him of my indignation toward the villain who had kept him prisoner for so long, he admonished me: "He with whom he had always been" was not bad, but his father, that is what he called that man, then, when I visited him, to whose care he had been handed over. It is only in the last two months, more or less, that it appears to have become clear to him that he was the object of an evil deed, and since then he expresses the greatest fear at the very thought of the possibility of falling into the hands of his jailer again.

He felt a deep sorrow about the fate of this boy, whose "key emotional state is a quiet melancholy" (*der Grundton seiner Gemütsstimmung ist eine stille Schwermut*). He told Elise von der Recke that nothing could be done any longer to discover the criminal responsible, because "I have reasons to believe that the barbarian in whose power Kaspar had been, taught him certain points, by means of terrifying threats that had as their goal the covering up of all clues to the discovery of the place or the person responsible for the deed."

Moreover, he realized that the attention Kaspar Hauser received—being stared at in his small room like an animal in a cage, being made the object of foolish experiments, was literally making him sick—in body and in soul. Kaspar would not survive unless he was removed. Feuerbach notified the *Regierungspräsident* (head of state) of Bavaria, Herr von Mieg, who traveled to Nuremberg and saw for himself what was happening. It was at their suggestion that Kaspar Hauser moved into Daumer's house on July 18, just a week later.

Daumer's interests were similar to Feuerbach's, but even more directly connected to education. He no doubt genuinely liked Kaspar Hauser and continued to support him throughout his short life. But Daumer also had a number of theoretical interests, and Kaspar Hauser proved a subject for experiments—benign ones to be sure, unlike those described by Feuerbach in the letter to Elise von der Recke, but experiments nonetheless. Daumer believed that some people are inordinately affected by certain substances, especially metals. Kaspar Hauser provided him with many examples, and he gave them at tedious length in his three books about Kaspar Hauser. He was an early disciple of Christian Samuel Hahnemann (1755–1843), the founder of homeopathy, who was himself fascinated by Kaspar Hauser's strange abilities.[108] He also believed that Kaspar Hauser's purity came, in part, from his vegetarian diet. And so he hypothesized that Kaspar Hauser began to lose this purity, including his sensitivity to other creatures, when he began to eat meat. Daumer even blames himself for this in one of the few directly personal passages in his 1875 book:

It is true, I cannot deny it, and I must take this opportunity to confess: In my treatment of Hauser I was guilty of one major error. Nobody has held it against me, and so I don't really need to mention it, but I cannot forgive myself, even though I acted with good intentions. Hauser's exaggerated irritability and sensitivity toward impressions from the external world were for him a source of unending pain and suffering: his relations with other people were especially made difficult in that he was so terribly sensitive to the effect animals had on him, which is nonexistent for ordinary people. I thought that this would be changed as soon as he became accustomed to eating flesh. . . . The aim I had of freeing him from those torturous sensitivities was in fact achieved; the physiological miracles disappeared, and they were really not necessary, and so it could have been a good thing. But at the same time his ability to understand and think suffered a regrettable reduction, and [there was] an extremely deplorable deadening of his moral sensitivities, both of which qualities he had formerly possessed in the highest degree. This was for me a significant experience with respect to the question of whether animal flesh is natural, useful to people, and to their advantage, especially with respect to higher considerations [*höherer Rücksicht*—that is, spiritual matters?]. I deeply regret that I accustomed the foundling Kaspar Hauser to meat.[109]

In contrast to Feuerbach, who at times seemed to believe that life was not unpleasant in Kaspar's prison, something that Kaspar Hauser himself seemed to have thought as well (at others, however, Feuerbach was well aware, as the title of his book indicates, what had been done to Kaspar), Daumer was exquisitely aware of how deeply Kaspar Hauser had been hurt, and seemed to think that this somehow gave him access to special powers. It is a not uncommon theme in mythology: The hurt person develops strange faculties. In Kaspar Hauser's case these faculties were primarily physical: keen hearing, keen sight, keen smell. Daumer did not believe these were miraculous powers, rather they were the direct result of his confinement, developed in compensation for his lack of normal abilities. Daumer himself believed in miracles, but he was always careful not to impose these beliefs on Kaspar:

> My friends and I have duly observed, valued and noted what was extraordinary in Hauser's being and appearance, but we never told him any stories of the supernatural [telepathic dreams, and the like] nor did we attempt to instill a belief in miracles in him. For Hauser, daily, ordinary occurrences were miraculous and amazing enough. It was important first to make him familiar with this ordinary reality.[110]

Why was the educated public so interested in Kaspar Hauser? I think that for them Kaspar Hauser was Rousseau's innocent child and an opportunity to see the role that education could play in the life of such a person. One is reminded of the "experiment" of Frederick II, 1194–1250, Holy Roman emperor, German king, king of Sicily, and king of Jerusalem, who called himself "lord of the world" and "one of the most arresting figures of the Middle Ages":

> Himself the master of so many tongues, he was anxious to discover by research what the primeval human speech had been. He, therefore, had a number of infants reared by nurses who were most strictly forbidden to speak to them. 'He wanted to discover whether the children could speak Hebrew, or Greek, or Latin, or Arabic as the original of all languages, or whether they would speak the speech of their parents who had borne them.' The experiment failed, for the children died.[111]

Michel de Montaigne (1533–92) had this to say on the topic:

> I believe that a child brought up in complete solitude . . . would have some kind of speech to express his ideas, for it is not likely that nature would deprive us of this resource when she has given it to many others . . . but it is yet to be found out what language the child would speak; and what has been conjectured about it has no great probability.[112]

One should note that this experiment was perhaps a deliberate repetition of one reported at the beginning of book 2 of Herodotus's *History:*

> He [Psammetichus] took two newborn children of just ordinary people and gave them to a shepherd to bring up among his flocks. The manner of their upbringing was to be this: the king charged that no one of those who came face to face with the children should utter a word and that the children should be kept in a lonely dwelling by themselves. At a suitable time the shepherd was to bring the goats to them, give them their fill of milk, and do all the necessary things. Psammetichus did this and gave these orders because he wished to hear from those children, as soon as they were done with meaningless noises, which language they would speak first. This, indeed, was what happened. For when two years had gone by, as the shepherd was performing his tasks, he opened the door and went in, and the children clasped his knees and reached out their hands, calling out "bekos." At first, when the shepherd heard this, he remained silent about it. But as he came constantly and gave careful heed to the matter, this word was constantly with them. So he signified this to his master and at his command brought the children to his presence. When Psammetichus himself had heard, he inquired which of mankind called something "bekos." On inquiry he found that the Phrygians called bread "bekos." So the Egyptians conceded and, making this their measure, judged that the Phrygians were older than themselves. I heard this story from the priests of Hephaestus in Memphis. The Greeks tell, among many other foolish stories, one to the effect that Psammetichus had the tongues of certain women cut out and made the children live with these women.[113]

But the interest in a natural state, a prelapsarian emotional and intellectual paradise, dies hard. Jean-Jacques Rousseau's *Émile, or On Education* was published in 1762, a few years after the *Discourse on the Origins of Inequality* (1754).[114] Rousseau's thesis is, to put it in the famous words of the first sentence of that influential book, *"Tout est bien, sortant des mains de l'auteur des choses: tout dégénére entre les mains de l'homme*

(All is well coming out of the hands of the author of all things; everything degenerates at the hands of man).[115] Many of the ideas in that book (for example, Rousseau's advocacy of vegetarianism) were on people's minds, certainly on that of Kaspar Hauser's teacher, who, we saw, berated himself severely for having weaned Kaspar Hauser from his vegetarianism. What was natural man like was for Rousseau a philosophical question that could be, and was, answered in great detail in *Émile*. But Kaspar Hauser represented an example from nature itself. *He* was what a natural man looked like. Was it good or bad? Rousseau's advice was "do not expose his eyes at the outset to the pomp of courts, the splendor of palaces, or the appeal of the theater. Do not take him to the circles of the great, to brilliant assemblies" (*Émile*, p. 222). But this is precisely what Stanhope did for Kaspar Hauser, and what Daumer and Tucher objected to. If, as Rousseau believed, man was born essentially good and was only corrupted by socialization, Kaspar Hauser provided a good example. In fact, he never did learn cruelty. We can see how those who believed in nurture as opposed to nature found the rumors of Kaspar's royal birth to be useful: After all, his relatives, the princes and princesses of the house of Baden, were killing one another with great frequency. If character was inherited, he too should have been cruel. Yet he was not: He had not "learned" how to be. People were struck, too, by the fact that Kaspar came out of his dungeon with no illnesses, outer or inner. Was language the demon? There are already hints of this early on. As long as Kaspar knew no language, he claimed that he felt no misery, or happiness. Language had not yet mediated his feelings. That is, he could not speak about what he felt, exposing his emotions to other people. (To do so always holds the danger of having one's deepest feelings rejected, mocked, or in some other way not accepted). Even at a more benign level, other people are always reflectors of what is inwardly invisible. We may not be certain what we feel until we see a reflection in the response of another human being. Is it possible that the essence of happiness is only a state of tranquillity, a lack of awareness of an "other"? Perhaps to see oneself reflected in another (with all the possibility for rejection that entails) marks the beginning of misery or at least the potential for it. This certainly seems to have been the case for Kaspar Hauser. Cruelty after all, requires two people. In fact, he only became deeply unhappy when he was in the world, faced with insensitivities he encountered once he was released from his prison. At least, Kaspar says in the autobiographical account of his imprisonment, his situation in prison was predictable. He knew what to expect and when. In contrast, once he was in the world he never knew what people were going to do to him.

A. F. Bance shrewdly points out that "absurdly inflated expectations were followed by an exaggerated hypocritical rejection, the pattern, *mutatis mutandis*, running remarkably close to the Europeans' experience with the "noble savage" of the South Seas in the 1780s:

> One only had to shift the evidence a little and one saw in place of idyllic love and natural goodness a world of thieves, voluptuaries, cannibals and idolaters—anarchy instead of Arcady, Sodom and Gomorrah rather than New Cythera. Civilization, it seems, had a clear duty to save these unfortunate people from themselves. (Alan Moorhead, *The Fatal Impact*, "Arcady Reformed," p. 79)."[116]

Like the educated public in general, Daumer was also greatly interested in the nature/nurture controversy. There had always been an interest in feral children, and clearly Kaspar Hauser was one version of a wild child. Dr. Preu, the first person to examine Kaspar Hauser, said that he was a "half-wild boy who had been raised in the woods," a judgment he was to rescind quickly, but obviously not before those very words got out and set up reverberations in the mind of the public.[117] Certain cases were well known in Germany: The wolf-child of Hesse who was found in 1344 running wild in the woods: "According to the story, a hole had been dug for him by wolves. They had carpeted it with leaves and at night would encircle him with their bodies in order to protect him from the cold."[118] Peter, the savage from Halin in Hannover (1724), had been abandoned by his father in the forest. He lived on plants and tree bark. When captured he would eat only the green bark from twigs and suck the sap from raw wood. He was sensitive to music, but never, in the sixty-eight years he was in captivity, learned to speak.

The underlying metaphor of the wild-children legend suggests a longing to be part of another world. This took a specific form in the case of Kaspar Hauser: the curiosity about his possible royal parentage. As we have just seen, for everybody, educated and uneducated, as well as for both Daumer and Feuerbach, one reason for the interest in Kaspar Hauser was the mystery of his origins: Who, really, was he? Connected to this issue was the sudden appearance on the scene of the earl of Stanhope. Why, the public wanted to know, was Stanhope, with his close ties to the houses of both Baden and Bavaria, so interested in this boy? Of course the attempt on Kaspar's life, and finally his murder, certainly increased the interest. That the king of Bavaria offered an immense sum of money for information leading to the arrest of the criminal proved that Kaspar Hauser's identity was hardly a matter of indifference to the princely houses.

At the same time, and also right from the beginning, voices were raised in opposition to Kaspar Hauser. As early as 1830, Johann Friedrich Karl Merker (1775–1842) wrote his notorious ninety-three-page treatise *Caspar Hauser, Most Likely a Fraud*[119] without ever having met Kaspar Hauser. The flavor of the debate is captured in a statement, typical of the anti-Hauser sentiment, by the Danish writer Dr. Daniel Friedrich Eschricht in his book *Unverstand und schlechte Erziehung:*[120] "When Hauser was given over to Professor Daumer, he was still a poor, very limited, but innocent child. Under Daumer's guidance he gradually turned into a vain fool, a charlatan, a liar. When he left Daumer's house he was a complete fraud, as only a simpleminded idiot knows how to be." Daumer responded: "I must have been able to take somebody who was, due to a brain defect at birth, a dull simpleton beyond any recovery, cure him completely, and magically turn him into a dangerous cunning devil who was, for mysterious reasons, able to dupe the entire world. I challenge anyone to do that!" For Eschricht, of course, Kaspar Hauser killed himself: "Hauser died as a liar and a fraud, and by his own hand as well."[121]

The story itself was utterly absorbing, and would prove fascinating to generations of writers, poets and playwrights. Golo Mann called the "case" of Kaspar Hauser "the finest detective story of all time."[122] Students of French will remember Paul Verlaine's haunting poem "Gaspard Hauser chante." Verlaine wrote his melancholy poem about a boy with no mother and no friends in 1873, while he was in prison for assault on his former companion, the poet Rimbaud. He wrote it, he said, because he was feeling as lonely and abandoned as Kaspar Hauser. The famous last stanza reads:

> Suis-je né trop tôt ou trop tard?
> Qu'est-ce que je fais en ce monde?
> O vous tous, ma peine est profonde:
> Priez pour le pauvre Gaspard!

> (Was I born too early or too late? / What am I doing in this world? / Oh, all of you: my sorrow is deep: / Pray for poor Kaspar!)[123]

The story had always intrigued writers. Herman Melville (1819–91) had already compared Billy Budd to Kaspar Hauser, when he declared that the "character marked by such qualities has to an uninitiated taste an untampered-with flavor like that of berries, while the man thoroughly civilized, even in a fair specimen of the breed, has to the same moral palate a questionable smack as of a compounded wine. To any stray inheritor of these primitive qualities, found like Caspar Hauser, wandering dazed in any Christian capital of our time . . ."[124] Kaspar was the ultimate "outsider." He was, to the admiration of many writers, unwilling or unable to be integrated into ordinary society, and his attempt to do so was seen as tragic. For many twentieth-century European writers, Kaspar Hauser was a kind of "secret stowaway," who, once they learned of his enigmatic appearance and inexplicable death, worked inexorably on their imagination. German writers, such as the poet Rainer Maria Rilke ("Der Knabe"), the novelist Jakob Wassermann, the Austrian writer Hugo von Hofmannsthal (Sigismund in his political drama *Der Turm* [The Tower] is clearly an echo of Kaspar Hauser); the poet Georg Trakl (1887–1914); the novelist Klaus Mann (1906–49), the son of Thomas Mann; and the journalist Kurt Tucholsky (1890–1935), were among those fascinated by the figure of Kaspar Hauser.[125]

There were also many elements from fairy tales: a secret dungeon; a simpleton with extraordinary abilities; a social outcast who was possibly of noble birth and would triumph in the end (he did not). Even his love of animals suggested the theme of the animal helper (hence the insistence, against the evidence, that he was an extraordinary horseman). The issues it raised for memory, for debates about nature versus nurture, and for the relevance of abuse in childhood seemed decisive. But there was a paradox: Kaspar Hauser was kept locked in a dungeon for at least twelve years of his childhood and perhaps more. Released at sixteen, he seemed not entirely human. Yet within a few months he developed into an engaging adolescent. He did not seem unduly damaged or unhappy—that is, he was not by ordinary standards "neurotic."

Our Interest in Kaspar Hauser

At least three threads are interwoven in the modern interest in Kaspar Hauser. First, the preceding interest is a historical phenomenon in itself. Then there is the influence of the Kaspar Hauser legend or story or case history on literature. A number of books have been written on this topic, most recently by Ulrich Struve in *Der Findling Kaspar Hauser in der Literatur.*[126] And, not least, is the fact that the interest in his real identity has by no means died down. We see it even in the latest film, the prizewinning 1994 *Kaspar Hauser,* by Peter Sehr. Based on a careful reading of many historical documents (the Kaspar Hauser scholar Johannes Mayer was the technical adviser), the film portrays Kaspar Hauser as without any doubt the prince of Baden. This is also the opinion of the most serious researchers in the field—Hermann Pies, Fritz Klee, and Adolf Bartning. I share this belief, though I am not persuaded that the matter has been "proved" in the strictest juridical sense of the term. But this is not really the source of my interest in the Kaspar Hauser mystery, nor will it be, I suspect, for many others who will nonetheless find the story intriguing. Regardless of who he really was, here is somebody who was abused.

Kaspar Hauser and Child Abuse

The Kaspar Hauser story is of considerable contemporary interest for another reason: because of the light it can potentially shed on an explosive current debate about what can and cannot be forgotten. At the moment in the United States and Germany, a great deal is being made of the so-called False Memory Syndrome (no doubt the name itself is meant to confer some semblance of medical dignity on what is after all only an idea), and proponents of this "theory" would almost certainly claim that Kaspar Hauser's memories were little more than fantasies put into his mind by well-meaning educators.[127] In Germany this same theory goes by the name of *Missbrauch des Missbrauches* (abuse of abuse). The question, put starkly, is this: Can a person undergo horrendous abuse in childhood over a prolonged period and simply forget it? Very little empirical research has been done on this topic. It has just been assumed that children do not forget traumas (or do not repress them—the distinction being that something can be forgotten for no particular reason, whereas if it is repressed, it is because it was unpleasant to remember, so that a psychological defense mechanism is in operation; Freud in fact considered repression the main defense mechanism). Recently in the United States there has been a spate of books maintaining that repression of sexual abuse is rare, or even nonexistent, and that anyone who claims to have recovered a memory of sexual abuse is either lying or has been manipulated by a therapist or other interested party.[128] This position is the backlash against the belief (prevalent in the 1980s) in the reality and pervasiveness of childhood sexual abuse. I, among others, am one of those blamed for creating the intellectual climate in which this "hysteria" could flourish.[129]

A history of my own interest in this topic may be pertinent here. In Toronto in the 1970s I was a candidate in training to become a psychoanalyst at the Toronto Psychoanalytic Institute. My training in philology and history and my interest in the etiology of misery led me early on to become intrigued by an unsolved puzzle: Why did Freud initially believe that all of the eighteen people (twelve women and six men) he had in analysis in 1896 were sexually abused, and then, some years later, maintain that he had been mistaken and that these people had only imagined the abuse? The actual process by which he changed his mind on this matter presented seemingly insoluble puzzles: These people were no longer in analysis with Freud. Did he suddenly, years later, have an "aha!" experience that allowed him to know in hindsight that what was reported as a memory of an event was in reality the memory of a fantasy, or a wish? Did he think that subsequent clinical experience applied by analogy to his earlier cases? Did he receive new information on all those eighteen cases? Was his retraction based on newly available data, or did theoretical considerations drive his decision? After all, one did not normally tell a person who summoned the courage to remember an occasion of being abused as a child that her (or his) memory was mistaken and that she (or he) was indulging in a wishful fantasy. Abuse quickly shifted from a universal phenomenon to a women's issue. What evidence was there that Freud was right?

Psychiatrists, psychologists, and psychoanalysts knew that the number of women who reported sexual abuse in childhood was high. As part of our clinical training, we were taught, however, that the actual incidence of such abuse was rare. One therefore had to conclude that these women (men had early on dropped out of the picture) were not remembering actual abuse. Fantasies, desires, wishes, impulses—in other words, internal events, not external ones—were at work here. Freud's experience in 1896 served as a cautionary tale of how easy it was to be misled by direct testimony.

But what, really, *was* Freud's experience in 1896 and the subsequent years? This question had not been answered by any historical or scholarly work, and I was left with a compelling desire to see if there was any way to come up with new documents that would point to where an answer might be found.

Fortunately Freud's daughter, Anna, granted me access to her father's private papers and letters, and there I was able to come up with new documents that shed some light on these questions. I have written on them in a series of books, and this is not the place to go into detail.[130] Suffice it to say that I developed the following hypothesis: As long as Freud maintained that the women (and some men) who told him about sexual abuse in childhood were telling him the truth—that they remembered events that actually happened—he was going up against received wisdom that such events did not happen, or happened so rarely that they were of negligible importance for psychology. When Freud, for a brief time, persisted in believing his patients, and telling colleagues about his views, he began to perceive himself as being shunned by his medical peers. This was no misperception on his part: He was considered at best naive, and at worst paranoid, to believe his "hysterical" women patients. In a letter Freud wrote to Fliess on May 4, 1896, two weeks after he gave a courageous paper about the reality of child sexual abuse, he said, "I am as isolated as you could wish me to be: the word has been given out to abandon me, and a void is forming around me" (a passage omitted from the first edition of the letters, and which I restored in *The Complete Letters of Sigmund Freud to Wilhelm Fliess*). When I asked Freud's daughter, Anna, why she omitted this letter from the collection she published, she told me that "it made him sound so paranoid." But of course Freud was perceptive, not paranoid. Since we now know that about 38 percent of women have been sexually abused by the time they reach the age of eighteen, and there is no reason to suppose that things were very different in Freud's time, we can assume that *some* of the men in Freud's audience (there were no women present to support Freud from their own direct experience, nor were women ever permitted to publish personal accounts of sexual abuse until very recently) were themselves guilty of sexual abuse. Not surprisingly they were not receptive to Freud's theories.

Freud's one close medical friend, Wilhelm Fliess, an ear, nose, and throat specialist from Berlin, was also putting pressure on Freud in a different direction to abandon this view (Fliess's son, Robert, became a prominent analyst and claimed, at the end of his life, that as a small child he had been abused by his father precisely at the point that Freud was communicating his belief in the pervasiveness of child abuse to his friend). Fliess had operated on Emma Eckstein, one of the major sources of Freud's views on sexual abuse, with disastrous results: She nearly bled to death as a result of the bungled operation. Fliess insisted that the bleeding was "hysterical," and that he was not responsible for it. The connection between hysterical bleeding and hysterical lying about sexual abuse was not lost on Freud.

It is my hypothesis that these two forces together—peer pressure and the need to protect Fliess—pushed Freud in the direction of conforming to the standard view that any such accounts must be mistakes, lies, or wishes.

But the letters in Freud's papers (which I later published[131]) indicate that Freud had considerable clinical data to support his initial view that these reports of abuse were real. These letters are particularly valuable in that they provide us with the most elaborate accounts available in the literature of Freud's actual clinical material. They permit a detailed look, too, at the climate in German-speaking countries, which was no doubt the same as it had been some sixty years earlier at the time of the case of Kaspar Hauser. Yet these letters had been omitted from the published record. One particularly poignant one, dated December 22, 1897, includes one of the rare fragments of Freud's clinical work—a case history of a two-year-old girl who was anally raped by her father and nearly died as a result of the loss of blood. At the end of this letter Freud has this *cri de coeur:* "A new motto: 'What have they done to you, poor child?' This is a line from a poem by Goethe, from his novel *Wilhelm Meisters Lehrjahre* (1795–96), and is put in the mouth of the strange, androgynous character Mignon. She sings a song to Wilhelm Meister that begins: "Do you know the country where the lemon trees flower, and the golden oranges glow in the dark foliage. . . ?" The line could serve as a motto to the story of Kaspar Hauser as well. But the sympathy Freud shows for the suffering of this patient was not permitted to stand. This passage was omitted from the published letters, and Freud's motto, along with it, was removed from the record. Freud meant it to be the rallying cry of his new science, but for whatever reason — a loss of personal courage, a change of mind — he caved in and adapted himself to the prevailing wisdom that such things simply could not happen in a civilized country.[132] Without these early letters, and their unedited version of what Freud really believed at the time, and what actual clinical material he had in front of him, we really did not have a history of Freud's views so much as an official account. Even if one disagreed (and almost all psychoanalysts do) with my interpretation of these documents, it is incontestable that the new letters and other documents I found in various archives in Europe raised important new questions for any complete history of the discovery of child sexual abuse. They were also of significance in the larger debate about trauma and memory.

For if sexual abuse was the primary subject of these "lost" letters, they raised the larger question of trauma, or abuse in general. Was physical, sexual, emotional, or psychological abuse (including neglect), and the myriad other ways a child could be deprived of the nourishment necessary for a happy adulthood, the source of all later human unhappiness? Was psychoanalysis a traumatogenic theory of the neuroses—in other words, was all later neurosis caused by early childhood experiences of abuse in some form or other? I thought it was. There is a sense in which Kaspar Hauser's case seems to prove the opposite: His early deprivations apparently gave him greater happiness (or, in any event, security) than did his later fame in the larger world, which brought him only unhappiness. But to speak of his "happiness" in his dungeon may have only been a device that enabled Kaspar to speak of how unhappy he was made later. He suffered a different series of deprivations once he was discovered, and different kinds of trauma, and it is always difficult to compare traumas. Moreover, we do not know the full extent of what Kaspar Hauser suffered in his dungeon.

The effects of trauma and deprivation are not a subject that could be tested in a laboratory. One could not subject a human being to various forms of deprivation in order to see if he or she would develop a neurosis as was inhumanely done with animals. Nonetheless a vast source of data was case histories of patients in therapy (as long as the recorder was not allowing bias to interfere with the recounting), as well as accounts of historical cases of abuse (to the extent that society permitted such stories to be published).[133]

Kaspar Hauser was of obvious psychiatric interest, and I am puzzled by the fact that Freud never refers to the case in any of his letters or published writings.

But other accounts *were* of particular interest to Freud, and raise issues similar to those in the case of Kaspar Hauser. One was the story of the "psychotic" Doctor Daniel Paul Schreber.[134] He was the presiding judge in an appellate court, who wrote a detailed account of his own illness, *Memoirs of My Mental Illness* (recently reprinted by Harvard University Press). On the basis of this work, Freud in 1911 published "Psychoanalytic Notes on an Autobiographical Account of a Case of Paranoia" (S.E. vol. 12), which was the first attempt to account in a serious manner for the genesis of paranoid psychosis from a theoretical point of view. It was the first and only time that Freud wrote extensively about a patient whom he had never met and who was still alive at the time of writing. Schreber believed that he was being "unmanned" that is, castrated and turned into a woman for the sexual enjoyment of God. Freud interpreted this belief as a fantasy—in fact a desire, and a homosexual one, directed at his psychiatrist, a surrogate for the father. But Freud ignored the fact that Schreber's psychiatrist, Emil Paul Flechsig, had in fact practiced castration on his female patients. Freud may also not have known that Schreber's father practiced a series of sadistic experiments on the child, almost all of which were later incorporated into the so-called psychotic delusions of the adult Schreber.[135]

All this is relevant to so-called false memories, or even false reports, because in fact very few data on the actual statistics of false reports have ever been collected. We are left with people's impressions. There were many who doubted, on no very solid ground, the story of Kaspar Hauser, and claimed that he fabricated his early life of trauma, just as there are people today who believe *no* account of abuse. I have no doubt that there must be *some* false memories, but I seriously doubt that the percentage of them, compared to genuine memories, is significant (just as there are, occasionally, recantations of rape accusations, but their number is minuscule). And just as false memories are rare, so too is fabrication rare.[136] They can only constitute a tiny minority of all accusations.[137]

On the other hand, there are actual data on the forgetting of real events that were traumatic and sexual in nature (too often the research on forgetting and remembering focuses on trivial matters that have little impact on the emotional lives of the subjects).[138] These data cannot be ignored if we wish

to consider the possibility that Kaspar Hauser did not remember everything that had happened to him while he was
in prison.[139] An important article appeared in 1994: "Recall
of Childhood Trauma: A Prospective Study of Women's
Memories of Child Sexual Abuse."[140] It was the first time
that a large number of women (129) could be interviewed in
adult life about experiences they had in childhood (according to hospital records). The results showed that a large proportion of the women (38 percent) did not recall the abuse
that had been reported seventeen years earlier. What Linda
Williams shows is that it is precisely repeated abuse, and especially abuse by a close family member, that is most likely to
be forgotten. She does not explore why this might be so, but
it is not difficult to perceive a psychological reason: The be-
trayal, the confusion, is much greater. A onetime abuse by a
stranger is more likely to be reported, because one can
count, to some extent, on being believed and being given
comfort. (To whom would Kaspar Hauser have turned? The
only experience he knew was his, there was nothing to contrast it to.) Sixteen percent of the women who recalled the
abuse stated that there had been a time in the past when they
did not remember that the abuse had happened. An example
of one of the cases is given: "In one instance, the young
woman told the interviewer that she was never sexually
abused as a child, and she repeatedly and calmly denied any
sexual abuse experiences throughout the detailed questioning. She was then asked if anyone in her family had ever gotten into trouble for his or her sexual behavior, and she said
no and then spontaneously added, "Oh, wait a minute, could
this be something that happened before I was born?" When
told that it could, she said, "My uncle sexually assaulted
someone." Later she said the following:

> I never met my uncle (my mother's brother), he died before I was
> born. You see, he molested a little boy. When the little boy's

mother found out that her son was molested, she took a butcher knife and stabbed my uncle in the heart, killing him.

The interviewer (unaware of the circumstances of this woman's victimization) recorded the details of this account of the uncle's death and completed the interview:

A comparison with the original account of the abuse recorded in 1974 revealed that this participant (at age 4), her cousin (at age 9), and her playmate (at age 4) were all abused by the uncle. The records of the earlier research revealed that when this participant told her mother about the abuse, her mother, in turn, informed the mother of the playmate, a little boy. This boy's mother, according to newspaper accounts available in the case files, armed herself with a knife and then went looking for the uncle. She stabbed him five times, killing him. The participant in the present study apparently did not recall that she was abused by this man.

The debate over the recovery of memories and the possibility of forgetting trauma is directly relevant to any study of Kaspar Hauser. It would be pure speculation to suggest what may have happened to him in his dungeon. We have almost no clues, and Kaspar Hauser himself provided few data. He remembered almost nothing. However, he did recover some memories, and might, over the course of a normal lifetime, have recovered many more. He was never given the opportunity. From his case, we know that language can act as a moderator. When there is no language, or language is poorly developed, forgetting is particularly easy. According to the authoritative work by Diana Russell, 38 percent of women spontaneously remember having been sexually abused before the age of 18.[141] The vast majority of these women have always remembered the abuse and did not require therapy to recover the memory. What we cannot know, of course, is how many of the other 62 percent of women, with no memory of abuse, have either forgotten the abuse or simply refuse to talk about it. Many women learn to their chagrin that society often simply turns a blind eye to their memories of pain, either genuinely disbelieving them or claiming to. Many people did not want to believe Kaspar Hauser, refused to believe him, and found it easier by far to claim that he was inventing, fabricating, that his fantasies had carried him away, that he was a hysteric—in short, he was treated like a woman.

Precious little research has been done on the memories of children who survived traumas—the Holocaust, for example. It is simply said that such experiences *cannot* be repressed. I find that idea implausible, but it is an empirical question and could presumably be answered by the necessary research. The importance of these questions to the veracity of memories of sexual abuse in childhood is obvious. Little is actually known on the topic of forgetting traumatic memories. How different, for example, is a three-year-old's memory of a traumatic event from that of a twelve-year-old? What difference does the extent of the trauma make? And is there something unique about a sexual trauma? Is it not possible that there are no general rules, and that each person will react differently, some forgetting permanently, some repressing, some remembering permanently, and some simply unwilling to talk about it, ever, with anyone? How can we be certain that Kaspar Hauser did not belong to this latter group, and simply elected not to talk about certain things he knew? After all, he emerged from his "cage" at sixteen. Just days before, he was locked up, experiencing things he could not have forgotten in just a day or two, even if he only acquired the necessary linguistic skills to speak of them some weeks or months or years later.[142]

I have long been intrigued by the term "soul murder" (found in Feuerbach's book about Kaspar Hauser), not because of the word, but because of the idea behind it: that a crime can be committed against a person's very being.[143] This was Feuerbach's idea, and it suggests that interest in the actual abuse of Kaspar Hauser may not be confined to the modern age. Perhaps fascination of the European world of the nineteenth century with the story of Kaspar Hauser represented a hidden acknowledgment of the reality of child abuse. Kaspar Hauser was abused by his parents or parent when he was abandoned as a newborn infant; abused by whoever kept him for twelve or fourteen or sixteen years locked in a dungeon; abused by Lord Stanhope for political reasons; abused by an unknown assailant who tried to murder him for reasons that could only have been obscure to Kaspar Hauser; and finally abused by the man who stabbed him to death. Because this death took three days to happen, he was abused one final time by his "teacher" Herr Meyer, who let it be known both to Kaspar himself and to anyone else he encountered that the wound was superficial, not in the least deadly, and when it was clear that Kaspar was dying from this superficial wound, that the wound was in fact self-inflicted in a misguided and unsuccessful attempt to bring attention to himself.

It was hard to be more abused than Kaspar Hauser. For all the thousands of children who were abused in more mundane ways—sometimes less deadly but at others equally murderous in intent and often in fact—who were invisible, here was a "case" that could not be ignored. It was like the return of the repressed. Kaspar Hauser represented, I believe, the objective proof of something that many suspected: Children were hated, hurt, and often murdered for reasons that made no sense. It was the most denied fact of the nineteenth century, just as child sexual abuse was the most denied fact of the twentieth.[144] In the nineteenth century it was claimed that nobody except a monster could harm a child, and that when it did occur, it would be so rare as to deserve mention in the newspapers. Indeed, French and German newspapers reserved sections for just this kind of report. Yet severe physical punishment was practiced, routinely, in families, where fathers felt it their prerogative to beat their children for any and all infractions of self-designed prohibitions. In schools, physical punishment was the rule, not the exception, and there is even a well-documented case of a girl who died, not from the beating but as a result of the humiliation she experienced during the caning of her bare bottom.[145] In the twentieth century the same thing has been said about sexual abuse. One in a million, perhaps, was the incidence rate the psychiatric textbooks claimed for incest as late as 1975.[146] Yet some of the people who denied such abuse were well aware that it happened, since they were in fact the perpetrators. Others, who possibly preferred not to think about it, were victims. Among the "public," then, were both victims and perpetrators, two classes of people, large in number, who *knew* that this denied fact was actual and real. Kaspar Hauser, like a symptom, allowed the public to dwell on and think about the consequences of child abuse without having to acknowledge what they were actually thinking about. Kaspar Hauser himself knew that people suffered for something they had never done. Meyer claimed that he simply could not get Kaspar Hauser to understand that suffering in this world would be compensated for in the next, and that Kaspar insisted that "there were people who suffered deeply, through no fault of their own."[147]

The modern reader (could it have been any different for readers in the last century?), including myself, desperately wants to reconstruct Kaspar Hauser's actual feelings, memories, and experiences while he was in his dungeon. We want to know if this story is true and, if so, what it says about human nature—that is, what does it mean for us? Do we all suffer from what Freud called "the family romance"—a feeling that our family of origin cannot possibly be the humble one we already know about, but must be a far more noble one that we do not know about? Freud thought this was a universal longing. We see it in the fantasies about children raised by wolves, and see, too, that it can be realistic: The Indian wolf-children, Amala and Kamala, of whom I write in the appendix on wolf-children, would have been better off among the wolves than in an Indian orphanage.

But not everybody wants to come from a different family. Those who do do so for good reasons: They have been hurt. All this means, then, is that one wishes one had not been hurt. "Dysfunctional families" merely translates the insight Tolstoy had long ago: Happy families are all alike, only the unhappy ones are interesting. They are interesting because they teach us about what happened to us that we have "repressed." We only repress what is intolerable. It was Freud's later belief that small children imagined, wished for, desired, and fantasized sexual assaults, and that these fantasies, when remembered in adolescence, caused a neurosis (since one could not acknowledge the desire behind the fantasy). It is not a very logical idea, and one that runs counter to ordinary experience. We do not wish for horrible things to happen to us. We do, however, often try to make those that *did* happen disappear, and one way to do this is to imagine that they never happened in the first place, to deny them any reality. Contrary to Freudian doctrine, then, I believe that it is not fantasies that make us ill, but memories that cannot or will not be remembered. Sometimes these memories cannot be remembered because they cover deep wounds that still hurt every time they are touched: The mind balks at any attempt to get close to them. On the other hand, I believe Freud was right when he claimed that ghosts can only be laid to rest when they are brought to the light of day. Until we can acknowledge and think about what has happened to us in the past, we cannot deprive the memory of whatever hurting power it still has over us. Every buried memory, then, contains, embedded in it, a *longing* for derepression—that is a wish or a need to remember, a kind of built-in self-healing device. We need to make ourselves whole by possessing our own memories. It is this desire to know what has happened to us, to remember it, and to think about it with ever decreasing pain that lies, I think, at the heart of the European obsession with *le pauvre Gaspard*. To think about the suffering of Kaspar Hauser and the mysteriousness of it is to think about our own past suffering in an attempt to undo that mystery, recover our past, and emerge scathed but whole.

But Kaspar Hauser was not just *any* hurt child. He was kept in a dungeon for twelve years, from the age of four to sixteen, the most important years of one's life. What, one cannot help but wonder, would have happened to me in such a situation? And who, exactly, is the me, the self, that then emerges? This case raises many issues of how we can discover the past. Suppose a good historian, or even a good psychologist (something of an oxymoron in my view), were to have had access to Kaspar Hauser and wanted to help him recapture his own past—what could he or she have done? Well, the first thing would be to shelter Kaspar Hauser from contamination from the outside. We would want *his* memories, not those others think he should have had. This is the complaint that Feuerbach lodged against Binder's proclamation—that suggestion could easily have been at the heart of Kaspar Hauser's memories. We could, as Daumer did, ask him to write down everything he could remember. But the difference is obvious: Writing was not his medium. He did it with great difficulty. Neither was speaking; this too was hard for him.

Nobody ever asked Kaspar Hauser how long *he* thought, *afterward*, he was kept in the dungeon. (It would not be accurate, but it would be interesting.) Did he have any sense of time? (For example, did he have a bowel movement once or twice a day?) The times when he was emotional, as when he said that the man with whom he had always been had not done anything to harm him, would have been the times to ask him exactly what the man *did* do to him. In contrast, when he was most frightened—for example, when he said that he saw a man lurking in the bushes and that frightened him—would have been the time to ask what he was frightened of. We *know* that Kaspar Hauser read the book by Feuerbach (but not if he read the book by Daumer).[148] However, we know nothing of his reaction. Did he read the "proclamation" by Mayor Binder? To learn more about Kaspar Hauser's earlier life is to learn more about what happens to memories under the influence of traumas.

Kaspar Hauser, too, asked himself in the passage from Daumer quoted above what he thought about in his prison, what he imagined, what he knew of a world outside. But he gave no answer. Or at least he could find none. He believed that he remembered no such thoughts. But he seemed uneasy with this notion, and so are we. There *were* thoughts, of course, and either they were repressed or forgotten. But given the poverty of his environment, the question must at least be asked whether this impoverishment had more than a psychological and a cognitive effect. Could it also have had a physiological effect, which in turn would have further impoverished his thinking? That the brain can be physically (as well as psychologically) hurt by trauma is clear.

Nonetheless, I think Kaspar Hauser was telling Daumer the truth here, and it was one of those moments when he told a deep truth—a truth that one does not expect to hear from the mouth of a sixteen-year-old. It was obvious that he suffered greatly. Where was that suffering? What happened to it? Where was it put? In his inability to learn like a normal person? In his melancholia, which struck everybody? In his compassion for all small creatures?

What happens to the memories of a person who suffers greatly? Are they obliterated? Distorted? Does it become dangerous to remember, either because one has been ordered not to (or knows without an order that one must not), as Feuerbach hints in his letter to Elise von der Recke, or because to remember is to relive the pain? Or is it even possible that the person recognizes that the memories will not be believed—that people will turn their backs on such suffering by denying their accuracy or in some other way minimizing their significance? For so many years society has refused to acknowledge the depth of human suffering caused by child abuse. Any memory that points to the authenticity of such experiences is bound to be received with the same cold rejection. Ultimately it is too dangerous for society to acknowledge the world it has created for children. Far easier to claim that the memories are specious, that their bearer is mentally ill, that such events cannot have taken place because otherwise the world we live in would be an intolerable place of injustice, crime, and suffering.

Conclusion

Why do we know so much more about Kaspar Hauser than about other children of his time? Is it only because it was suspected that he was the legitimate heir to the throne of Baden? Why, actually, would that have such a deep effect on people? Though at the time it had serious dynastic consequences, it is *interesting* but not more. And it was *much* more interesting closer to its own time than it is to us today. Yet Kaspar Hauser still holds the modern reader in thrall. Hardly a year goes by without a new book appearing about him. True, fashions change, and whereas his story was once the touchstone for thinking about "nature" versus "nurture," a few years ago it was more likely to be a means of testing the limits of language, as in Peter Handke's 1967 play *Kaspar Hauser*,[149] and today it is a crucial document in the debate over memory and reconstruction. What has not yet been noticed is the extent to which the abuse to which Kaspar

Hauser was subjected, while practically unique, is not really so foreign to our own experiences. Therein, I believe, lies the key to the endless fascination.

Kaspar Hauser may or may not have been the prince of Baden, but it is worth noting that the world today knows more about, and is more interested in, Kaspar Hauser than in any prince of Baden who ever lived. Something about his perplexity in the face of the world touches a chord deep in everyone: *Kaspar Hauser, c'est moi!*

TRANSLATION

Anselm Ritter von Feuerbach's

Kaspar Hauser

Heaven, I beseech you,
What crime did I commit by being born
That you treat me in this abominable fashion?

—Sigismund, in Calderon's *Life Is a Dream*[1]*

Ansbach, 1832

To his Lordship, Count Stanhope,[2] Earl of Great Britain, etc.

Your Lordship: Nobody has greater claims on this book than you do. Providence has sent you to the young boy with no childhood and no youth, to be his paternal friend and all-powerful protector. On the other side of the ocean, in beautiful Old England you have prepared a safe haven for him, until such time as the rising sun of truth will drive away the darkness which lies over the mysterious fate of this human being. Perhaps, in what remains of his half-murdered life, some days await him in which he will no longer lament having seen the light of this world. For such a deed, only the genius [?] of mankind can reward you.

In the vast desert of our time, where the blazing sun of selfish passion parches and turns dry our hearts, to have finally found a true human being is one of the most beautiful and unforgettable experiences I have had in the evening of my life.

With love and deepest respect, from your Lordship's most devoted servant: von Feuerbach.

———————

*The notes to this translation appear at the end of the section. The notes by the translator are in brackets and are preceded by the words "translator's note." All other notes are original notes by Feuerbach. Similarly, anything in the text within parentheses is by Feuerbach. What is in brackets has been added by the translator. All emphases are Feuerbach's own.

Chapter I

The second day of Pentecost belongs, in Nuremberg, to those major holidays on which the inhabitants find diversion in the countryside or in neighboring villages. Nuremberg was very spread out, given how few people lived there at the time. On this beautiful spring day it was so quiet and empty that it seemed more like an enchanted city in the Sahara than the busy trading and commercial center it is. Especially in the more outlying areas of the city, many a secret thing could easily happen in public yet remain secret.

And so it happened that on the second day of Pentecost, May 26, 1828, between four and five o'clock in the evening, the following occurred:

A resident[3] of what people call Unschlitt Square (close to the infrequently visited small Haller Gate) was lingering in front of his house, about to go to the so-called New Gate, when, looking around, he noticed not far away a young boy dressed like a peasant, standing in a most remarkable posture, who, like a drunkard, was trying to move forward without really being able to stand straight or control his feet. The resident approached the stranger, who held a letter out to him. The letter was addressed as follows: "To the well born captain of the Fourth Squadron of the Sixth Regiment of Light Horses in Nuremberg."

Since the captain in question[4] lived near the New Gate, the resident took the young boy, a stranger, with him to the guard and from there to the nearby house of Captain W., the commanding officer of the Fourth Squadron of the above-mentioned regiment.[5] Keeping his hat on his head, and holding his letter in his hand, the boy approached the servant[6] of Captain von W. as the door of the house opened and said: "I want to be such a one as my father was." The servant asked him what he wanted, who he was, where he came from. But the stranger did not seem to understand any of the questions and only continued to repeat the words: "I want to be such a one as my father was." Or: "Dunno!" According to the deposition of the captain's servant, the boy was so exhausted that he did not so much walk as "staggered." Weeping, and expressing severe pain, he pointed to his feet, which were beginning to give way on him. He seemed to be suffering both from hunger and thirst. He was given a small piece of meat, but no sooner did the first bite touch his mouth than he began to shake and his facial muscles went into violent spasms. He spat it out with obvious disgust. He displayed the same signs of revulsion when he was given a glass of beer and tasted a few drops. He devoured a piece of dark bread and drank a glass of fresh water eagerly and with the most apparent relish. In the meantime, every effort to find out something about him and how he made his way there was in vain. He seemed to hear without understanding, to see without taking anything in, to move his legs without being able to walk. His language consisted primarily of tears, groans of pain, unintelligible sounds, or the frequently recurring words: "I want to be a rider the way my father was." In the captain's house he was at once taken for a wild man, and led to the stable until the master returned. There he promptly stretched himself out on the straw and fell into a deep sleep.

He had been sleeping for several hours when the captain returned home and went to the stable immediately to see the wild man, of whom his children had, on greeting him, told him so many strange things. He remained in the deepest sleep. They tried to awaken him. They jiggled him, they shook him, they poked him, but all in vain. They picked him up off the floor and tried to get him to stand on his feet, but he continued to sleep as if he were dead. The only thing that distinguished him from somebody truly dead was the fact that he was still warm. Finally, after many exertions, which had their effect on the sleeper, he opened his eyes, woke up, saw the captain in his colorful shining uniform, and seemed to admire it with childish delight. Then he moaned his usual "Rider," etc., etc.[7]

Captain von W. did not know the young stranger; neither was he able to explain why the letter was addressed to him. Finally, as no more could be gotten out of the boy by questioning him, beyond his repeating over and over "Want to be a rider," etc., etc., or "Dunno," there was nothing more to do but to leave the solution to the riddle and the care of the unknown stranger to the municipal police. Consequently he was taken there. Captain von W. was to say in his later court deposition: "From what I was in a position to observe of this man's mental state, I would have to say that he appeared to have been totally neglected, or he was behaving like a small child, which contrasted with his size."

The trip to the police station was made around eight o'clock in the evening; in his condition the walk was sheer torture. Apart from some low-level officials, several members of the military police were present in the police station. The strange youth also struck all of them as a very odd apparition. They could not decide in which of the usual judicial categories to place him. Official policelike questions were directed to him: What is your name? What is your social class and occupation? Where are you from? Why are you here? Where is your passport? These and similar questions had absolutely no effect on him. "Want to be a rider like my father was," or "Dunno," or something he would often repeat with tears in his voice: "Take me home!" These were the only words with which he would respond to all and sundry inducements.[8] He did not seem to know or even grasp where he was. He betrayed neither fear nor puzzlement nor embarrassment, but rather an almost animallike apathy. He either took no notice of his surroundings or stared without thought, allowing everything to pass by without being affected. His tears, his whimpers while pointing to his wobbly feet, his helplessness, his childlike and childish personality soon won the compassion of all of those present. A soldier brought him a piece of meat and a glass of beer, but just as he had in W's house, he pushed them away with revulsion and ate only bread and drank fresh water. Another soldier gave him a coin. He displayed a small child's joy over it, and played with it and made hand gestures, saying over and over, "Horse! Horse!" which seemed to indicate that he wanted to hang this coin on some "horse." His behavior, his whole being, showed him to be barely a two- or three-year-old child in the body of an adolescent. Most of the policemen there were divided only as to whether he should be considered an insane idiot or a half-wild man. There were a few, however, who thought that it was actually possible that a clever imposter was hiding in the person of this boy, an opinion that earned itself a not-inconsiderable plausibility from the following circumstance: It occurred to somebody to see if perhaps he could write. So he was given pen and ink, paper was placed in front of him, and he was told to write. He seemed to display pleasure at the idea, took the pen between his fingers in a manner that was anything but clumsy, and wrote, to the astonishment of everybody present, in firm, legible letters the name:

Kaspar Hauser[9]

He was then further asked to write down the name of the place from which he came. But he did nothing but repeat in a moaning tone his "Rider want to be," etc. etc., his "Take me home," and his "Dunno."

Since for the moment nothing else could be done with him, the rest was left to time. He was handed over to a policeman who took him to the Vestner Gate Tower, which is set aside for minor criminals, vagabonds, etc., etc.[10] This is a relatively short walk—yet he collapsed, groaning at almost every step he took—if his staggering could even be called

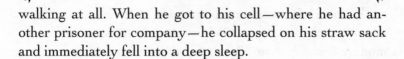

walking at all. When he got to his cell—where he had another prisoner for company—he collapsed on his straw sack and immediately fell into a deep sleep.

Chapter II

Kaspar Hauser—the name he has kept to this day—arrived in Nuremberg wearing on his head a round felt hat lined with yellow silk and stitched with red leather. It was a somewhat common town hat, in which one could still make out a half-scratched-out picture of the city of Munich. You could see the toes of his bare feet sticking out from torn high-heeled half-boots that did not fit him, their soles hammered together with horseshoe nails. A black silk scarf was tied around his neck. He was wearing a gray cloth jacket that country folk call a Janker or a Shalk over both a coarse shirt[11] and a linen vest with red dots that showed signs of many washings. Only later, on closer examination by experts, did it turn out that the tailor did not fashion this as an ordinary peasant jacket but rather, as the collar showed, as a *tail-coat*. The back part had been cut out and the top half had been stitched together clumsily by somebody who knew nothing about sewing. The somewhat more refined gray cloth pants were reinforced with the same gray cloth material between the legs, much as *riding pants* are; they must originally have belonged to a servant, a stable boy, a forester, or someone in that category rather than to a peasant. Kaspar was carrying with him a white-and-red-checked handkerchief with the initials K.H. embroidered in red. He was also carrying some rags in his pockets with blue and white flowers on them, a German [?] key, and a small envelope with some *gold dust* in it, which one would not expect to find in a peasant's hut. He also had prayer beads made of horn, and a substantial supply of spiritual objects. Besides Catholic prayers, several were printed religious texts of the kind gen-

❖──────────────────────────────────────❖

erally found in Southern Germany—especially at pilgrim sites—which are sold to pious crowds for a good bit of money. Some had no place of publication on them, others were from *Altöttingen, Burghausen, Salzburg,* and *Prague.* They had such edifying titles as: "Spiritual Sentry"; "Spiritual Forget-me-not"; "A Very Powerful Prayer by Means of Which One Can Participate in the Benefits of All Holy Masses"; "Prayer to the Holy Guardian Angel"; "Prayer to the Holy Blood"; and so on. One of these precious little spiritual works, entitled "The Art of Replacing Lost Time and Years Badly Spent" (n.d.), seems to allude cynically to this young man's life as he later told it. It can hardly be doubted, to judge from the religious objects he brought with him, that more than worldly hands played a role in this matter.

The letter that was in Kaspar's hand when he got to Nuremberg, addressed to the unnamed captain of the cavalry of the fourth squadron of the sixth regiment of light horses, read in form and content as follows:[12]

From the boarder of Bavaria. The place is unnamed. 1828.

To the High and Well Borne Captain of the Cavalry!

I'm sanding yous a boy who would like to faithfully serve his king he beggs, this boy was laid on me on the 7th of Oktober, 1812, and I, myself a poor day laborer, I myself have ten children, I have enough to do to get by myself, and his mother laid the boy only for being raised, but I was not aeble to find his mother, and now I have also said nothing to the Provincial Court that this boy was given to me. I thught to myself that I must have him for my son, I raised him as a Christian, and I have sinc 1812 not allowed him to take a single stepp out of the house so that nobody knows the place where he was brought up, and he himself doesn't know what my housse is called and the place he doesn't know also, so you ken ask him as much as you like, but he can't tell you, reeding and writing I have already taught him and he can write my handwriting like I write it and wen we ask him what he wans to become, he said he wants to be a Schwolische wich his father was, he also wants to be, if he hade parents whiche he had none he wuld have become a learned boy. You only haf to show him something once and he can do it,

I only pointed him to Nuemark, and from there he had to walk to you on his own I told him that when he is a soldier, I would come right away and take him home, otherwise I would have been in trouble. [? meaning unclear]

Best Captain: you shudn't terture him with questions: he doesn't know my plaace where I am, I tok him away in the middle of the night he doesn't know any more how to go home. Truley yours, I don't make my name nown because I coud be punished.

And he doesn't have a single cent on him because I myself have nothing, so if you can't keepe him, you will have to butcher him [?] or hang him up in the chimney.[13]

Enclosed was another note, this one handwritten in Latin letters, although probably by the same hand. It read:

The child is already baptized she is called Kasper you'll half to give him a last name yourself the child you will half to raize his father was a Schwolische wen he is seventeen years old send him to Nuremberg to the Sixth Schwolische Regiment that is where his father was too I ask you to raise him until his seventeenth year borne was he on the thirtieth of April, in the yeer 1812 I am a poor little girl I canot fead the boy his father is dead.

At the time of his appearance in Nuremberg, *Kaspar Hauser*[14] was four feet nine inches tall, and appeared to be around sixteen or seventeen years old. His chin and lips were covered with a very fine down, his wisdom teeth were still missing, and only broke through in 1831. His light brown, very fine hair, cut in peasant fashion, was frizzled in little curls. He was stocky with broad shoulders, and perfectly well proportioned with no visible physical defects. His skin was very fair and delicate; his complexion was not exactly glowing but not sickly either; his limbs were of delicate build; his small hands were beautifully formed. This is true of his feet, too, which showed no signs that any shoe had ever cramped or squeezed them. The soles of his feet were without calluses, as soft as the inside of a hand, though covered all over with fresh blisters, traces of which could be seen for months. He had a vaccination scar on both arms;[15] on his right arm a wound with a fresh scab was clearly visible. Kaspar was later to say that this came from a blow with a cane (or a piece of wood) administered by the man "with whom he had always been" when he once made too much noise. His face was very ordinary at that time, and almost without expression when he was in repose; the lower part of his face protruded slightly, giving him an animallike appearance. The vacant stare from his bluish, otherwise clear and light-colored eyes, betrayed an expression of animallike apathy.[16] His facial features changed completely in the next few months. His eyes took on expression and life, the protruding lower half of his face receded, and his earlier physiognomy could hardly be recognized. In the early period his weeping consisted of an ugly contortion of his mouth; but if something pleasant touched his spirit, a lovely friendly smile took over his features, a smile that could not but win over everyone's heart. It was the irresistible charm of the joy of an innocent child. He could barely be said to know how to use his hands or fingers. With the exception of his index finger and thumb, he kept his fingers straight, stiff, and spread far apart. He generally kept the tips joined together in such a way that they made a circle. Where other people used only a few fingers, he would use his whole hand in the most clumsy and awkward way. When he moved it was like a child learning to take its first steps under constraint of a child's leash. It was not so much a walk as a waddling, swaying, groping, an awkward compromise between falling down and standing up. When he tried to walk, instead of putting his heel down first, and raising his legs, he would put both his heel and the balls of his feet on the ground at the same time and then, his feet facing inward toward each other; his chest thrust out, his arms straight out, which he seemed to use as if they were balancing poles, he would stumble slowly and clumsily forward. If he encountered the slightest obstacle in his little room, he would often fall flat on the floor. Long after he arrived in Nuremberg, he still had to be taken up and down the stairs. Even now it is not possible for him to stand on one foot and lift, bend, or hold out the other one without falling.

During a forensic examination of Kaspar Hauser's physique that was carried out in the year 1830, the following highly unusual peculiarities, among others, were noted, which shed some clarifying light on his life and fate. According to the expert opinion of Dr. Osterhausen,[17] "his knees show a peculiar deformity. Generally when the lower leg is extended the kneecap becomes visible. But in Hauser's case the kneecap remains considerably depressed. Ordinarily the four extensor muscles of the lower leg, the *vastus externus*, the *vastus internus*, the *rectus femoris*, and the *cruralis*, are attached to the protuberances of the shinbone by a common tendon after they have been interwoven with the kneecap. But in Hauser's case the tendon is severed, and the tendon of the large external and internal thigh extensor *(m. vastus externus et internus)* proceed downward at the external and internal side of the protuberance of the knee and are inserted into the shinbone underneath. Between them lies the kneecap. By this means—and because these tendons are very strongly affected—the depression I spoke of ensues. When he is sitting on the floor, with his femur and shank stretched out in a horizontal position, his back forms a right angle with the flexion of the femur, and his knee joint extended straight in front of him is so close to the floor that there is no elevation to be seen between the floor and his knee. Even a playing card could hardly fit into the hollow of the knee."

Chapter III

The strangeness surrounding Kaspar Hauser in his first appearance in Nuremberg transformed itself, during the next few days and weeks, into a dark and terrifying mystery whose solution one tried in vain to find with one guess after another. He was far from being an idiot or insane. In addition he was so gentle, obedient, and good-natured that nobody could even be tempted to believe that this young stranger was a savage, or a boy who had been raised by animals in the forest. And yet, except for those expressions I have already referred to, which he used over and over, he was so completely devoid of words and concepts (comparable only to the state of an Indian from Tierra del Fuego [*Pescheräh*]); he had such a total lack of acquaintance with the most common objects and the most everyday occurrences of nature, he had such an indifference, contempt even, for all habits, comforts, and necessities of life; and at the same time gave evidence of so many peculiar traits in his entire mental, moral, and physical being, that observers could actually believe themselves in a position to choose whether he should be taken as an inhabitant of another planet miraculously transported to earth, or as one of those men about whom Plato had written that they are born and grow up under the earth and only when mature emerge into our world and see the light of day.

Kaspar consistently displayed extreme aversion toward all food and drink except dry bread and water. Not just the taste, even the mere smell of our common foods nauseated him or worse; a small drop of wine or coffee, secretly mixed in with his water, caused him to break out in a cold sweat or be seized with vomiting and violent headaches.[18] At some point somebody to get him to drink some brandy under the pretext that it was water. When the glass was brought to his mouth, he turned pale and fainted. He would have fallen backward into a glass door if someone had not caught him. Another time he was forced by the jailer to drink some coffee. He had barely swallowed a few drops when he was seized by diarrhea. From a few drops of beer that had been strongly diluted with water he developed terrible stomach cramps, his whole body felt feverish, he began sweating profusely, followed by chills with headaches and burping. Even milk, boiled or unboiled, did not please him and caused him unpleasant burpings. Once somebody concealed some meat in his bread; he smelled it immediately and expressed his strong aversion to it. When he was nevertheless forced to eat it, it made him very sick.

At night, which generally began for him when the sun set and ended when it rose, he lay on his straw sack; during the day he sat on the floor, his legs stretched out straight in front of him.

In the first few days, when he saw a burning candle in front of him for the first time, the bright flame delighted him and he innocently reached out to it, burning his hand and finger, which he withdrew too late amid screams and crying. When, to test him, somebody ran at him with a naked saber and pretended to stab him and beat him, he remained completely motionless, did not even blink his eyes, and seemed completely unaware of the fact that this object could cause him harm.[19] When a mirror was held in front of him, he reached for his own reflexion and then made for the back of it to find the person [he thought was] hiding there. Whenever he saw a shining object, he reached for it like a small child. When he couldn't grab it or was denied it, he wept.

A few days after his arrival in Nuremberg, Kaspar was being led around the city by two policemen in the hope he might recognize the gate through which he had been led. As one might well have anticipated, he was unable to distinguish one gate from another; in fact he seemed to take no notice of anything that passed before his eyes. He stared dully at any object that was brought close to him, betraying only once in a while a puzzled curiosity. He had only two words with which from time to time he would designate whatever living creature he became aware of. The human figure, regardless of gender and age, he would call *"Bua"* [boy]; any animal he happened to see, four-footed or two-legged, dog, cat, goose or chicken, he would call *"Ross"* [horse]. If the horses were white, he displayed pleasure; dark animals aroused in him repugnance or fear. A black hen that ran up to him terrified him; he screamed and made the greatest efforts to run away on those legs of his, which refused to serve him.

His soul seemed at first completely rigid, and so also some of his senses, only very gradually awakening and opening to the conditions around him. After a few days he became conscious of the striking of the clock tower and the ringing of the bells. This put him in a state of awe reflected in an expression of intense listening and amazement, but soon his eyes returned to a dull stare that had something wistful about it. A few weeks later he heard the music from a peasants' wedding procession as it passed under the window of his little room in the tower. He stood there suddenly listening, like a statue, his face transfixed, his eyes radiating delight. His ears and eyes were continuously fixed on the gradually fading music; even when the last notes were completely inaudible he stood there motionless trying to catch them. It was as if he hoped to incorporate these last sounds—like heavenly vibrations to him—into himself. Or as if his soul had abandoned his body to a state of numbness in order to draw nearer to these sounds. It was certainly not to test Kaspar's musical sense that somebody, knowing full well his extraordinary sensitivity to nervous arousal, had positioned him right next to the big regimental drum during a military parade. The first beat on the drum upset him so much that he fell into convulsions and had to be taken away immediately.

Among the many unusual reactions of Kaspar Hauser in the first days and weeks, it was noticed that the idea of *horses*, particularly *wooden horses*, held a special significance for him. The word "horse" seemed to take up the greatest space in his dictionary of barely a half dozen words. It was uttered most frequently, on the most varied occasions, and for the most varied objects. He often spoke in a pleading, melancholy tone, with tears in his eyes, as if he were expressing a longing for a horse. When somebody gave him a present of some small trivial item, say a shining coin, a ribbon, a little picture, and so on, he would say: "Horse! Horse!" He made clear by expression and gesture that he wanted to put these pretty things around the neck of a horse. Kaspar was taken every day to the police station, which was not exactly to the advantage of his mental development or in the service of accurate observation, although the singularity of his person would surely demand it. There, amid the din and the hustle and bustle, he would generally pass a good part of the day. In fact he felt at home there, and soon won the affection and love of the denizens of the police station. Here, too, he would often repeat his "Horse! Horse!" This gave one policeman,[20] who had the most to do with the strange half-youth half-child, the idea of bringing a white toy wooden horse to the police station. Kaspar, who until then had almost always shown himself to be unresponsive, indifferent, detached, or even depressed, was as though transfigured as soon as he saw this wooden horse and behaved as if he had found in this little horse an old friend he had long been yearning to see. Controlling his joy but weeping with a smiling face, he immediately sat down on the ground next to the horse, stroked it, petted it, kept his eyes glued to it, and attempted to hang on its neck all the colorful, shiny, tinkling little objects he had been given by well-wishers. Only now that he could decorate the little horse with them did these objects seem to reach their true value for him. When the time came for him to leave the police station, he tried to pick up the horse in order to take it home with him. When he realized that his arms and legs were too weak to carry away his beloved horse over the threshold of the door, he wept bitterly.[21] After that, whenever he visited the police station, he would immediately sit down on the ground next to his beloved horse paying not the slightest attention to the people present. Later one of the policemen was to say, in an official deposition, first before the police and then before the court, that "Kaspar would sit for hours beside the oven playing with his horse, without paying the slightest attention to what was going on around him or near him."

In the tower, too, in his small bed- and living room, he was soon provided with not one but several different kinds of horses. These horses were, from then on, as long as he was home, constant companions and playmates that he never let out of his sight or presence. Whenever he was observed, through a hidden hole in the door, he was continually occupied with them. One day, one hour, was like any other. Kaspar would sit on the ground next to his horses, legs stretched out straight in front of him, constantly adorning them this way or that with ribbons, strings, colorful bits of paper, or hanging coins, small bells, or gold sequins around their necks. Sometimes he seemed lost in the deepest thought about how best to improve their finery by putting something here or rather placing it there. He would also often push them back and forth by his side, without moving from his place or changing positions, but very carefully and quietly — as he later explained, so that the rolling of their wheels did not give rise to any noise for which he might be beaten. He would never eat his bread without first holding up each and every bite to the mouth of the little horses; never did he drink his water without first dipping their mouths into it, which he carefully wiped each and every time. As one of these little horses was made of plaster, its mouth soon became soft from dipping into the water. He did not know what caused this, since he remarked that the mouths of the other horses got wet without affecting the form of their mouths. Weeping, he showed this misfortune with the little plaster horse to his jailer, who, in order to calm him down, helped him understand that this little horse did not like water. After this he ceased dipping its mouth in water, since he believed that the horse was showing him by this visible deformity in its mouth that it did not want to drink. The jailer, who often saw how hard Kaspar sought to feed his horses bread, tried to help him understand that these horses could not eat. But Kaspar attempted to refute him by pointing to the bread crumbs on the muzzle of his horse. One of his horses had a bridle in its wide-open mouth; Kaspar constructed a bridle out of gold spangles and tried in every possible way to get his other horse to open its mouth so that he could put the bridle inside—an attempt he tirelessly took great pains with for two days running. Once when he dozed off on a rocking horse and fell down and hurt his finger, he complained that the horse had bitten him. One day he was pushing one of his other horses across the floor when its back legs got caught in a crack in the floor and its front legs reared up. This caused Kaspar such enormous delight that he constantly repeated this marvelous spectacle for the entertainment of all his visitors. Since the jailer showed displeasure over Kaspar's always displaying the same thing over and over to everybody, Kaspar stopped, but cried over the fact that he could no longer show how his horse reared. Once when it was rearing the horse fell. Kaspar ran to help, showing great tenderness and expressing his sorrow that the horse had hurt itself. He became completely inconsolable when once he saw the jailer hammer a nail into one of the horses.

From this and many other circumstances it was possible to infer—an inference soon proved completely correct—that the notion of living and dead, animate and inanimate, organic and inorganic, natural objects and artificial ones, were all strangely intertwined in his childlike soul.

He differentiated animals from humans merely by their shape, men and women by their clothes. He preferred the varied, eye-catching colors of female clothing to those of the male, because of which he later on often expressed a desire to become a girl, in order to be able to wear women's clothes.

That little children might become adults never seemed plausible to him. When assured that he too had once been a child, after all, and that he himself would probably grow significantly taller than he already was, his denial was most emphatic. After many attempts he became convinced a few months later, only after observing his own rather quick growth by marking his height on the wall.

Not the slightest spark of religion or the most minute notion of [church] dogma was to be found in his soul. In the very first weeks after his appearance in Nuremberg several clergymen tried preternaturally to find and encourage it in him. No animal could have understood and grasped less of their questions, speeches, and sermons than Kaspar did. What he brought with him of religion—if it would not blaspheme the word to say it—consisted only in [the religious pamphlets that] had been put into his pockets, with whatever malice disguised as piety tinged with stupidity, when he was abandoned in Nuremberg.

Since the jailer Hiltel was able to closely observe him for several weeks, perhaps it would not be without interest to listen to the deposition of this simple but understanding man, concerning Kaspar Hauser's behavior during his stay in the tower. Among other things, he made the following official declaration:

> Shortly after I was able to observe the so-called Kaspar Hauser
> quietly for some time, I reached the conclusion that he is not so

much simple or deprived by nature, as, for unfathomable reasons, forcibly deprived of all education and opportunities for mental development. To relate all the proofs and experiences based on observations of Hauser that led me to this unquestionable position would take me too far afield. In the first days that he stayed with me, he behaved exactly like a small child, displaying a great natural innocence in everything he did. On the fourth or fifth day he was moved from his small cell on the upper floor of the tower prison down to the lower floor where I live with my family and put in a small room equipped so that I was able to observe him at all times without his noticing it. It was here that, under the mayor's order, I observed him frequently and found that when he was alone, his behavior was unaltered. He took just as much pleasure in his toys when he was by himself as he had when he played with them in the same natural and unaffected way in my presence. In the first days, when he was avidly occupied with his toys, anything could take place around him and he would take no notice of it. Nevertheless I must point out that this pleasure in childish toys was of short duration. As soon as his attention was diverted to more serious and useful objects, and he was made receptive to them, he took no more pleasure in playing. His entire behavior was, one might say, a perfect mirror of childlike innocence. He had nothing false in him. Whatever he felt in his heart, he simply said it straight out, so far as his sparse vocabulary permitted. A sure proof of his innocence and ignorance was provided by the occasion when my wife and I took off his clothes for the first time and washed his body. His behavior on this occasion was that of a child, completely natural and without embarrassment.[22] After he had received the toys and when other people were allowed to visit him, I sometimes let my eleven-year-old son Julius visit him too. He virtually taught him to speak, drew the letters of the alphabet for him, and attempted to communicate ideas to him insofar as he understood them himself. At the same time I sometimes permitted my three-year-old daughter Margareta to go into his room. In the beginning he played with her happily, and she taught him to string glass beads. As he began to tire of his inanimate toys, he no longer found this entertaining. Toward the end of his stay with me he took the greatest pleasure and diversion in drawing and etching, the results of which he hung on the walls of his little room.

Chapter IV

After his first few days in the tower, Kaspar was treated not as a prisoner but as an abandoned, neglected child in need of care and education. The jailer took him along to his own table, where he did not partake of the meals but learned to sit properly, to use his hands in a civilized way, and to imitate the good manners of educated people. He played happily with the jailer's children, who also took pleasure in amusing themselves with the good-natured youth whose ignorance and naïveté they found entertaining. Kaspar was particularly fond of the oldest of the children, eleven-year-old Julius. It flattered Julius's incipient vanity to be able to teach the rudiments of language to Kaspar—this young vigorous adolescent on whose chin a beard was already beginning to sprout.

Soon curiosity led crowds of people to him on a daily, even an hourly, basis, only a few of whom were content just to stare at the tame wild man. Most of them attempted, each in his own way, to engage him in various ways. For some he was just an object of amusement or the subject of experiments that were anything but scientific. Still, there were also many who attempted to communicate sensibly with him, to awaken his mind, and encouraged him to communicate with them. One person would tell him words and figures of speech, which he would then have him repeat; another would attempt through signs and pantomime or whatever else worked to make Kaspar know what he did not know, understand what he did not understand. With each thing, with each toy with which, in human sympathy, the good citizens of Nuremberg approached the unfortunate young man, he gained new material for thought; he enriched his vocabulary and store of ideas. The most advantageous aspect of this lively human interchange was the fact that his mind, gradually awakening to a clearer consciousness, was stimulated in a variety of ways to observe, to reflect, and to think.

Through his ever-increasing need to communicate, which grew in ability from day to day, the well-known language teacher creatively and instinctively at work in the spirit of man was kept constantly busy.

About two weeks after Kaspar's arrival in Nuremberg, good fortune brought him the worthy Professor Daumer, a young, bright scholar who found it in his kind heart to devote himself to the mental development, education, and instruction of this unfortunate person, to the extent that the boisterous crowds of the curious and other disturbing and inhibiting circumstances permitted. To everybody's astonishment, Kaspar was found to have an active mind, extreme diligence in grasping everything new to him, and a lively, powerful, youthful memory for remembering once he had grasped something. In a short time he managed to learn as much as he needed to barely express his thoughts. It is true, however, that for the longest time his attempt at speech was nothing but a fragmentary, sorry, childishly awkward jumble of words, such that one was never sure what his bits of convoluted speech intended to express. It was always necessary for the listener to guess much and suppose the rest. At that point it was impossible to expect any fluency of speech or narration from him.

The first mayor of the city, Mr. Binder, as chief of the municipal police, had to concern himself with Kaspar not only out of pure human interest but primarily for official reasons. He gave his particular attention and sympathy to this extremely rare subject of police inquiry. It was crystal clear that ordinary official procedures could not handle this case, which was anything but commonplace,[23] and that to solve the mystery at least to some extent, he could not content himself with formal depositions, hearings, and other such official procedures, at least for the moment. For the time being, therefore, Mr. Binder was absolutely right to choose the path of a less constrained extrajudicial approach. He had Kaspar brought to his house on an almost daily basis, made him feel at home in his presence as well as that of his family, spoke to him and let him speak, no matter how well or badly this went, and took pains, through abundant questions repeated many times, to discover some information about his life and arrival in Nuremberg. Mr. Binder did, in the end, after much effort, succeed, or at least think he succeeded, in distilling from Kaspar's various answers and statements the material for an account that, on July 7 of the same year, 1828, was announced to the world in the form of a public declaration.[24]

This official story, if one wants to call it that, contains some unbelievable and contradictory things. Many details were also given with such completeness and assurance that it is hard to ascertain what came from the questioner and what from Kaspar Hauser—how much really flows from his dim memories and how much he was unwittingly talked into, or how much was adapted from the many questions; what was added to or created through suppositions; what was grounded in simply misunderstood comments he made, since he was an animallike man barely capable of speech, still unacquainted with the most commonplace natural phenomena, and impoverished in everyday concepts. Nevertheless the story told in [Binder's] declaration agrees by and large—that is, with respect to the *essential major circumstances*—with what Hauser himself, duly sworn, was to write later in an essay, incorporated into official court depositions that were taken in the year 1829, as well as with what he has told me and many other people on different occasions, all of them in essential agreement.[25]

In brief, here is what Kaspar Hauser told Daumer (which Daumer recounted in the third person):

He does not know who he is or where he comes from. He first "came into the world" in Nuremberg.[26] It wasn't until then that he learned for the first time that apart from himself and "the man with whom he had always been" there were other people and creatures in the world. As far back as he could remember, he had always lived only in a hole (a small, humble room he would sometimes call a *cage*), where, dressed only in a shirt and leather pants cut with a hole in the back, barefoot, he sat on the ground.[27] In his room he never heard a sound, either from humans or animals, nor anything else. He never saw the sky nor was he aware of the brightness of sunlight as in Nuremberg. He never experienced any difference between day and night, even less did he have occasion to see the beautiful "lights in the heaven." Next to him on the ground was a hole (probably with a bucket) in which he relieved himself. Whenever he woke up, there was bread and a pitcher of water next to him. From time to time the water had a very bad taste. At those times, shortly after drinking some of it, he was not able to keep his eyes open and had to fall asleep.[28] When he was once more awake, he noticed that he was wearing a clean shirt and that his nails had been cut.[29] He never saw the face of the man who brought him food and drink. In his hole, he had two horses made of wood, and several ribbons. It was with these horses that he played continuously when he was awake. His only activity was to push them by his side and to place or tie the ribbons he had—first one way and then another. One day passed him by like the next. He never missed anything, was not sick, and, except for a single exception, had never experienced physical pain. In fact, things were much better for him there than in the world where he had to suffer so much. Since he had no knowledge of time, he knows nothing of how long he lived in that world. He could not say when and how he had been brought there. Nor did he have any memory of ever being in any other circumstance or in any other place. The man with whom he had always been never hurt him. But one day, which must have been shortly before he was taken away, when he had dragged his horse on the floor too hard and made too much noise, the man came and hit him on his arm with a cane or a piece of wood. This was the wound he brought to Nuremberg.

About the same time, the man showed up in his dungeon one day, placed a little table over his feet, spread out something white in front of him, which he now recognizes to be paper, and standing behind him so that he could not be seen by him, held his hand, and with a thing that he put between his fingers (a pencil), moved it back and forth on the paper. He (Hauser) did not know what it was, but was immensely pleased when he saw the black figures suddenly appear on the white paper. When he felt his hand free once again, and the man let go of him, in joy over his new discovery, he never tired of drawing these figures over and over again. So engrossed was he in this new task that he almost neglected his horses, even though he did not know what those lines meant. On several occasions, the man repeated his visits in the same way.[30]

After this the man came another time, lifted him off his pallet, set him on his feet, and attempted to teach him to stand up, which he repeated on several occasions. He accomplished this by way of holding him firmly around the chest, placing his legs behind Kaspar's, and raising them so that they could move forward.

Finally the man appeared for the last time, put Kaspar's arms around his shoulders, tied them together, and with him on his back in this manner, dragged him out of the hole. He carried him up or down a hill.[31] He does not know what was happening to him. It went completely dark, and he was placed on the ground. As became clear from several occasions in Nuremberg, in Kaspar's vocabulary "going dark" meant "losing consciousness" as well.

The account of his further voyage is confined essentially to the fact that on more than one occasion he put his face on the ground and lay down when it grew dark, that he ate bread and drank water a number of times, that the man "with whom he had always been" often took pains to teach him to walk, which always hurt him very much, and so on.

This man did not say anything to him beyond constantly prompting him to repeat the words: Reutä wähn, etc. etc. On this voyage he (Kaspar) saw this man's face as little as he did earlier in prison. Every time he led him, the man sternly ordered him to look in front of him at the ground and his feet. He strictly obeyed, partly out of fear, partly because he had more than enough to do with himself and his feet. Before he was found in Nuremberg, the man put the clothes on him in which he appeared in Nuremberg. Having his boots put on hurt him very much. The man had put him down on the ground, seized him from behind, pulled his feet up with great force and pushed his feet into the boots. Then they set forth again, only this time it hurt more than before. Now he took in as little of anything around him as he had before. He observed nothing and saw nothing, so that he was unable to say from which area, from which direction, from which road he had come into Nuremberg. The only thing he was conscious of was the fact that the man who led him finally pushed the letter into his hand and disappeared, whereupon a citizen of the town saw him (Kaspar) and brought him to the police station in the New Gate.

This story of the mysterious captivity and abandonment of a young man is indeed not just gruesome, but also a strange and dark puzzle. It gives rise to an extraordinary number of questions and conjectures, but nothing that can be answered with any certainty. And naturally, as long as there is no solution, it has, in common with other puzzles, the quality of being puzzling. The *soul-condition* of Kaspar during his life in the dungeon was one of a human being who as a child sank into a profound slumber, a dreamless sleep or at least one during which he had no succession of dreams. He just slept on in a stupor, until the day he suddenly awoke in terror and pain, to the wild clamor of a colorful world. Now in a daze, he does not know what happened to him. Anybody who would expect such a person, waking to full consciousness, to thereupon provide a complete, detailed, utterly convincing historical account of his sleep and his dreams would be demanding nothing less than that a sleeping person be awake while asleep and a waking person be asleep while awake.

In certain parts of Germany, which a second Dupin[32] in his map of the Enlightenment could shade in dark gray, such accounts as the one Hauser told about himself are anything but unheard of. For example, Dr. Horn,[33] just a few years ago, saw in the Salzburg Infirmary a not unattractive twenty-two-year-old-girl who was raised in a pigsty among pigs and forced to sit there with her legs crossed until she was sixteen years old. One of her legs was completely crooked, she grunted like a pig, and behaved without manners when appearing as a person. Compared to such cruel acts, the crimes committed against Kaspar can be counted among the more caring acts of humanity.

It really is no wonder that Kaspar is unable to say anything at all about the way and manner he reached Nuremberg, that he can furnish so little about his adventures on the trip, about the places through which he came, and about all other matters we are generally able to observe on our trips by coach or on foot. The real wonder would be if he were able to do so. Had Kaspar already been awakened to a completely clear, reasonable state of self-awareness in his dungeon, had he, in his tomb, like Sigismund in his tower,[34] been able to grow into the mental maturity of an adolescent through good upbringing and education, he would, as a result of sudden emergence from his narrow, dank dungeon into the open air, still immediately have fallen into unconsciousness, or at least into a state resembling complete inebriety. The unaccustomed exposure to external air must have stunned him, and the bright sunlight must have blinded his eyes. But even if his eyes had not been blinded, had they seen, he still would not have seen or at least would not have *noticed* or *taken in* anything. At that time nature and all its phenomena could only have appeared to him as a colorfully spotted confused mass, from which he would not have been able to distinguish any particular thing that flitted momentarily in front of his face. This, as we shall presently demonstrate on the basis of incontrovertible experiences, can be proved to have been the case even when he reached Nuremberg.

From what general area Kaspar was brought to Nuremberg, what road he took, through which gate he came, whether he arrived on foot or by wagon, or whether he made his trip by both foot and wagon, these things and others remain questions, even if they could be answered with certainty, that would be of interest only to an investigating magistrate pursuing the truth, and less to the general public. Kaspar himself remembers only that he walked. There is nothing in his account to establish how long he walked or approximately what distance he covered. The fact that he has no memory at all of riding does not prove in any way that he may not actually have been driven, possibly even the greater part of the way. Even today, when Kaspar rides, especially in the fresh air, he soon falls into a virtual deathlike sleep. He cannot be awakened whether the wagon moves or stands still. When he is in that state, he can be picked up and put down, no matter how roughly, without his taking the slightest notice, as if he were nothing but an inanimate bundle. Once sleep has taken hold of him, no noise, racket, or din, no thunder is loud enough to wake him.

Since, as one can conclude from his own account, Kaspar lost consciousness as soon as he was in the fresh air, he was probably once again given the foul-tasting water (opium diluted with water) as a precaution. One could then throw him into a carriage with some confidence and take a few day-trips, even many such trips, without having to be concerned that he would wake up, scream, or in some way make himself disagreeable to his abductor.

Mr. Schmidt von Lübeck, in an astute essay entitled *Über Kaspar Hauser* (Altona, August 1831) attempts to substantiate his conjecture that *Kaspar* was brought from a place *very close* to Nuremberg. For this, as for many other conjectures, the account given above provides ample room. It is certain that the person who brought Hauser to Nuremberg had to have been closely acquainted with Nuremberg and its neighborhoods. It is also highly probable that he had once served as a soldier in one of the regiments stationed there.

The crimes committed against the person of Kaspar, as far as they have been charged, are to be judged according to the Bavarian Criminal Code[35] as follows:

(1) The crime of *illegal confinement* (Criminal Code, Part I, Articles 192 to 195). This is doubly aggravated, first with regard to *duration,* insofar as the imprisonment is concerned, begun, from earliest childhood and continued, so it appears, until adolescence; secondly by its *manner,* insofar as it was accompanied by particular *"abuse."* In the latter case we must take into account not only the bestial lair that crippled the unfortunate child's body, not only the miserable food that was barely acceptable for a dog, but above all, the cruel denial of all those gifts, even the smallest, which nature extends to the poorest with a generous hand, the withholding of all means of mental development and education, the unnatural retention of a human soul in a state of bestial unreason.

(2) That also objectively meets the requirements of the crime of felonious *abandonment,* which, according to the Criminal Code, Part I, Art. 174, can be committed not only against children but also against *adults,* if they "are incapable, due to illness or feebleness, of taking care of themselves," in which category Kaspar certainly belonged, since at that time he was as stupid as an animal, practically blind, and barely able to walk upright. The abandonment of Kaspar was at the same time an abandonment that should be classified as *exposing his life to danger.* This person was, by virtue of his mental and physical condition at the time, in danger of falling into the Pegnitz River, near where he was abandoned, or of being run over by a horse or a carriage.

Were the customary law or the Bavarian Criminal Code to recognize a special *crime against the powers of the mind,*[36] or more precisely a *crime against the life of the soul,* then this would have to occupy the first rank in legal judgment next to the crime of imprisonment—or rather, the crime of imprisonment would have to be subordinated to this crime. The deprivation of freedom of movement, though in and of itself an irreparable injury, cannot possibly be compared to the incalculable totality of irreplaceable and inestimable benefits which were completely taken away from this unfortunate victim. Robbed of his freedom in this way, his capacity for the enjoyment of these benefits was destroyed, or at least crippled, for the rest of his life. This grave offense, this murderous assault, was carried out not only on a person's external physical self, but aimed at his innermost essence, his spiritual being, the holy temple which houses natural reason itself. Our writers classify such crimes only as a *deprivation of reason (noochiria)*, and, with [Carl August] Tittman[37] make them dependent in essence upon *"effectuating a loss of reason or insanity."* But the example of Kaspar Hauser shows that this concept is far too narrow. A legislator who would increase the reach of his system by including a category of crime such as this one really needs to adopt a much broader and all-encompassing point of view. Kaspar was imprisoned for his entire childhood, but he did not fall into dementia or go crazy. Once freed he emerged, as we shall see more clearly in the following pages, from the state of bestiality that he was in *and has developed to the point where he can be considered everywhere, with certain reservations, as a reasonable, sensible, ethical, and civilized person.* Nonetheless, nobody will fail to recognize that it is primarily the criminal assault on the mental life of this person, the sin against his higher spiritual nature, that constitutes the most outrageous aspect of the violation against him. To deprive a human being of nature and the company of other sentient beings, through artificial means; to remove him from his human destiny; to withhold from him all the spiritual nourishment that nature has provided for the growth and prosperity of the human soul, for its training, development and education. Such a deprivation, independent of its consequences, deserves in and of itself the most serious punishment as an invasion into what is most holy, most unique to a human being, an invasion of the freedom and destiny of the human soul. Yet added to this is the following: Kaspar, submerged in a bestial slumber of the soul during childhood, wasted [*verlebt*] the most beautiful part of his whole life without having lived it [*gelebt*]. He was like a dead man during this period. He slept through his childhood, it passed him by, without his really having had one, since he could never become conscious of it. Torn out of his life by the terrible deed done to him, this gap cannot be bridged. The time that was not lived cannot be called back to be lived over. He cannot catch up on the childhood that escaped him while his soul lay asleep. No matter how long he might live, he remains a person without a childhood and without a youth, a monstrous being, who, contrary to the laws of nature, has begun his life only in the middle of it. Insofar as his entire earlier life was thus taken away from him he was the victim of what I may be permitted to call a partial soul-murder [*Seelenmord*]. The act committed against Kaspar is to be distinguished from a crime committed against a person whose reason is healthy and who is later driven into dull idiocy, or into a state without consciousness or reason, by virtue of the fact that the soul murder was committed at a different period of life. In the first case the life of a human being's soul is snuffed out before it has even begun, in the second case, at the end of that life. Moreover, we should not forget a major consideration. Childhood and youth have been designed by nature as the time for development and education, both of the physical self and of the spiritual life, since nature does not allow for omission of these stages. Kaspar emerged into the world as a child at the age of early manhood. Now and for all time the stages of his life have been jumbled and displaced. Because he could not begin his childhood until he was physically mature, his mental development will lag behind his physical age for the rest of his life, and his age will always outdistance his mind. Mental and physical life, which in the natural stages of development keep pace with each other, in Kaspar's person have been as it were torn apart and placed in unnatural opposition to each other. The childhood that he slept through, precisely because he slept through it, will never have its day. He will have to repeat it, and, always untimely, it will follow him in later years not as a smiling spirit but as a frightening apparition. If we take into consideration, in addition to all this, the devastation that fate has brought upon his youth and spirit, which will become clear later in this account, we can conclude from this example that the idea of *theft of the intellect* does not by any means exhaust the notion of a crime against the life of the soul.

What other crimes could possibly remain hidden behind the wrong committed against Kaspar? What purpose could the secret imprisonment of Hauser have been designed to further? These questions would lead us too far into the giddy heights of speculation, or into certain hallowed halls that could not tolerate such illumination.[38]

This remarkable crime, scarcely believable in the history of human atrocities, presents yet another strange aspect to the scholar of law as well as to the forensic medical doctor. The examination and judgment of states of mind usually looks only at the criminal to determine whether or not he can be considered responsible for his actions. But here we have before us a case that is by its very nature unique, in which, for the most part, the *evidence for the crime lies hidden in the human soul.* The facts of this case, therefore, can only be investigated by purely psychological means and can only be based on, and determined through, observation of the mental and emotional expressions of the victim.

As for the history of the crime, we have at present no information other than the account of that person against whom it was committed. But the truth of the narration is vouched for by the personality of the narrator upon whose body, spirit and emotions, as we will learn in greater detail, the crime itself is clearly written, in a way that cannot be misunderstood. Only he who has experienced and suffered what Kaspar did can be like Kaspar. Whoever shows himself to be like Kaspar must have lived under identical circumstances to those Kaspar related. Thus does our evaluation of the trustworthiness of the narrator of an almost unbelievable event rest once again almost exclusively on psychological grounds. Events supported this way acquire authenticity which outweighs any other kind of proof. Witnesses can lie. Documents can be falsified. But no other person, unless he were at the very least an omnipotent and omniscient magician, could lie in this fashion, so that no matter how carefully examined, the lie resembles the purest truth, indeed would seem to be the very personification of truth itself. He who doubts Kaspar's story must doubt Kaspar's person. But then such a skeptic, were he faced with a man lying in front of him bleeding from a hundred wounds, convulsed in his death throes, must wonder with equal logic whether the man is really wounded and dying. Maybe he is just pretending to be wounded and dying.?[39] But it won't do for me to anticipate the reader's judgment. My description of Kaspar's person has just begun.

Chapter V

When Kaspar Hauser had already been in Nuremberg well over a month, I heard tell of this foundling among the latest gossip. The highest authorities of the province had not yet received any official notice of this event. It was therefore purely in my capacity as a private individual, out of human and scientific interest, that I traveled to Nuremberg on June 11, 1828, to observe this phenomenon, which was in its own way unique.

At that time Kaspar was still living in the Luginsland Tower at the Vestner Gate. Anyone who wanted to have a look at him was given permission to do so. In truth, Kaspar enjoyed from morning until night hardly less clientele than the kangaroo or the tame hyena in Mr. von Aken's celebrated menagerie.[40]

I, too, made my way to him, accompanied by Colonel von D., two ladies, and two children. Fortunately we arrived during a time when nobody else was there at the spectacle.

Kaspar's dwelling was a small but neat and bright little room whose windows opened out onto a country scene, offering the eye an expansive and friendly landscape. We found him barefoot, dressed in an old pair of long pants, and nothing else on but a shirt.

As far as he could reach, Kaspar had decorated the walls of the room with sheets of painted pictures, gifts from his many visitors. Each morning he would glue them onto the wall. For glue he would use his own saliva, which *at that time* was as thick as glue.[41] As soon as it began to grow dark, he took them back down and folded them up next to him. There was a built-in bench against all four walls of the room, and in one of its corners was his bed, a straw sack with a pillow and a woolen blanket. The entire rest of the surface of the bench was covered with a large quantity of every kind of toy: hundreds of tin soldiers, little wooden dogs, horses, and other toys made in Nuremberg [the city was famous for such toys]. During the day he no longer [as he had earlier] played with them very much, but in the evening he took considerable pains to put all these things, big and small, away carefully, just so he could take them out again and put them next to one another in rows in a certain order when he woke up. Moreover, the good citizens of Nuremberg, out of a sense of charity, had given him various items of clothing that he kept under his pillow and showed us with a childlike pleasure, not without a little vanity. On the bench, among the toys, different kinds of coins lay strewn around, which he favored with no attention. I took a dirty silver *Kronentaler* [crown] and a brand-new *Vierundzwanziger* [twenty-four-penny coin] in my hand and asked him which he liked best. He chose the smaller, shiny coin. He said the larger one was nasty and made a disgusted face. When I tried to make him understand that the bigger coin was worth more, that one could buy far more pretty things with it than with the smaller coin, he listened to me carefully, true, but soon looked bewildered, and finally gave me to understand that he didn't know what I meant.

When we entered his room, he seemed anything but shy or timid. Quite the contrary, he ran up to us trustingly with pleasure at our visit. At first he was preoccupied with the bright uniform of the colonel. He could not stop admiring his shining golden helmet. But then he turned his attention to the colorful clothes the women were wearing. At first, I, in my modest black frock coat, was deemed unworthy of a single glance. We introduced ourselves to him one at a time, each with name and title. At each introduction Kaspar came right up to the person being introduced and stared at him, taking in every feature of the face in a quick glance: forehead, eyes, nose, mouth, chin, and so on. I clearly noticed that it was only after he had read them one by one that he was able to put the parts of the features into a whole. He thereupon repeated the names of the people to whom he had been introduced. As later experiences would demonstrate, now that he knew that person, he knew that person forever.

He turned his eyes away from the bright light as much as possible. He very carefully avoided every ray of sunlight that came through the window. If such a ray accidentally hit his eyes, he blinked rapidly, wrinkled his forehead, and showed obvious pain. In addition, his eyes were slightly inflamed and on the whole showed great sensitivity to light.

At that time the left side of his face, which was later to be perfectly symmetrical, was strikingly different from the right. The left side was conspicuously twisted and contorted. Frequent spasms struck it like lightning. The left side of his entire body, especially his arm and hand, was visibly involved. If he was shown anything that stimulated his curiosity, if a word was spoken that he took notice of and did not understand, he immediately went into spasms that ended more often than not in a kind of rigidity. Then he stood motionless. No facial muscle moved, his eyes stared lifelessly without blinking. It was as if he were a statue, unseeing and unhearing, which could not be stimulated to life. This state could be observed whenever he was in deep thought, whenever he sought the appropriate word for a new object, when he tried to connect something unknown with something already known, or tried to understand something as a result of something else.

Those words he was able to speak he enunciated distinctly and clearly without pausing or stammering. But he was still far from being able to speak in coherent sentences, and his vocabulary was as poor as his supply of concepts. It was therefore difficult to make oneself understood. No sooner had one spoken a few sentences which he seemed to understand, than one added something that was foreign to him, when he would fall prey to spasms in his efforts to understand. Conjunctions, particles, and auxiliary verbs were lacking in almost everything he said. His verbal forms comprised little more than the infinitive. The badly tousled and jumbled syntax was the worst. His normal manner of speaking was to say, "Kaspar very good," instead of, "I am very good." Or: "Kaspar already say Juli" instead of "I want to tell it to Julius" (the son of the jailer). He hardly used the pronoun "I" but spoke nearly always of himself in the third person. When he spoke to other people he did not use the pronoun "you" but addressed them in the third person. Instead of "you" he would use the third person: Mister Colonel, Mrs. General [the wife of the general], etc. If you wanted him to understand that you were referring to him, you could not say "you" but had to say "Kaspar."[42] One and the same word was frequently used in various different meanings, which often led to a ridiculous and funny Quiproquo [confusion]. Sometimes he would use a word that referred only to a species for the whole genus. For example, he employed the word "mountain" for any curve or elevation, so that a large-bellied gentleman whose name he could not remember was called "the man with the big mountain." A woman whose shawl hung down so low that the end trailed on the floor he called "the woman with the pretty tail." It will certainly be expected of me not to have failed to give him every opportunity, through various questions, to tell me the story of his life. But what I was able to get out of him was such an indeterminate, jumbled, confused gibberish that I could only guess what most of it meant, and much I could not understand at all since I was not yet familiar with his way of talking.

It seemed to me not unimportant to put his taste in *colors* to the test. In this respect he exhibited the same disposition as children and so-called savages. He liked the *color red* best of all, especially a loud red. He disliked yellow, except in the form of gold striking the eye, in which case he could not make up his mind between this yellow and the loud red. He was indifferent to white, but green was almost as abhorrent to him as black. This predilection, especially his preference for red, stayed with him for a long time, as the later observations of Professor Daumer were to show, even after his education had progressed considerably. If he had a choice, he would have dressed himself and those he liked in scarlet or purple from head to toe. He took no pleasure in nature because the primary color of its garment was green. To find nature beautiful, he would have had to see her through red-tinted glasses. In Professor Daumer's house, which he exchanged for the Luginsland Tower shortly after I visited him, he was not very pleased. He explained this by the fact that there his view was of the garden, and of its many, as he said, "nasty" green trees and plants. On the other hand, he was immensely taken by the dwelling of a friend of his teacher, which was on a narrow unappealing street, because the view from there looked out on the pretty red-painted houses opposite and all around it. When somebody pointed out to him a tree full of red apples, he said he liked it enormously, except that the tree, he thought, would be even prettier if the leaves were red as well. When he, who drank only water, saw somebody drinking red wine, he said: "If only I could drink things that are so pretty to look at!" He only wished that his favorite animal, the horse, were scarlet red instead of black, brown, or white.

The *curiosity,* the *thirst for knowledge,* as well as the steadfast tenacity he showed for things he had made up his mind to learn or comprehend, were beyond all imagining and were deeply moving to watch. As I noted earlier, he no longer occupied himself with his toys during the day. He filled the daytime hours with writing, drawing, and other studious activities that Professor Daumer busied him with. He complained bitterly to us that his many visitors left him no peace and that he was unable to study at all. It was touching to hear his often repeated complaint that other people knew so much and there was so much he still had to learn. Besides writing, one of his favorite occupations was drawing, to which he brought as much talent as tenacity. For the last several days he made it his task to copy a lithographic portrait of Mayor Binder. A whole package of half-folio sheets were filled with copies he drew. He laid them out in rows on top of one another in the order in which he finished them. I went through them one by one. The first attempts looked exactly like the drawings of small children who think they have drawn a face when they have scrawled something on paper supposed to be an oval figure by drawing a couple of round flourishes next to some long and cross strokes. But progress was evident in almost every subsequent attempt, so that eventually those lines resembled a human face more and more, and in the end, while still somewhat imperfect and crude, they showed some similarity to the original lithograph he was copying. I expressed my admiration for his last attempts to him, but he declared himself not yet satisfied and gave me to understand that he would have to draw the picture many more times until it was completely right, and then he would give it to the mayor as a present.

He was by no means happy with his life in the world. He longed to go back to the man with whom he had always been. "At home (in his hole)," he said, "I never had so many headaches, and nobody tormented me the way they do now in the world." He was referring to the discomforts and pain of the many new impressions that were completely unfamiliar to him, to the many different smells which were disgusting to him, as well as to the numerous visits by the merely curious, their ceaseless questions and some of their thoughtless and not entirely humane experiments. Moreover, the only thing he had to complain about with respect to the man with whom he had always been was the fact that he had not yet come to take him back home, and that he had never shown him or even spoken to him at all about so many of the beautiful things in the world. He wants to live in Nuremberg until he has learned what the mayor and the professor (Daumer) know. Then let the mayor bring him home and he will show the man what he learned in the meantime. When I said to him at this point: "Why would you want to return to this bad, awful man?" he retorted, mildly angered: "The man not bad, the man me no bad done."

We soon acquired the most extraordinary proof of his astonishing *memory*, which was as quick as it was tenacious. For each and every thing in his room, big and little, for each and every picture and drawing, he was able to tell us the name and title of the person who gave it to him as a present. If some of them shared the same last name, he would distinguish them either by their first names or by some other attribute. About an hour after we had left him, we met him again in the street as he was being taken to the mayor's house. We greeted him and when we asked him if he remembered our names, he greeted each one of us, without thinking or hesitating, with our full names, including all our titles, which could not have meant anything to him. Dr. Oster-hausen (the medical doctor), on another occasion, made the following observation: Kaspar was shown a bouquet of flowers and was told the name of each flower. Several days later he recognized each and every flower and was able to give its correct name. But this memory diminished later on, seemingly in inverse proportion as his mind became enriched, as it had greater tasks to perform.

His *obedience* toward those who exercised fatherlike authority over him, especially the mayor, Professor Daumer and his jailer, Hiltel, was strict and without limits. "Because the mayor or the professor said so" was for him the only reason for doing or not doing something, and made all further questions or considerations unnecessary. When I asked him why he believed that he had to obey so completely, he gave the following answer: "The man with whom I have always been taught me that I had to do everything I was told."[43]

However, Kaspar Hauser's subjection to external authority was confined exclusively to doing or not doing something. It did not extend to *knowledge, beliefs*, and *opinions*. In order to accept something as certain and true, he had to be personally convinced, either through direct sensory mediation or through any other means that was compatible with his still almost totally empty head and his capacity for understanding. If one was unable to convince him by sensual experience or other means, he did not exactly object, but he would allow the matter to rest until he had learned more, as he was in the habit of saying. Among other things, I spoke to him of the coming winter, telling him that the roofs of the houses and all the streets of the city would often look totally white, white as the walls of his little room. He thought this would be quite lovely but made it clear that he would not really believe it until he had seen it. When the first snow fell the following winter, he displayed great joy that now the streets, the roofs, the trees, were so nicely "painted" and rushed down to the courtyard to get some of the "white paint." He quickly returned crying and bawling to his teacher, fingers outspread, screaming that the white paint had "bitten" his hand.

Most noticeable and completely inexplicable was his love of *order* and *cleanliness,* carried to pedantic extremes. Each of the many hundreds of things in his little household had its preordained place and was meticulously put away or carefully spread out, symmetrically arranged, and so forth. Uncleanliness, or what he took to be unclean, he found disgusting in himself just as in others. He noticed virtually every speck of dust on our clothes, and when he saw some grains of snuff tobacco on my collar, he indignantly drew my attention to it, hastily letting me know that I should get rid of those awful things.

Only some years later was I able to understand fully the importance of the most extraordinary experience of all. It came about through a test I am about to describe, which occurred to me through an obvious association between Kaspar, who spent his early years in a dark cellar and only emerged into the light of day when he was an adolescent boy, and the famous case of a blind man related by Cheselden. This man was blinded a few weeks after birth, and only when he was an adolescent did a fortunately successful cataract operation allow him to see again. In my experiment I told Kaspar to look in the direction of the window and pointed to the wide expansive view of beautiful summer landscape, resplendent and jewellike. I asked him whether what he saw outside was a beautiful sight. He obeyed, but immediately turned away from the window with obvious disgust, crying out: "Nasty! Nasty!" Then he pointed to the white wall of his little room and said: "There not nasty!" When I further inquired: "What there nasty," nothing came out beyond "Nasty, nasty!" At the time there seemed nothing to do but carefully notice this circumstance and wait for later explanation when Kaspar would be better able to make himself understood. I believed I clearly determined that his turning away from that landscape could not be explained solely by the irritating impression that the light made on his optic nerves. This time his facial expressions did not just reflect pain but disgust and horror. Moreover, he was standing at some distance from the window, to the side, so that he could see the scenery, but no direct ray of light could have fallen upon him. In 1831 Kaspar came to my house as a guest for a few weeks, when I had the uninterrupted opportunity to observe him in the closest possible way and so could complete or correct my earlier observations. Among other things I was able to return to this topic. I asked him if he still remembered my visit to him in the tower, and in particular the time I asked him how he liked the landscape outside the window? I reminded him that at the time he had turned away from this view with a look of disgust, and had repeated: "Nasty, nasty!" Why had he done that, I asked him. What had occurred to him? "It is true," he answered me,

that what I saw at that time was nasty. When I looked toward the window, it was always as if a window blind had been pulled down right in front of my eyes, and a painter had taken his brushes, and shaking them, provided a colorful mix of white, blue, green, yellow, red. Things I now see as separate and individual, then I could not recognize and distinguish. At the time, it was terrible to look at. I felt anxious because I thought that the window had been closed with these gaudy shutters to prevent me from being able to look out freely. The fact that what I was looking at were fields, mountains, houses, that something that then seemed to me bigger than something else was actually much smaller, that is, that something big was actually small, all of this I was easily able to convince myself of only later when I was able to walk outdoors, and I finally saw nothing of that shutter.

When I inquired further, he remarked: "In the beginning I was unable to distinguish what was really round and triangular, from something that was only painted round or triangular. The horses and men that were painted in my pictures appeared to me to be just like those horses and people carved in wood. The former seemed as round as the latter, and those appeared as flat as these." Still, when he was putting his things away, or taking them out, he soon *felt* a difference and so he rarely confused things in this way, and finally not at all.

We have here in Kaspar, then, a reincarnation of the blind man of Cheselden, blind from childhood, who regained his vision. Let us hear what Voltaire[44] (and Diderot,[45] who in this is at one with Voltaire) has to say about this blind man:

The young man whose cataracts were removed by the skillful surgeon Cheselden was unable to distinguish sizes, distances, situations, even figures for a long time. An object just one inch tall held before his eyes, which concealed a house from his view, appeared to him as tall as the house. All objects were present to his eye, and appeared to him to apply to that organ, as objects of touch apply to the skin. He could not distinguish (by sight) an object he had determined to be round by touching it with his hand, from objects he had determined were square; nor could he distinguish whether what he had determined to be above or below (by feel) was in fact above or below. He was finally able, with difficulty, to become convinced through his senses that his house was larger than his room, but he never grasped how his eyes could give him this information. It took many repeated experiences for him to convince himself that paintings represented real objects. As a result of repeatedly studying paintings, when he was fully convinced that he was not looking at just flat surfaces, he reached his hand out to touch them and was surprised to find a plane surface with no projections. Then he asked whether his touch or sight deceived him. Painting had the same effect on savages: The first time they saw them, they took the painted figures for living men, questioned them, and were surprised to get no answer! This error certainly did not derive from being unaccustomed to seeing [Translator's note: my translation from the French].

Children, too, in the first few weeks and months after their birth, see everything as if it were close up. They reach out to seize the shining ball of a distant church steeple, cannot distinguish what is really large or small from what is only apparently so, nor can they distinguish painted objects from real ones. This is because when it comes to objects of sight and touch, both senses must interact, one with the other, so that what is touched, or comprehended with the eyes can be recognized for the object that it really is. This experience is based on the elementary law of sight, about which the renowned Englishman Berkeley said the following:

It is, I think, agreed by all that *distance* of itself, and immediately cannot be seen. For *distance* being a line directed end-wise to the eye, it projects only one point in the fund of the eye. Which point remains invariably the same, whether the distance be longer or shorter. — I find it also acknowledged, that the estimate we make of the distance of *objects* considerably remote, is rather an act of judgment grounded on *experience*, than of sense. For example: When I perceive a great number of intermediate objects, such as houses, field, rivers, and the like, which I have experienced to take up a considerable space; I thence form a judgment or conclusion, that the *object* I see beyond them is at a great distance. Again, when an *object* appears faint and small, which at a near distance I have experienced to make a vigorous and large appearance, I instantly conclude it to be far off. And this, it is evident, is the result of *experience*, without which, from the faintness and littleness, I should not have inferred any thing concerning the distance of objects [Translator's note: original English from Berkeley].

The application of this optical law and its underlying experience to Kaspar's delusion of the senses is obvious. Since Kaspar had never gone any farther than from the tower to the mayor's house, or at most one or two other streets, and since his eyes were so sensitive, and since he was also afraid of falling, when he walked he kept his eyes always focused on his feet and constantly avoided looking directly into the ocean of light because he was hypersensitive to light, he therefore had no occasion to experience seeing objects in perspective and at a distance for a long time. All the various things in the world around him, including the somewhat small strip of blue sky that filled the window frame from bottom to top, must have seemed to him formless appearances, close to, next to, or on top of one another. He must have seen it to be like a blackboard covering his window, upon which multicolored objects, big and small, indistinguishable from one another, appeared as formless colorful blots.

Chapter VI

Kaspar Hauser became acquainted with a great variety of things and words in a short time. Soon he was making relatively good progress in speaking and understanding. This was the undeniable advantage of the almost constant company of the many people who thronged to see him all day long. Nonetheless it became clear that the medley of people to whom Kaspar Hauser was exposed in droves was probably not really suitable for furthering the natural development of this neglected youth.

Hardly an hour of the day went by without its bringing him something new from one person or another. But what he learned this way did not form even a small whole. On the contrary, it formed one disorderly, scattered, and colorful heap of hundreds and thousands of ideas—really only half ideas, or even quarter ideas carelessly piled on top of one another.

If the blank slate of his soul was soon written upon in this way, it was at the same time all too quickly marred and muddled, overflowing as it was with things that were, at least in part, worthless.

The unaccustomed effect of light and fresh air, the strange and often painful variety of impressions that crowded his senses constantly and all at once, the massive effort of his soul, thirsting for knowledge, to create a self out of itself, his attempt to grasp everything new that was offered (and everything was new!), to seize it, to take it in as if he were starved to the point of exhausting himself—all this was more than a frail body and a fragile, constantly excited and overexcited nervous system could bear.

From my visit to Kaspar on July 11, I took with me the conviction, which I attempted to convey to the appropriate authorities, that Kaspar Hauser would die of nervous fever, or would descend into insanity or idiocy, if his situation were not changed soon. After a few days my concerns proved largely justified. Kaspar became sick, or at least so sickly that a dangerous illness was feared.

His physician, Dr. Osterhausen, wrote in his first court-ordered expert opinion, reporting to the municipal magistrate on the current condition of Hauser's health, as follows:

Kaspar Hauser has been until now buried alive in a dungeon, isolated from the whole world, and left entirely to himself. Suddenly he was thrown into the world among people and found himself assaulted on all sides by a vast multiplicity of impressions which affected him not singly but all at once, impressions of the most diverse kind, fresh air, light, objects that surrounded him, all of which were new to him. Then the growing sense of an inner self, his aroused hunger for learning and for knowledge, his altered way of life, all of these impressions must necessarily have violently shaken him. Finally, because of his very sensitive nervous system, they must prove damaging to his health. When I saw him again, I found him completely changed. He was sad, very discouraged, and worn out. The excitability of his nerves had abnormally increased. His facial muscles were convulsing constantly. His hands shook so much that he could scarcely hold anything. His eyes were inflamed, could not bear the light, and hurt him considerably whenever he tried to read or observe an object more closely. His hearing was so sensitive that any loud talking caused him severe pain to such an extent that he could no longer even listen to the music he loved so passionately. He lacked the desire to eat, had infrequent, incomplete, and difficult bowel movements, complained about pains in his abdomen, and felt real discomfort. I was more than a little worried about his condition because it was not possible to deal with it through medicine, partly because he had an insurmountable disgust for everything except water and bread, and partly because even if he could have been convinced to take some medication, it was to be feared that even the most mild remedy could have too severe an effect upon him in the highly excited state of his nerves, etc.

On July 18, Kaspar Hauser was liberated from his room in the tower and handed over to the high-school teacher Daumer for board and education. Daumer was a man outstanding in both heart and mind, who had already taken the fatherly responsibility of instructing and molding Kaspar. Indeed, in the family of this man, in his dignified mother and sister, Kaspar Hauser found some compensation for what nature had given and human evil had taken away.

Some conception of the huge number of curious people to whom Kaspar Hauser was formerly exposed can be formed from the single circumstance that the mayor's office in Nuremberg found itself obliged, as soon as Kaspar was handed over to Professor Daumer, to publish the following public announcement in the newspapers on July 19 [1828]:

> The homeless Kaspar Hauser has been committed by the office of the city of Nuremberg to the care of a teacher who is particularly well qualified to promote the development of his mental and physical powers. So that they may proceed in their work without disturbance, so that Kaspar Hauser may enjoy and continue to enjoy the rest he so badly needs in every respect, the educator has been directed to permit no more visits to Hauser. The general public is therefore hereby put on notice to stay away from him and thereby avoid the humiliation of being sent away, if they intrude, through the intervention of the police.[46]

Instead of the pile of straw he had been given in the tower as a mattress, Kaspar Hauser was for the first time given a proper bed at Professor Daumer's house, which pleased him enormously. He would often state that the bed was the only nice thing that happened to him in this world, that everything else was just awful. Only since he slept in the bed did he begin to dream. *However, at first he did not recognize them as dreams.* When he awoke he told his teacher about them as if they were real events. Only later was he able to distinguish between dreaming and waking.[47]

One of the most difficult tasks was to get him used to normal food, which only succeeded slowly and with great effort and care.[48]

At first he consented to watered-down soup, which he seemed to like more as the days passed. Each day he imagined that it was better prepared, at times asking why it could not have been made so well from the start. He also liked anything made of flour or leguminous plants, and whatever resembled bread. When a few drops of meat broth were mixed into his water soup, he was able to eat a few small pieces of overcooked meat. As these offerings increased, little by little he became gradually accustomed to eating dishes with meat.

In the notes he put together on Kaspar Hauser, Professor Daumer makes the following remarks: "After Kaspar Hauser finally learned to eat enough meat, his intellectual alertness diminished. His eyes lost their shine and expression, his lively drive for activity slackened, and the intensity of his being turned into a need for distraction and finally indifference. His ability to comprehend also lessened significantly."[49] The possibility that all this was not the direct result of eating meat, but a consequence of the fact that his almost painful overexcitation had turned into a kind of dullness, cannot be decided, and rightly so. On the other hand, it can be assumed more reliably that eating cooked foods and various meat dishes must have affected his growth significantly. In just a few weeks in Daumer's house he grew more than two inches taller.

Since his inflamed eyes and the headache that resulted from any effort to use his physical senses made reading, writing, and drawing impossible, Mr. Daumer occupied him with things to do with pasteboard, in which he achieved no small measure of skill. He also taught him chess, which he learned quickly and practiced with delight. Moreover he was given easy garden work to do and was introduced to the many creations, the manifold appearances, and the wonders of nature. No day passed without his having been taught an untold number of new things, acquainting him with objects that made him disconcerted, admiring, or astonished.

Not a little effort and frequent correction was required to make him understand and become familiar with the distinction between organic and inorganic, something alive and something dead, as well as a voluntary movement and one occasioned from the outside. Many things that appeared to be men or animals—whether cut in stone, carved in wood, or painted—he still took to have a soul, endowed with all the qualities he perceived in himself or in other living creatures.

It seemed very strange to him that the horses, unicorns, ostriches, etc., which were chiseled in stone or painted on the walls of the houses of the city stayed in one place and did not run away. He expressed his indignation with one statue in the garden of his house, saying it looked so dirty, why didn't it wash itself? When he saw for the first time the large crucifix by Veit Stoss on the outside of the Saint Sebaldus Church, the sight sent him into outrage and despair. He implored that somebody take down the tortured man hanging there. Although somebody tried to explain to him that this was not a real person, but only an image and did not feel anything, he was not satisfied for the longest time. He took every movement he perceived in any object to be intentional, and the object displaying it alive. A sheet of paper that the wind carried off had run away from the table. If a baby carriage rolled down a hill, it had decided to take the trip for its own pleasure. For him a tree manifested life in that it moved its branches and leaves, and spoke when the wind whispered through its leaves. He was indignant with a boy who struck a tree trunk with a stick, saying he was hurting the tree. To judge from what he would say, the balls in a bowling alley rolled on their own, hurt the other balls, and finally stood still when they were tired of running. For some time Professor Daumer attempted in vain to convince him that the balls did not move voluntarily. He only succeeded when he got Kaspar to form his bread into a ball and roll it back and forth in front of himself. He was only able to understand that a humming top he had kept dancing for a while did not spin on its own when his arm was sore from pulling the string so many times. This made him conscious of the fact that it was his own physical power that had set the top spinning each time.

For the longest time he ascribed the very same qualities to animals that he did to people, and seemed only able to distinguish one from another by their different appearances. He was annoyed at the fact that the cat ate only with her mouth, without using her hands. He wanted to teach her to eat with her paws, tried to make her walk standing up, spoke to her as if she were an equal, and displayed indignation that she did not pay any attention to him and did not want to learn anything. On the other hand he greatly praised the obedience of a certain dog. When he first saw a gray cat, he asked why she did not wash herself so that she could become white. When he saw oxen resting on the pavement of the street, he asked why they did not go home and lie down there. It disgusted him greatly that horses, oxen, etc., dirtied the street and did not go to the outhouse like him. If he were told that something he asked an animal to do was beyond its capacity, he had a ready reply: They should just learn to do it, just as he too had learned a great deal after all, and still had much to learn.

At first he had even less concept of the origin and growth of objects in nature. He always spoke as if someone had stuck all the trees in the earth, human hands had made all the leaves, flowers, and blossoms and hung them on the trees. He first got some conception of the origin of plants when his *teacher* insisted that he plant some beans in a flowerpot with his own hands. He did so and saw them germinate and make leaves almost as he watched. He regularly asked about almost every new natural object that struck his attention: Who made that thing?

He had almost no sense of the beauty of nature. Nature seemed to mean something to him only when it made him curious and gave rise to the question: Who made this or that thing? The first time he saw a rainbow, he did, it is true, display pleasure for a few moments but shortly thereafter turned away from what he had seen. Asking who had made it seemed to touch his heart far more than its magnificent appearance.

One sight was a strange exception, and became a great and unforgettable occasion in his ever-growing mental life. It was in the month of August (1829), that his teacher showed him for the first time the star-studded sky on a clear, beautiful summer evening. His astonishment and rapture beggar any possible description. He could not get enough of looking at it, kept coming back to this view, kept looking in this way at the different constellations of stars and remarked on the particularly bright stars with their different colors. "That," he cried, "that is really the most beautiful thing I have seen in this world. But who put the many beautiful lights up there? Who lights them, and who puts them out again?" When he was told that just like the sun, which he already knew about, they always shine, but are not always visible, he asked all over again who put them up there, so they are always burning? At last he lapsed into a deep and genuine meditation, unmoving, his head bent, his eyes fixed. When he came back to himself, his rapture had turned to melancholy. Trembling, he sat down in a chair and asked: "Why did that bad man keep me locked up all the time and never showed me any of these beautiful things? I never did anything bad." At this point, he broke into uncontrollable sobbing difficult to still, and said that one should lock up the "man with whom I have always been" for a few days just for once, so that he would know how hard it is. Kaspar had never expressed any indignation toward that man before seeing this great heavenly spectacle, far less had he been willing to countenance any kind of punishment for him. Only weariness and sleepiness calmed him down. He went to sleep around eleven, something that had not happened before.

It would seem that only in Daumer's family did he begin to reflect upon his fate, to realize more and more how he had been deprived and how much had been taken from him, and to actually feel the pain of this recognition for the first time. It was only here that the concepts of family, of relationships and friendship, of the human ties between parents, children, and siblings, were brought home to him. It was only here that the words "mother," "sister," "brother," took on meaning for him, in that he saw how mothers, sisters, brothers, were bound together by mutual love, cared for one another, and lived to make each other happy. He wanted to know what, really, does one mean by "mother," by "brother," by "sister"? People attempted to satisfy him as much as possible with an appropriate answer. Soon thereafter he was found sitting in his chair, tears in his eyes, seemingly buried in thought. Asked what was wrong now, he answered, weeping: "I was thinking, why it is that I don't have a mother, a brother and a sister; it would be so beautiful."

Since his high degree of excitability at this time demanded complete rest from every mental effort, and since above all his weak body required exercise and strengthening, it seemed that along with other physical activities, horseback riding especially would be able to benefit his health, since he showed such particular eagerness for it. As with wooden horses formerly, living horses had become his favorite animal by far. Of all animals he considered the horse to be the most beautiful creature, and when he saw a rider playing with his horse, his heart swelled with the wish: "If only I too could have such a horse under me!" The riding master in Nuremberg, Mr. von Rumpler, was soon kind enough to gratify this deep longing: He accepted our Kaspar among his pupils. Kaspar took in all that the teacher showed and demonstrated to the scholars of riding, observing everything with the most intense attention. In the first few hours he had not only memorized the principal rules and elements of the art of riding, but mastered them in the first few attempts. In a few days he was already so far advanced that the other scholars, old and young alike, who had already had several months of instruction, were forced to recognize him as their master.

His bearing, his courage, his correct management of his horse amazed everybody; he felt confident of doing what no one but he and his teacher dared to do. Once when the riding master was breaking in a willful Turkish[50] horse, the sight so little alarmed him that he asked permission to ride that very horse himself. After he had practiced for a certain amount of time, the riding school became too confining and he insisted on taking his horse riding in the open fields. It was here that he demonstrated, alongside his skill, an inexhaustible bodily endurance, toughness, and stamina that the most experienced rider could barely match. He preferred spirited and hard-trotting horses. He often rode for many hours without stopping, without becoming tired, without getting sore from riding, or without feeling any pain in either his thighs or in his seat. One afternoon he rode, almost the entire time at a full trot, from Nuremberg to the so-called

Old Fort and back. This weakling, who would become so tired after a few outings in town that he had to go to bed a few hours earlier than usual in a state of exhaustion, came back home from that immense ride as fresh and strong as if he had only ridden at a walk from one gate of the city to the other. Every once in a while he joked about the lack of sensitivity in his seat: "If everything about me were as good as my behind, things would be very good for me." It is certainly not improbable, as Professor Daumer assumed, that the many years of sitting on a hard floor was responsible for this insensitivity in his seat. From Hauser's love of horses and his almost instinctual skill in horseback riding, one could just as easily draw the not entirely unacceptable conclusion that he may well have belonged to a nation of horsemen by birth. For it is not unknown that skills that can only be acquired originally through practice, when they are continued through many generations, can finally be transmitted as a habitual inclination or a particularly excellent predisposition. The talent that residents of the South Sea Islands show for swimming, the sharp-sightedness of the North American hunter nations, and so on, can serve as examples. A certain wily policeman[51] was misled, as a result of Kaspar's striking talent as a rider, to the conclusion that Kaspar is probably a young English rider who ran away from his gang to make fun of the good-natured Nuremberg citizens for his own advantage. Surely it would not be easy to find somebody eager to claim for its inventor the honor of this hypothesis.

Besides his unusual talent as a rider, what was particularly noticeable in Kaspar Hauser during his stay with Professor Daumer was the almost miraculous acuteness and intensity of all his senses.

With respect to *sight,* there *was no such thing* for him as twilight—no night, no darkness. One first became aware of this when it was noticed that at night he could stride ahead anywhere with the greatest confidence and that whenever he was in a dark place he would refuse any light offered him. It surprised him or made him laugh when he saw people — for example, when they came into their houses at night or started to climb the stairs, trying to help themselves in dark places by stopping and groping their way. In fact he saw far better in twilight than in broad daylight. For example, he could read a house number after the sun set, which by day he would not even have been able to recognize from such a distance, at about 180 yards. On one dark, dusky evening, he drew his teacher's attention to a fly caught in a spider's web far off in the distance. At a distance of a good 60 yards, he could distinguish grapes from elderberries, elderberries from blueberries. According to careful testing, he could distinguish colors in the dead of night, even dark colors such as blue and green. If, at dusk, a normally sharp-sighted person could distinguish only three or four stars in the sky, he could already recognize the constellations, and knew the individual stars in them, and was able to distinguish them by size and particular coloration. From the Nuremberg Castle Tower he could count a series of windows in the castle at Marloffstein, and from its fortress the series of windows in a house beneath Rothenberg Fort. His eye was as sharp in distinguishing nearby objects as it was in penetrating the distance. When flowers were dissected, he noticed subtle distinctions and delicate particles that completely escaped the observation of others.

His *hearing* was hardly less sharp and far-reaching. When he went walking in a field, he could hear the footsteps of several hikers at a relatively great distance, and distinguished each footstep by its strength. Once he had had occasion to compare the sharpness of his hearing at that time with the even sharper one of a blind man, who was able to hear the quietest footstep of someone walking barefoot. On this occasion he said that his hearing earlier had been just as sharp, but from the time he began to eat meat, it had diminished significantly, so that he was no longer able to hear such subtle distinctions as the blind man could.

Among all his senses, his sense of *smell* proved the most painful and intrusive to him and more than anything else turned his life in this world into torture. What for us is odorless was not so for him. The most delicate, pleasant scent of flowers, for example a rose, was for him a stench, or painfully affected his nerves. What for the rest of us announces itself by smell only when it is close, if at all, he smelled from a vast distance. With the exception of the smells of bread, fennel, aniseed, and caraway seed, to which he assured us he had become already accustomed in his prison (since his bread was baked with these spices), every kind of smell was for him more or less repulsive. When he was once asked what scent he found most pleasant, he answered: "None at all." He was put off his walks or horseback rides because they took him past flower gardens or tobacco fields or nut trees, and he had to pay for these relaxations in the fresh air with headaches, cold sweats, and attacks of fever. He could smell tobacco blooming in the fields from more than 50 yards away. The bundles of dry tobacco leaves commonly hung on houses in villages around Nuremberg he could smell at 100 yards.

From a great distance he was able to distinguish apple, pear, and plum trees by the mere smell of their leaves. The various coloring matter on the walls, tools, clothes, etc., the pigments with which he illuminated his paintings, the ink and pen with which he wrote—everything that surrounded him or came close to him wafted revolting or painful scents in his direction. If on the street a chimney sweep walked a few steps ahead of him, he turned his face away from the smell with a shudder. He felt unwell at the smell of old cheese and had to vomit. Once when he smelled vinegar, which was a good yard away from him, its sharpness affected his olfactory and optical nerves to such an extent that his eyes began to water. If decanted wine was placed on a table a short distance from him, he complained of a repulsive smell and a sensation of heat in his head. An open bottle of champagne was sure to drive him from the table or make him ill. What we term a bad smell seemed to affect him far less unpleasantly than did our good smells. He would say, for example, that he would far rather smell cat shit, since it hurt his head less than pomade, and by far any kind of excrement than eau de cologne or spicy chocolate. The smell of fresh meat was the worst of all. Even the stink of cat shit and the smell of dried cod were more bearable to him. When Professor Daumer (in autumn 1828) approached, with Kaspar, the cemetery of the Johannis Church in Nuremberg, the smell of the dead, which Professor Daumer himself did not sense in the least, affected him so strongly that he immediately began to freeze, shuddering violently. His freezing soon turned into the heat of a fever that finally broke into violent perspiration, drenching his shirt through and through. Such heat, he said later, he had never felt before. On the way back, near the city gate, he felt better again, yet he complained that it had become darker in front of his eyes. He had a similar experience (on September 18, 1828) when he happened alongside a tobacco field.

Professor Daumer first became aware of Kaspar's special *ability to feel,* and his sensitivity, especially for the effects of metal, when Kaspar was still in the tower. There a stranger once gave him the present of a small toy horse and a small magnetic wand with which he could drag it around, swimming in the water, since it was mounted in metal. When Kaspar started to use the magnet according to instructions, he felt himself immediately affected by it in the most unpleasant way. He quickly locked it away in the little wooden box it came with, and never took it out of its box again to show his visitors, as he was accustomed to doing with his other toys. Later on, when asked the motive of his behavior, he explained that the little horse caused him a pain that he felt through his whole body and in every limb. When he had moved in with Professor Daumer, he kept the little box with the magnet in a suitcase. One day when he was tidying up his things, it accidentally reappeared. It occurred to Professor Daumer, who remembered the earlier phenomenon, to make an experiment involving Kaspar and the magnet of the little horse. Kaspar immediately felt the most amazing effects. If Professor Daumer pointed the positive side of the magnet toward him, Kaspar grabbed his chest and pulled his vest out, saying: *"It is dragging me, there is a draft coming out of me."* The negative side of the magnet had a less powerful effect on him, and he said of the magnet that *it was blowing on him.* Because of this Professor Daumer and Professor Hermann[52] conducted various similar experiments with him, which were also designed specifically to *fool* him. But each time, his feelings revealed to him correctly, even when the magnet was at a significant distance, whether the negative or the positive or neither was directed at him. Such experiments could not be continued for long because sweat soon broke out on his forehead and he felt ill.

Concerning his sensitivity to other metals and his ability to distinguish them by merely feeling them, Professor Daumer has gathered many facts of which I will emphasize only a few. In the autumn of 1828 he happened to come into a warehouse filled with metal, especially brass merchandise. Barely had he *entered* when he rushed back out into the street showing great revulsion and saying: "In there it pulls on my whole body from all sides." Once a stranger pressed a small gold piece, about the size and thickness of a Kreuzer, into his hand, without Kaspar being able to see it. Nonetheless Kaspar said immediately that he felt gold in his hand.

Once Professor Daumer, in Kaspar's absence, put a golden ring [and] a compass made of metal and brass alongside a silver drawing pen under a piece of paper so that it was impossible to see what was hidden underneath. Daumer instructed Kaspar to move his finger over the paper without touching it. He did so and was able to identify correctly both the material and the form of objects through the difference and strength with which the metals "pulled" on his finger-tips.

Once when *Doctor* Osterhausen and the Royal Tax Collector Brunner from Munich were present, in order to test him, Daumer led Kaspar to a table covered with a wax tablecloth on which a sheet of paper lay. He demanded that he say whether any metal was under the paper. He moved his finger at some distance over it and said: "Here it's pulling!" Daumer retorted: "Now this time you are really wrong. Just look, there is nothing under it," and he lifted the sheet of paper. Hauser at first seemed shaken, but again moved his finger right at the place where he claimed to have felt the pull. He asserted again that he felt a pull right there. The wax tablecloth was raised, the table carefully examined, and a needle came into view.

He described the sensation that minerals aroused in him as a "pulling," accompanied by chills that ran up his arm. How far up the arm these chills ran depended on what the object was. Apart from that there were other strange effects. The veins in the hand exposed to metal irritation would become visibly swollen. Toward the end of December 1828 — when the pathological excitability of his nerves had almost completely subsided — his sensitivity to metal irritation gradually diminished as well and finally disappeared entirely.

The manifestations of *animal* magnetism were no less striking in him. This receptiveness he retained much longer than the one for metal irritation. Since this phenomenon in Kaspar corresponds with other similar well-known cases, it is superfluous to go into detail. It should perhaps only be noted that he called the sensation of magnetic fluids that poured into him as being "blowed at." He felt these magnetic sensations not only when human beings touched him with their hands, or even stretched their fingertips in his direction from some distance away, etc., but also felt them from animals. Whenever he touched a horse, "coldness ran up his arm," as he put it. If he sat on the horse, it felt as if a draft was going through his body. These sensations disappeared as soon as he had exercised his horse a few times on the riding trail. If he grabbed a cat by the tail, he would be overcome by chills and shivers, and felt as if someone had hit his hand.

In March 1829, he was taken for the first time to a circus tent in which foreign animals were displayed, and asked to be given a place in the third row. As soon as he entered he felt a feverish chill that grew much stronger as the aroused rattlesnake began to rattle its tail, and soon turned into heat with a great deal of sweat. The snake's gaze did not face the direction in which he was standing. He insisted that he was not conscious of terror or even fear at the time.

Now we leave the physical and physiological side of Kaspar to take a look at a deeper part of his being. Once the sharpness of his natural understanding is revealed, we are able to draw valid conclusions about his fate and about the total neglect to which human depravity had subjected him.

The childlike goodness and gentleness of his soul made him incapable of harming a worm or a fly, not to mention a human being. It proved spotless and pure as the reflection of eternity in the soul of an angel. As mentioned earlier, when he left his dungeon he took with him no idea, no notion of God, no shadow of belief in any higher invisible existence into the world of light. Fed like an animal, sleeping even when awake, unresponsive to anything in the desert of his narrow dungeon room except his animal needs, occupied with nothing but his feed and with the eternal monotony of his toy horses, his inner life could be compared to the life of an oyster, glued to its rock, feeling nothing beyond its food, not hearing anything beyond the eternal uniform crash of the waves, and there, in the narrow space of its shell, the most limited conception of a world outside of itself can find a place, not to mention any ability to fathom what is *above* the earth and then above all worlds [God in heaven].

And so Kaspar arrived in the higher world without preconceptions, but also without any sense whatever for the invisible, the incorporeal, the eternal. He was caught and tossed into the dizzying whirlpool of external objects. Visible realities occupied him too much for him to readily feel a need for invisible ones. At first nothing was real to him except what he could see, hear, feel, smell, and taste. His awakening and ruminating mind did not take in anything ungrounded in his sensual awareness, nothing beyond the realm of his senses, nothing that could not be brought into conformity with his obvious and simple mental categories. For a long time all efforts to awaken religious notions in him by the usual methods were in vain. He complained to Professor Daumer with complete naïveté that he just didn't know what on earth these priests wanted with all these things he couldn't grasp. To win him somewhat away from his shallow materialistic ideas, Professor Daumer attempted to make him receptive, at least in the meantime, to the conceivability and possibility of an invisible world, especially a godhead, in the following way. Daumer asked him whether he had thoughts, conceptions, and a will within himself. When he answered that he did, he was then asked whether he could see, hear, etc., them? When he answered no, his teacher made him aware of how, indeed, according to his own understanding, there were things that one could not see nor have access to from the outside. Kaspar admitted this was true and was very astonished to discover the spiritual nature of his inner being. Daumer continued: A being that can think and desire is called a spirit. Now God is such a spirit, and stands in relation to the world just as Kaspar's own thinking and desiring stands to his body. Just as Kaspar can produce invisible changes in his mind through invisible thinking and desiring, for example, can move his hands and feet, so can God do the same in the world. He is the life in all things. He is the active spirit in the whole world.

Now Professor Daumer ordered him to move his arm and asked him whether he could at the same time also lift up and move his other arm. "Certainly." "Well then," Daumer continued, "from that you can see, then, that your invisible thinking and desiring, that is, your spirit, can be effective at the same time in two of your limbs, that is, in two different places at the same time. The same applies, then, equally to God, but in the large, and now you will be able to understand a bit what it means to say God is omnipresent." Kaspar displayed great joy when this became clear to him, and said to his teacher that what he had just told him was something real, whereas what other people told him about it was never right. Teaching such as the above had, for a long time, no result except that Hauser no longer showed himself recalcitrant toward the idea of God, so the way was found to make his soul familiar with religious concepts.

Meanwhile, his inborn *Pyrrho* [a skeptical philosopher] appeared over and over again in different forms and from different directions. Once he asked whether he was permitted to ask God for something specific, and if he would be granted what he asked, for example, if he were to ask God to relieve him of his (recent) eye infection. "Of course," was the answer, he could ask; only he had to leave it to the wisdom of God whether He thought it good to grant the wish. "But," he retorted, "after all, I want my eyes back to learn and work, and that after all has to be good for me, so God can't have anything against it." It was explained to him that God sometimes has his own unfathomable reasons for refusing what seems good for us, in order to test us, for example, by making us suffer, to exercise our patience, etc. But this teaching always left him cold, and found no acceptance with him. His doubts, questions, and objections often put his teacher in embarrassing situations. For example, when the discussion was about God's almightiness, he asked whether God the Almighty could turn back time—a question that had bitter and ironic connection to his earlier fate, concealing the question whether or not God could give him back the childhood and youth he lost while buried alive in a grave. From the little bit I have recounted here, one can deduce what it would be like to instruct him in positive religion, with Christian dogmatics, the secrets of the teaching of Christ's expiatory death, and other such doctrines. I am happy to stay far away from his comments on these matters.

For a very long time Kaspar could not overcome his loathing for two kinds of people: doctors and clergymen. The former because of the disgusting medicines they prescribed in order to make people sick, the latter because they frightened and confused him with incomprehensible blah, blah, blah, as he put it. If he saw a priest, he would become frightened, even terrified. When asked for the cause he answered

> becuse these people have already tortured me so much. Once, four of them came to me when I was in the tower [after leaving the dungeon], and told me things I could not understand at all at that time. For example, that God created everything out of nothing. When I requested an explanation, they all began to shout at the same time, each saying something different. When I said to them that I don't yet understand any of that, that I have to learn to read and write first, they replied that these other things have to be learned first. They did not go away until I let them know I wanted them to just leave me alone.

This is why Kaspar did not feel at all well in churches. The crucifixes there caused him a horrible fright, since for a long time after these representations took on spontaneous life. The singing of the congregation seemed to him a repulsive scream. He said one time after a visit to a church that first

the people scream, and when they stop, the priest begins to scream.

Chapter VII

Under the careful nursing of the honorable Daumer family, through well-chosen exercises and suitable occupations, Kaspar's health flourished considerably. He learned eagerly, acquired all kinds of knowledge, progressed in arithmetic and writing, and soon reached a point where he could undertake, as his teacher requested, to put the memories of his life into a written essay. This was at some point[53] in the summer of 1829. This first attempt at representing his own thoughts for himself—even if, to be sure, it could only be taken as evidence of his long suppressed development and the poverty and clumsiness of his childlike mind—he looked upon with the eyes of a young writer who watches the first product of his quill pen coming off the press. In his excitement at being an author, he took to showing what he called his *autobiography* to local visitors as well as foreign ones. Soon it was announced in several newspapers that Kaspar Hauser was working on his autobiography. *It is very probable* that it was precisely this rumor that led to the catastrophe that soon after, in October of the same year (1829), was meant to bring his short life to a tragic end. Kaspar Hauser, if I am permitted to intersperse suppositions here, had finally become a dangerous burden to the one or ones who had concealed him. The child who had long been fed grew into a boy and finally a young man. He became restless, his strength began to stir. He sometimes even made noise and had to be forced into silence by the considerable beating of which he still carried the fresh traces when he came to Nuremberg. Why was Kaspar not gotten rid of in some other way? Why was he not killed? Why was he not removed from the world as a child?

Perhaps he was handed over to his jailer with the intent of having him murdered, but the jailer—out of compassion, waiting for more favorable times for the child who had been put aside, or from some other easily imaginable motive—kept the child and fed him in spite of the danger to himself. Each reader must judge these suppositions for himself. Meanwhile, the time had come, or rather had not come, when the secret of the child could no longer be kept hidden. They had to find a way, somehow, to get rid of him. So he was brought, dressed as a beggar, to Nuremberg. It was hoped that there he would be confined to a public institution as a vagabond or a lunatic or, should the recommendation he brought with him to become a cavalry soldier be taken into account, he could have disappeared as a soldier into some regiment. Against all expectations, not a single one of these calculations turned out as intended. The unknown foundling won for himself human sympathy, and became the subject of general public interest. The newspapers filled up with news and questions about the puzzling young man. At first the adoptive child only of Nuremberg, as the mayor of this town had made clear in his public announcement, he became finally the *child of Europe.* Everywhere people speak of Kaspar's mental development. The public is told of miracles in his progress. And now this half-man is even writing his autobiography! Whoever writes down his life, must have something to say about it. Therefore those who had all the reason in the world to remain in the darkness they had created around themselves, and around the traces that could lead to them, must have felt their chests tighten somewhat at the news of Kaspar's autobiography. The plan to bury poor Kaspar alive under the waves of a strange world had failed. Only now, as the clandestine criminals might have supposed, did the killing of Kaspar become a sort of self-defense.

During the morning, from eleven to twelve, Kaspar usually attended an arithmetic lesson away from home. But on

Sunday October 17, feeling unwell, at the insistence of his guardian, Kaspar stayed home. Professor Daumer was taking a walk at the time. Apart from Kaspar, who was known to be in his room, no one was left in the Daumer household but Daumer's mother and his sister, who at that time was busy cleaning the house.

Daumer's house, in which Kaspar lived, lies in a remote and rarely visited part of town, in an extremely large, desolate square that was nonetheless easily visible. The house, built with extreme irregularity according to the old-fashioned Nuremberg style, full of corners and angles, consisted of a front building, which the landlord occupied, and a rear building in which the Daumer family had their rooms. A separate entrance led to the stairs of the Daumers' quarters. To get there one passed through an open passageway bounded on both sides by the yard. Along this passageway, in addition to a wooden stall, a place for poultry, and other similar enclosures, in a corner, under a winding stairway, a very low, small, narrow outhouse pressed itself. The already small space in which the outhouse was to be found was made even narrower by a screen that was standing in front of it.

Whenever Kaspar wanted to visit this secret place, it was his habit, out of his love for cleanliness, to take off his jacket and his vest while still in his room and go, undressed except for his pants and an undershirt, with his throat exposed, to that room. It should be further remarked that whoever happens to be in the corridor I just described, on the ground level anywhere near the wooden stall, can easily observe who is coming down the stairs and going to the outhouse.

When, around twelve o'clock, on the day mentioned above, Katharina, the sister of Professor Daumer, was busy sweeping the apartment, she became aware of several spots of blood and bloody footprints on the stairs leading from the first floor to the backyard. She wiped them away right away without thinking that anything was wrong. She thought Kaspar might have had a nosebleed on the stairs. She went up to his room to complain to him about it, but she did not find Kaspar. She noticed, however, that in his room, close to the door, was yet another pair of bloody footprints. When she went back down the stairs to sweep the corridor in the yard that I mentioned earlier, she noticed yet again some traces of blood on the stone pavement of this corridor. She reached the outhouse, and there lay a thick clump of dried blood. At that moment the daughter of the landlord arrived and she showed it to her. The daughter thought it was the blood of a cat who had just had babies there. Daumer's sister, having immediately washed away this blood, was all the more certain of her opinion that Kaspar had made the mess on the stairs. He must have stepped into this pool of blood and gone upstairs without having cleaned his feet.

It was already past twelve, the table was set, and Kaspar, who otherwise always came to eat punctually at this time, was not there. Daumer's mother therefore came down from her room to call Kaspar, but could no more find him in his little room than her daughter could before. Mrs. Daumer saw his jacket hanging on the wall and his shirt collar and vest on the piano. From this she drew the certain conclusion that Kaspar would be found in the secret room, and so went down there to look for him. She did not find him there either. She started to go back to her room when suddenly she became aware of a wet spot on the trap door to the cellar, which looked to her like blood. Fearing the worst, she lifted up the trap door, noticed on all the steps of the cellar some drops and some larger spots of blood. She now climbed down to the lowest step and from there saw something white shining in a distant corner of the water-filled cellar. Mrs. Daumer hurried back and asked the landlord's maid to go into the cellar with a light to see what was the white thing lying there. No sooner had she shined the light on the object described to her than she cried out: "Kaspar is lying dead over there!" The maid, as well as the landlord's son, who in the meantime had also just arrived, lifted Kaspar off the floor and carried him out of the cellar. His deadly pale face was covered in blood, and he showed no signs of life. When they got upstairs, he gave his first sign of life, an enormous groan. Then he called out in a deep voice: "The man, the man!" He was immediately put to bed, where, with his eyes closed, from time to time he sometimes shouted, sometimes murmured to himself the following broken words and sentences: "Mother! — Tell professor — outhouse — man hit — black man, like kitchen[54] — mother say — not found — my room — hide in the cellar." Following this he was seized by a powerful febrile shivering, which soon turned into violent paroxysms, and finally resulted in a raving fit. Several strong men had a difficult time holding him down. In his attacks of rage he bit a large chunk out of a porcelain teacup from which they were trying to get him to take a warm drink. He swallowed it along with the drink. He remained mentally gone for nearly forty-eight hours. In his deliriums during the night, from time to time he would murmur the following sentence fragments to himself:

Tell the Mayor. — No imprison! — Man gone! — Man comes! — Bell gone! — I ride down to Fürth. — Not to Erlangen in Wallfisch.[55] — Not murder, not hold the mouth, not die! — Me sit on the toilet; not murder! Hauser where have been; not to Fürth today; no more leave; already headache. Not to Erlangen in Wallfisch. The man murder me! Go away! Not murder! I love all people; no one does nothing. — Mayor's wife help! Man also loves you, not murder! Why man me murder? I too want live. — Why you murder me? I to you never anything done. Me not murder! Because I beg, that you not be imprisoned. You never let me out of my prison, you even me murder! You have first killed me, before I understand what life is. You must say why you have imprisoned me.

And so on. He continuously repeated most of these sentences incoherently and out of order. At last the police authorities handed over the Kaspar Hauser case to the Court of Inquiry. On October 20, with the help of the forensic physician, Dr. Preu, this court deposed Hauser with the following result: Hauser was lying in a bed. In the middle of his forehead was a sharp wound, of the size and shape of which the forensic physician reported his findings as follows:

> The wound is located on the forehead, ten and a half lines above the bridge of the nose, running diagonally in such a way that two-thirds of the wound is on the right half of the forehead, and the last third on the left. The entire length of the wound, which runs in a straight line, is nineteen and a half lines. The left end of this gap is somewhat wider than the rest of it. From this it follows that the wound was deepest here. As for the origin of the just-described wound to Hauser, it is unmistakably the result of a stab or a blow (?) with a sharp instrument. The sharp edges of the wound are testimony to the sharp blade of the instrument; the symmetrical ends of the wound demonstrate that it was caused by a slash or stab (?), since if it had been the result of a cut on the forehead, the beginning and end of the wound would have been narrower and more superficial, but the middle would have been deeper and therefore would have appeared more gaping. It is most probable that the wound originated from a slash, since a stab would have shown great contusion in the neighboring flesh, etc.

The wound was, as the doctor explained, in and of itself, insignificant, and could easily have healed in six days, if it had been any other person. But because Kaspar had such an irritable nervous system, it took him twenty-two days to recuperate after he had been wounded. Kaspar recounts the substance of what happened this way:

> On the seventeenth I had to cancel my arithmetic lesson that I usually have every day from eleven to twelve with Mr. E. The reason is that one hour before, while I was visiting Dr. Preu, he gave me a walnut, and although I had barely eaten a quarter of it, I immediately felt very sick. Professor Daumer, to whom I reported this, ordered me not to go for my usual lesson this time but

to stay at home. Professor Daumer left the house and I retired to my room. I wanted to occupy myself in writing, but abdominal pains prevented me, and a natural need forced me to go to the outhouse. Because of a tearing pain in my stomach, I had to stay there for more than half of a quarter of an hour. Finally I heard a noise coming from the wooden stable, similar to the one that occurred whenever this door was opened and very familiar to me. Also, from the outhouse I perceived the soft tone of the bells on the door to the house which seemed to me to come less from being rung than from some kind of indirect contact. Right after that I heard light footsteps coming from the other end of the corridor. At the same time I saw through the spaces of the wall-covering (wooden screen) in front of the outhouse and the circular stairs leading to the house, a man sneaking along the corridor. I noticed the very dark hat on him and thought he was the chimney sweep. I stayed a moment longer on the toilet so that the chimney sweep would not see me as I got up. But when I straightened myself up from sitting on the toilet, sticking my head out of the narrow outhouse, as I tried to pull up my trousers, suddenly this black man was standing in front of me and hit me on my head, as a consequence of which my whole body fell down and hit the floor in front of the outhouse. (There follows the description of the man, which cannot be reproduced.)[56] I could see nothing of the face or hair of this man, for he was veiled by what I think was a black silk scarf that covered his whole head. I must have lain there unconscious for a considerable time. When I finally regained consciousness, I felt something warm trickling down my face, and grabbed my forehead with both hands, which were then covered in blood.

Terrified by this, I wanted to go upstairs to Mother,[57] but in my confusion and fear (since I was afraid that the man who had hit me was still in the house and would come after me a second time), instead of going to Mother's door, I found myself in front of the door to the closet next to my room.[58] At this point I felt I was beginning to lose consciousness and tried to stay upright by grabbing the closet with my hand.[59] When I had recovered, I again wanted to go upstairs to mother, but in my further confusion, instead of going upstairs, I went downstairs, and found myself, to my horror, back down in the corridor. When my eyes fell on the trap door to the cellar, fear gave me the idea of hiding in the cellar. The trap door to the cellar was closed. It is incomprehensible to me to this very moment how I found the strength to lift the heavy trap door. But I did and slipped into the cellar.[60]

Because of the cold water in the cellar that I had to wade into, my consciousness improved. I noticed a dry spot on the floor of the cellar and sat down there. I had barely sat down than I heard the church bells chime twelve, and I thought to myself: Now you are here, completely abandoned. Nobody will find you here, and you will die here. These thoughts filled my eyes with tears until I started to vomit. At that point I lost consciousness. When I had come to I found myself in my room on my bed with Mother sitting beside me.

As for the nature of the wounding, this author cannot bring himself to share the opinion of the forensic physician. I have several reasons—though they cannot be published[61]— to believe that the wound to Hauser was caused neither by a slash nor a blow, not by a saber nor by an axe, nor by a chisel, nor with any other ordinary knife meant for cutting, but with another well-known sharp cutting instrument. Moreover, the stabbing was not aimed at his forehead but his throat. For as soon as Kaspar saw the man with the weapon in his fist suddenly directed at his throat, he instinctively ducked his head, and in so doing covered his throat with his chin, thereby causing the blow to glance from his throat to his forehead. The perpetrator probably thought his work was accomplished, since Kaspar immediately collapsed bleeding. And he may well have feared, given the nature of the place, that someone could find him at any moment and it was best not to linger next to his victim any longer to see whether everything had succeeded and, if not, to complete the job. And so Kaspar escaped with just a forehead wound.

Soon several more clues were provided that proved to be traces of the perpetrator.[62] Among them for example, were that on the same day, at the very same hour when the crime took place, the man Kaspar described had been seen leaving

Daumer's house; moreover, the same well-dressed person described by Kaspar had been seen washing his hands, probably covered in blood, in the water trough that was on the side of the road not far from Daumer's house. About four days after the crime, outside the gate of the town, an elegant gentleman wearing clothes such as those Hauser described as being worn by the black man, joined a common-looking woman on her way into town. He urgently asked her in detail as to whether the wounded Hauser was alive or dead, and then walked with her up to the gate, where an official notice with respect to Hauser's wounding could be read. When he read it, without entering the town, he stalked off in a highly suspicious manner, and so on and so forth.

If the reader, in his curiosity, wants to learn more from me, should he ask me the results of the usual judicial inquiry, should he like to know in which direction those clues have led, in what places the divining rod really began to vibrate, and what happened next: I must answer that according to law and in the nature of the subject, I cannot, in my capacity as a writer, speak publicly of matters for which for the present I am allowed to know, or rather to suspect, only in my capacity as a state official. Moreover, may I express the certainty that the authorities in charge of this investigation, using all means at their disposal, even the most unusual ones, have made a tremendous effort to fulfil their duty without rest and without mercy—and, may I add, not entirely without success.

However, not all far, deep, and high places are accessible to the reach of civil justice. With respect to certain places in which justice would have reason to search for the giant responsible for such a crime, it would have to have the power of Joshua's trumpets, or Oberon's[63] magic horn, in order to do battle, tooth and nail, with the high and mighty colossuses armed with a flail who stand guard in front of certain golden castle gates, and thresh so intensely that between blows no ray of light can penetrate without being dispersed, and so render them for some time, impotent.[64]

> Nonetheless, dark midnight's evil deeds
> Will at last, at daybreak, be brought to light.[65]

Chapter VIII

Were Kaspar, who must now be considered to belong to polite society, to enter a room full of people unrecognized, he would soon strike everybody as some strange apparition. Blended into his face are the soft features of a child with the angular ones of a man, a few lightly drawn wrinkles as early signs of age, heartwarming friendliness with deliberate seriousness and a slight tinge of melancholy. His naïveté, his trusting openness, and his often more-than-childlike lack of experience, coupled with a certain kind of precociousness and a distinguished but still informal gravity in speech and behavior; and then the awkwardness of his speech, which sometimes strains for the right words, at other times is hard and sounds strange; the stiffness with which he carries himself and the ungainliness of his movements, all make it apparent to every eye capable of observation that here is a mixture of child, youth and man, but without being able to come to any conclusion as to what age group this lovable hybrid really belongs.

In his intelligence there stirs nothing at all of genius, not even any particular outstanding talent.[66] What he learns he owes to persistent, tenacious diligence. As for the zeal of burning enthusiasm with which, in the beginning, he seemed to wish to storm the gates of all knowledge, that has long been muted, almost extinguished. In everything he undertakes, he gets no further than the beginning or remains only mediocre. Without a glimmer of fantasy, unable to make any kind of joke, or to understand even a metaphorical way of speaking, he has a dry but completely healthy common sense. With respect to everything concerning his own person, or within the narrowly circumscribed sphere of his meager knowledge and experiences, his judgment and sharp intellect are so right that he could shame and embarrass many a pedant.

In common sense a man, in insight a small boy, in many things less than a child, his speech and behavior display a strange contrasting mixture of man and child. With a serious expression, and in a tone of great moment, he not infrequently makes statements that in anyone else his age would be called stupid or banal. From his mouth, however, there always forces itself a melancholy smile of compassion. He appears especially droll when speaking of his future life projects, of how he would, once he had learned an honorable profession and earned some money, settle down with his wife and treat her as a necessary piece of furniture. He is only able to think of a wife as a housekeeper, or as a kind of chief maid, whom you keep only as long as she does her job but dismiss if she puts too much salt in the soup, or does not do a good job sewing up the holes in shirts, or who does not brush the clothes properly, etc.

Mild, soft, without vicious inclinations, without passion and emotion, his even temperament is like a placid, mirror-like lake illuminated by a full moon in the still of night. Incapable of harming an animal, compassionate toward a worm, which he is afraid of stepping on, at the same time he is fearful to the point of being a coward.[67] Nonetheless, he would insist on his own principles recklessly, even mercilessly, as soon as it became a question of fighting for truths he decided were right and should be carried through. If he felt himself oppressed, he would put up with it silently for a long time, hoping to avoid the difficulty or attempting to change the situation though mild objections. But, in the end, if nothing helped, as soon as the opportunity presented itself to free himself from the constricting bonds, he would calmly do so, showing no anger toward the person who was hurting him. He is obedient, willing, compliant. But if you falsely accuse him of something, or claim something to be true which Kaspar thinks is not, do not expect him, just to be nice or for any other reason, to put up with injustice or a lie. He will modestly but resolutely insist that he is right, and if the other person stubbornly puts up a fight, he will silently leave.

As a mature youth who slept away his childhood and youth, too old to be considered still a child, too childishly ignorant to be considered a youth; with no companions his own age, a citizen of no country, with no parents or relatives, the only creature of his species: Every moment reminds Kaspar of his loneliness amid the bustle of a world that overwhelms him; of his powerlessness, weakness, and helplessness against the power of the circumstances that rule his fate, especially his personal dependence on people's goodwill or the lack of it. This is the origin of his accomplished ability to observe people, a measure forced upon him for self-defense, as it were, his vigilant perspicacity with which he quickly takes in their peculiarities and weakness; his intelligence, which his enemies have called slyness or shrewdness, which helps him to come to terms with those who have the power to hurt or help him, to avoid attacks, to please, to skillfully further his wishes, and to take advantage of the goodwill of his friends and well-wishers. Childish pranks, vandalism, practical jokes, are as foreign to him as meanness and falseness: For the former he is too serious, and has too much cool common sense; for the latter he is too goodwilled and has an almost pedantic sense of what is permissible.

Without doubt, one of the biggest mistakes in the education and formation of this person was that, instead of giving him a general humane education appropriate to his idiosyncrasies, he was sent for the last few years to a classical high school. Even worse, he had to start in a higher grade.[68] This

This is a contemporary portrait of Kaspar Hauser that Feuerbach used as the frontispiece to the book translated in this volume. Kaspar sent signed copies of this portrait to various friends. The one reproduced here was sent to Elise, one of Feuerbach's daughters. (Reproduced with permission from *Kaspar Hauser: Das Kind von Europa,* by Johannes Mayer. All illustrations here are from this source unless otherwise noted.)

This is a contemporary picture of the Unschlittplatz in Nuremberg, where Kaspar Hauser first appeared on May 26, 1828. It was about four o'clock in the afternoon when he suddenly turned up looking lost, dazed, confused, and helpless.

A contemporary photograph of the dungeon at Schloss Pilsach in which Kaspar Hauser was probably imprisoned. The novelist Klara Hoffer bought the castle and discovered the dungeon in 1924.

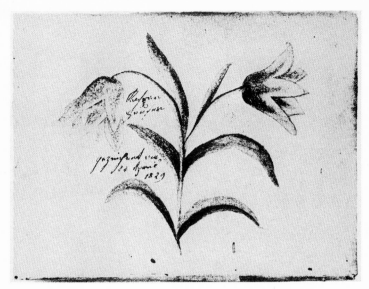

This tempera drawing by Kaspar Hauser is the earliest one to have survived. Dated April 22, 1829, it bears an astonishing resemblance to the ironwork around the window in the dungeon of Schloss Pilsach *(below)* where it is now believed that Kaspar Hauser was imprisoned and isolated for twelve years.

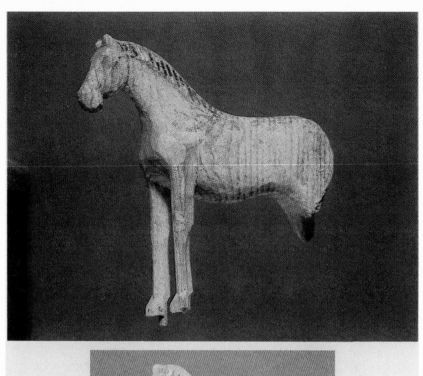

This small white wooden horse was found recently during renovations made in Schloss Pilsach. It answers almost perfectly to the description of the horse Kaspar Hauser played with in his dungeon and is probably the original.

A portrait of Anselm von Feuerbach (1775-1833) done in 1831, two years before he died. He was a German judge (renowned for outlawing torture in Bavaria) who first investigated Kaspar Hauser's "case," wrote a famous book about him, and became his staunchest ally, protector, and friend.

Georg Friedrich Daumer (1800-1875) was Kaspar Hauser's first teacher and remained his steadfast friend to the end. He wrote a series of books defending the authenticity of Kaspar Hauser, the first in 1832 while Kaspar was still alive, the last published shortly before Daumer's own death. His contemporary notes about Kaspar Hauser were found only in 1994.

Philip Henry, 4th Earl of Stanhope (1781-1855), is the most mysterious figure in the drama of Kaspar Hauser's life. He befriended Kaspar, offered to take him to his castle in Chevening and adopt him, and handed over large sums of money for his upkeep. Recent research has clearly demonstrated that he was in the pay of the house of Baden and was involved, directly or indirectly, in the murder of Kaspar Hauser.

A contemporary portrait of Stéphanie (Beauharnais) of Baden. She was adopted by Emperor Napoleon, who arranged her marriage to Karl of Baden. She is widely believed by historians to be the real mother of Kaspar Hauser. When she read Feuerbach's book on January 24, 1832, she asked Stanhope to bring Kaspar Hauser to her. He promised to do so but did not fulfil his promise. Although many people even at that time thought Kaspar Hauser was her son, she appears either not to have believed it or to have been unable to bear the thought.

Gottlieb Freiherr von Tucher (1798-1877) in old age. He was Kaspar Hauser's benefactor and attempted in vain to protect him against Stanhope.

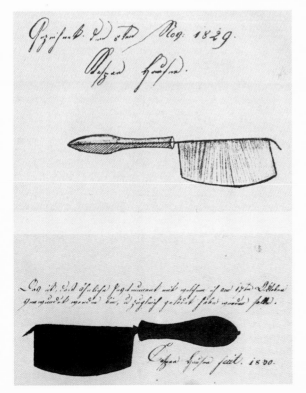

These are two drawings made by Kaspar Hauser of the weapon with which an attempt was made on his life on October 17, 1829. He made the first drawing on November 5, 1829, and did the second in 1830. The handwriting on the page is by Kaspar Hauser and reads, "This is an instrument similar to the one with which I was wounded on October 17, and which was supposed to have killed me." (Drawing after Pies, "Eyewitness Accounts," 1925. Drawing and photo: Germanic National Museum, Nuremberg)

A contemporary colored lithograph of Ansbach, the small city where Kaspar Hauser was sent for his safety. He lived here with a rigid schoolteacher, Johann Georg Meyer. On the right is the "Orangerie," the grove where he was lured by a promise that he would receive news of his mother, and then murdered at the age of twenty-one, on December 14, 1833, a few years after he arrived in Ansbach.

This is one of the most unusual of Kaspar Hauser's drawings, done in 1831. The original, which I saw in Ansbach, has amazing colors.

poor neglected youth, who only recently got his first glimpse of the world, and still has to catch up with what our children learned at their mother's breast and in the laps of their nurses, suddenly had to break his head over Latin grammar, Latin exercises, with Cornelius Nepos and finally even Caesar's *The Gallic Wars*. Squeezed in Latin thumbscrews, his mind suffered a kind of second imprisonment. Now the dusty walls of the classroom are keeping him from nature and from life, just as the walls of his dungeon did so earlier. Instead of useful things, he was given words and phrases whose meaning and relevance he could not understand, and so his childhood was once again perversely prolonged.

While his time and his in any case limited strength were wasted on shallow school nonsense, he was continually starved of the most simple basic knowledge of things that could feed and delight his soul, that could somewhat compensate his injured nature for his lost youth, and which could prove useful as a basis for some future profession. "I really don't know," he said more than once, in despair and half angry, "what am I supposed to do with all this Latin stuff, since I cannot become a priest and don't want to become a priest." When a pedant once replied to this by saying that learning the Latin language is essential for learning the German language, and that to learn German properly, one has to have learnt Latin thoroughly, his healthy common sense retorted: "Did the Romans have to learn German in order to speak and write Latin thoroughly?" One can judge how well Latin suited Kaspar and vice versa, by the fact that this bearded student of elementary Latin, when he was living with me in the Spring of 1831, had still not understood the fact that objects seen at a distance appear smaller than they actually are. He was puzzled by the fact that the trees on the side of a quiet avenue we were walking along, are smaller and shorter, and the road in the distance gets more and more narrow, so that when we reach the end it will be too narrow to walk through at all. He had not yet seen anything like this while he was in Nuremberg. He was as astonished as if he had seen a magic trick, when he at last found as he walked down the avenue with me, that each of these trees was equally high, and the path equally wide everywhere.

He had a depressing feeling of his own ignorance, help-lessness, and dependency, the conviction that he would never be in a position to recall his lost youth, to catch up with boys his own age and become a useful member of society; with his youth taken away, not only was he robbed of the most beautiful part of a person's life, but also the whole rest of his life was stunted and crippled. Finally, added to all this, was the terrifying thought that the atrophied rest of his allotted days was threatened at every moment by an invisible murderous ax and a hidden bandit's knife. Such is the heavy content of the dark clouds that shadow his forehead, which when external circumstances cause them to thicken, fre-quently pour down in tears and melancholy lamentations.

At the time he was staying with me, I often took him on my walks. One bright sunny morning I took him to one of the so-called mountains from which there was a beautiful clear view of the lovely tiny city at its feet, and of the sweet little valley surrounded by hills. Kaspar, at first delighted with this view, soon became quiet and sad. In response to my question as to the cause of his changed mood, he answered:

I was just thinking about how there is so much beauty in the world, and how hard it is for me, to have lived as long as I have, and not seen any of it. How fortunate are the children who were able to see all this from their first years, and can still see it. I am already so old, and I still have to learn what children have already known for so long. I wish I had never come out of my cage. Who-ever put me in should have left me there. For then I would have known nothing of all this beauty, and would not have missed it, and would not have been miserable over the fact that I was never really a child, and have come into the world so late.

I tried to provide him solace when I told him that, with respect to the beauty of nature, he really had no cause to complain, compared to our children and to those people who have been in this world since their childhood. Most people who have grown up amid these wonders look upon them with indifference, as something ordinary, everyday, and carry this apathy with them through their whole life. In general they feel for the wonders of nature nothing more than does the beast in the pasture. But for him (Kaspar), who stepped, as an adolescent, into a world that was to him brand-new, these pleasures retained all their freshness and purity. This provides him with a not-inconsiderable replacement for the loss of his early years, whereby he gains a significant advantage over other people. He didn't say anything to me in reply, and seemed, if not convinced, at least to some extent comforted. Nonetheless he will never at any time be completely reconciled to his fate. He is a small, tender tree, whose foliage has been removed and whose deepest root has been eaten by a worm.

In such moods, when he felt that way about his situation, it was religion, the belief in God and religious faith in His providence, that had to find access to his soul so in need of comfort. He is now, in the real sense of the word, a pious person. He speaks with devotion of God and happily occupies himself reading sensible, edifying spiritual tracts. On the other hand, he certainly would not swear by any of the symbolic books, and even less would he feel comfortable in a pious society of Hengstenberg[69] & Co.[70] Removed early on from the superstitious tales of a wet-nurse, buried as a child; as a mature adolescent resurrected to a new life, he brought with him into the world of light a soul devoid of categories, but also one without prejudices, free of any superstition. He for whom at first it was so difficult to become aware of his own spirit is even less capable and inclined to imagine ghostly spirits. He ridicules the belief in ghosts as the most incomprehensible of all human stupidities and fears nothing except the invisible, the secret, the uncanny, whose murderous weapon he has already felt. If he were to be given assurance that he would be safe from this man, he would go at any hour of the night to a cemetery and sleep on the graves without any fear.

His way of life is almost entirely like that of other ordinary people. He enjoys every kind of food except pork, but of course, without hot spices. His favorite spices are still caraway, fennel, and coriander. His drink still consists of water. Only in the morning does he drink a cup of healthful hot chocolate. All alcoholic drinks, beer, wine, as well as tea and coffee, continue to repel him, and should somebody try to force a drop on him, it would certainly make him sick.

The extraordinary, almost supernatural development of his senses has also at present completely diminished, and is almost reduced to the common level. True, he still sees in the dark, so that there is no real night for him, only twilight, but he is no longer capable as he once was of reading in the dark or of being able to recognize the smallest objects at a great distance. Where he used to see in darkest night far better and sharper than by day, now it is the reverse. Just like other people, he can now bear the sunlight and even loves it, for it no longer, as it once did, injures his eyes. Of the great power of his memory and other astonishing qualities not a trace is to be found. There is no longer anything extraordinary about him, except for his extraordinary fate and his indescribable gentleness and loveableness.

—End.—

Notes to von Feuerbach's *Kaspar Hauser*

1. [Translator's note: *La vida es sueño* (*Life Is a Dream*) is the title of one of the great plays of Spanish literature, by Pedro Calderón de la Barca (1600–81). The main character is Sigismund, a prince who is locked up in a tower. No doubt this is Feuerbach's way of hinting to his readers that he considers Kaspar Hauser to be a prince.]

2. [Translator's note: Philip Henry, fifth earl of Stanhope 1805–75). At the time that Feuerbach dedicated his book to him, he knew him only as the wealthy English lord who was paying the city for the upkeep of Kaspar Hauser and who offered to adopt him and take him to his palace in England. Feuerbach did not live to see Stanhope turn into the greatest enemy of Kaspar Hauser.]

3. [Translator's note: Georg Leonhard Weickmann, fifty-three at the time, a shoemaker. His deposition is published by Pies in *Die Wahrheit über Kaspar Hausers Auftauchen und erste Nürnberger Zeit.*]

4. [Translator's note: Friedrich von Wessenig, fifty-two, captain of the Cheveauxlégerregiment, commander of the Fourth Squadron. He seems not to have liked Kaspar Hauser, and was responsible for a cruel joke, telling Kaspar that he had a letter from his mother. His deposition can be found in Pies, *Augenzeugenberichte und Selbstzeugnisse* (Eyewitness accounts and personal statements), 2 vols. (Stuttgart: Robert Lutz Verlag, 1925), reprint edited by Johannes Mayer (Stuttgart: Urachhaus, 1985).]

5. I feel entitled to be brief in giving the above account. This is because the documents that give the exact circumstances under which Kaspar was taken by the citizen I mentioned from the Unschlitt Square to the Guard and from there to the house of Captain von W. are both incomplete and unsatisfactory as well as being open to critical and historical doubts with respect to the alleged circumstances. For example: the citizen in question claims that while he was walking along with K. he tried to start up a conversation and asked him several questions. Finally he noticed that K. *knew nothing about anything and had no conception of what he was talking about and therefore no longer spoke to him* [emphasis in original]. This is how K. appeared then, and also the same evening at Captain von W's and later at the Guard Station, as well as during the next few days and weeks. Nevertheless, this same citizen maintains that K., when asked the question: "Where are you from?" answered: "From Regensburg." Moreover, he claims that K. told him when they got to the New Gate: "This must just have been built, since it is called the New Gate," and so on. I do not doubt that the witness *believed* that he heard this and similar things from K. Nor do I doubt that K. *did not say* them. Everything that follows provides the irrefutable proof. What probably happened is that Kaspar had a stock phrase for everything: "Rider want to be like my father was." The man who was guiding him took him for a simpleton and didn't pay all that much attention to his answers, so he be-

lieved he was able to make out the words he quoted him as saying. In general, however, the police files that accumulated over this affair were compiled in such a manner, contain so many contradictions, treat so much so lightly, and are so completely anachronistic in some of their most important details, that as a historical source they can only be used with the greatest of caution.

6. [Translator's note: Johann Mathias Merk.]

7. [Translator's note: Kaspar Hauser, in his autobiography, a fragment of which was published by Daumer in 1832, says about this: "I saw the captain's uniform and his saber, and was amazed and delighted by it, and wanted to have one for myself. I said: "I would like to be such a rider as my father was." By this I meant to say that I should be given such a shining beautiful thing." (Text reproduced in Pies, *Augenzeugenberichte und Selbstzeugnisse*, p. 430).]

8. These phrases, namely, "Want to be rider," etc., held no particular meaning for him, as we found out later. They were nothing but sounds he had memorized just parrot fashion, with which he gave general expression to all his ideas, feelings, and desires.

9. [Translator's note: How Kaspar Hauser received this name is not clear. Undoubtedly it was given to him by his jailer, but why, and what significance it has, is not known. Stéphanie de Beauharnais intended to name her first son Gaspard. Kaspar's jailer claims that both the shirt Kaspar wore and the handkerchief he carried had the initial K sewn in them. When, at the beginning of a deposition of October 28, 1829 (reproduced in Pies, *Augenzeugenberichte*, p. 474) Kaspar was asked his name, he replied: "As far as I know, my name is Kaspar Hauser."]

10. [Translator's note: Kaspar was to remain in the tower for eight weeks. His jailer there was Andreas Hiltel, fifty-one years old, who took an enormous liking to his prisoner. Hiltel's eleven-year-old son, Julius, and his three-year-old daughter were to become Kaspar's constant companions during that time. Hiltel had eight children and said that had it not been for that, he would have liked to adopt Kaspar. He further said that Kaspar was so terrified the first few days he was in the tower that he even asked him whether his two-year-old child would hurt him. In 1830 Hiltel told Daumer that even if God himself were to say that Kaspar Hauser was a fraud, he would have to contradict him. He *knew*, and there could never be any doubt for him, that this child was completely innocent. He said that nobody who saw Kaspar Hauser in those first few days could possibly believe otherwise. See his comments, quoted in Hermann Pies, *Kaspar Hauser: Eine Dokumentation,* p. 20.]

11. All of this, including the boots, were thoughtlessly thrown out right away, allegedly because they were in such bad condition! This is how objects were treated that could have been of the greatest importance in terms of *evidence!*

12. [Translator's note: the following letter is written in poor German with many spelling and grammatical mistakes. Not all of it is entirely intelli-

gible. I have tried to reproduce the errors in English so that the reader has some idea what the letter actually looked like to a native speaker.]

13. [Translator's note: The original reads: *"so müssen Sie im abschlagen oder in Raufang auf henggen."* The meaning is unclear.]

14. The following personal description does not come from the police files, since it cannot be found there, but from my own observations and from written comments made by other trustworthy people.

15. [Translator's note: This is not certain. The first person to examine Kaspar Hauser, the physician Dr. Preu, wrote, in an article published in *Archiv für homöopathische Heilkunst*, in 1832: *"Doch ist er geimpft, wie man am rechten Arm deutlich sieht."* (But he is vaccinated, as one can clearly see on his right arm.) But Daumer, on p. 170 of the manuscript I found, writes: *"Geimpft ist Hauser nicht. Gleich anfangs behaupteten dies 2 Aerzte (Medizinalrat v. Hoven und Dr. Osterhausen). Auch Dr. Preu nimmt jetzt seine Behauptung zurück."* (Hauser is not vaccinated. Right from the beginning two physicians, von Hoven and Dr. Osterhausen, claimed this. Dr. Preu also now retracts his claim.)]

16. The author of this book expressed at the time the desire to see Kaspar's face painted by a skilled portraitist, because it would almost certainly soon change. The wish was to remain unfulfilled, but my suspicion [that the face would change] soon proved true.

17. [Translator's note: Johann Karl Osterhausen. His observations on Kaspar Hauser are reprinted in Mayer and Tradowsky, *Kaspar Hauser,* pp. 38–41.]

18. It is an unfortunate circumstance that in the whole city of Nuremberg there was not a single person who displayed sufficient scientific interest to want to undertake physiological examinations of Kaspar Hauser. Even just a chemical analysis of the urine, saliva, and other bodily discharges of this young man who had been raised exclusively on bread and water would have yielded considerable scientific material of some consequence. This scientific material in turn would have proved of judicial significance: It would have confirmed to the point of graphic certainty the fact that Kaspar until now really had been raised on bread and water. But when the judicial system finally, after many fruitless efforts on its part, was in a position to take up matters connected to Kaspar Hauser, the opportunity to undertake such examinations was long gone.

19. Apparently, though I cannot vouch for it, somebody is supposed to have shot at him with a rifle, to test him, as a joke.

20. [Translator's note: Joseph Blaimer, thirty-three at the time, who accompanied Kaspar Hauser on his walks through the city. He was deposed several times, and his remarks can be found in Pies, *Die Wahrheit über Kaspar Hausers Auftauchen und erste Nürnberger Zeit.*]

21. His arms and legs remained extremely weak. Only in September 1828, when he had begun to eat meat, did his strength progress, through re-

peated exercise, to the point where he could just about lift a weight of about thirty pounds slightly off the ground with both hands.

22. Not long after that, however, the feeling of shame was awakened in him; and he became as bashful as the most chaste and delicate girl. Taking his clothes off now is for him something horrible. When the wild Brazilian girl, Isabella, whom Mrs. Spix and Maritus brought back with them to Munich, had lived for some time among civilized people and worn clothes, she could only be forced with enormous efforts, by threats and beatings, to take her clothes off in front of a person who was to draw her.

23. One ought not even *later* to have made the questionable attempt to cloak the purely private investigations in the *apparent form* of an official interrogation, which only gave the increasingly large police files an odd appearance.

24. This public declaration is the document that has served as the source of all the many brochures and fliers that have appeared up to now about Kaspar. [Translator's note: The proclamation is translated in full in appendix 1].

25. [Translator's note: See appendix 3 for a translation of Kaspar Hauser's autobiography.]

26. He is still in the habit of using this expression to mean his abandonment in Nuremberg and the awakening of his mental life.

27. According to Kaspar's more detailed account, he never, not even when he was sleeping, lay with his whole body stretched out, but rather, whether awake or asleep, *sat with his back straight*. This is completely confirmed by several facts: by the unmistakable traces that have remained on his body; by the shape, peculiar to him alone, of his knees and the hollow beneath his knees; and by the very odd way, peculiar to him, he had of sitting on the floor with both legs outstretched. It is probable that the way his lair was constructed and some particular contrivance made him take this position. He himself is unable to give any further information on this point.

28. This account allows us to assume that his water was mixed with opium. Later the assumption was completely confirmed in the following circumstances: When Kaspar had long been living with Professor Daumer, his doctor once tried to get him to drink a glass of water that contained one drop of opium. Barely had Kaspar taken a single swallow of this water than he said: "This water tastes awful. It tastes just like the water that I sometimes had to drink in my cage."

29. From this and other circumstances it is clear that Kaspar was always treated with a certain primitive care during his imprisonment. This would then explain his devotion, which he retained for a long time, to the man "with whom he had always been." Only very recently is this beginning to diminish, though not yet to the point where he would like to see him punished. He would only like to see those who ordered his imprisonment punished; but the man himself, he said, had never done anything bad to him.

30. As early as on the first morning after his appearance in Nuremberg, Kaspar proved before people's very eyes that he had really had writing lessons, in fact *regular elementary lessons*. When the jailer Hiltel came to him in his prison that first morning, he gave him, either to keep him busy or to give him pleasure, two sheets of paper and a pencil. Kaspar hastily grabbed both of them, put the paper on the bench, sat himself down on the floor in front of it, and immediately began to write. He wrote continuously, without looking up or allowing himself to be disturbed by anything at all, until he had completely covered all four sides of the folio sheets with writing. These sheets of paper which are still to be found in the police files, don't really look any different than if Kaspar had had in front of him a sample of the kind children use as a model during their first writing lessons, though it was clear that he was writing from memory. In fact these sheets contain rows of letters and syllables. Each row consists of repetitions of the same letter or the same syllable. At the end of the page there are even to be found all the letters of the alphabet, just as one usually finds them in a sampler for children, one right after the other, all put together in one line, and then on another line the Arabic numbers from 1 to 10, again completely in order. One side of the sheet repeats over and over the name "Kaspar Hauser." On another the word *reiðer* (rider) is frequently found. But it is clear from the appearance of these sheets that Kaspar's writing had never progressed beyond the most elementary stage.

31. It is clear and can be demonstrated from other circumstances that Kaspar could not, at that time, distinguish between a rising motion and a descending one, high from low, even in his own feelings, let alone was he capable of correctly indicating this difference in words. What Kaspar called a "hill" was most probably *steps*, as became clear from other comments he made. Kaspar thinks he can remember being scraped on his side as he was being carried.

32. [Translator's note: André-Marie Jean-Jacques Dupin, 1783–1865, French lawyer and member of the French Academy.]

33. In his *Reisen durch Deutschland* (see the *Göttingsche gelehrte Anzeige,* July 1831, p. 1097).

34. In Calderón's *Life Is a Dream.*

35. [Translator's note: Feuerbach was the author of the Bavarian Criminal Code.]

36. See [Julius Friedrich Heinrich] Abegg, *Untersuchungen aus dem Gebiete der Strafrechtswissenschaft,* Part III.

37. *Handbuch der Strafrechtswissenschaft,* Part I, Paragraph 179ff.

38. [Translator's note: This is Feuerbach's first hint, apart from the quotation from Calderón that opens the book, that Kaspar Hauser's imprisonment may have had a dynastic purpose. His use of the words *"geheiligte Räume"* (hallowed halls), suggesting palace rooms, was clearly intentional.]

39. [Translator's note: Remember that Feuerbach wrote this in 1831. It is ironic in light of what happened: In 1833, when Kaspar Hauser was lying wounded and dying, both Meyer and Stanhope said he was only pretending. Even after he died of the wound, they both maintained their position.]

40. [Translator's note: There is a passage on page 69 of Daumer's unpublished diary that is relevant to this remark. Daumer writes that when Kaspar Hauser "saw monkeys doing all kinds of tricks, he was thrilled. But when he realized that they had to begin all over again to satisfy a new audience, he begged piteously to be led away. He said later that out of compassion he could no longer bear to watch, for he himself had experienced how disgusting it was to have to start all over again after what he had already told and demonstrated to curious onlookers a thousand times."]

41. His saliva was so much like glue that when he removed the pictures, parts of them remained on the wall, and parts of the plaster stuck to the pictures.

42. Professor Daumer's notes agree with this observation. [Translator's note: Feuerbach could have inserted this note at many points in his book. Why he does so precisely here is not clear; he is correct however. For on page 5 of the unpublished Daumer diary there is the following note: "At first he did not understand 'I' and 'you.' He spoke of himself in the third person, like a child, and called himself Kaspar, which when speaking with him, one had to do as well if one wanted to be understood. The word 'you' he is supposed to have used as the proper name of the unknown man with whom he had earlier lived, calling him the 'You.'"]

43. [Translator's note: One can't help wondering if Feuerbach's quote is correct here. Is Kaspar Hauser referring to the few times the man taught him to read and write, or perhaps to the time he was beaten for making noise with his horse? Otherwise it is hard to see how the man taught him anything at all, and by what means.]

44. In his *Philosophie de Newton (Oeuvres complètes* [Gotha: 1786], vol. 31, pp. 118ff).

45. *Lettre sur les aveugles à l'usage de ceux qui voyent* (Londres: 1749), pp. 159–64. Moreover, Diderot wrote down Voltaire's account word for word.

46. Nonetheless this public announcement did not entirely have the desired effect. Just as a stranger could not easily visit Nuremberg and not be taken on a visit to the grave of Saint Sebaldus, the paintings on glass in the Church of Saint Lawrence, [the statue of] the little boy herding the geese, so, too, now nobody could feel he had properly visited Nuremberg if he did not at least get to see the mysterious adopted child of this city. From the time Kaspar arrived in Nuremberg to the time of my writing, several hundred people of almost every European nation, from all social ranks, scholars, artists, statesmen, officials of every kind, high and the highest, have seen and spoken with him.

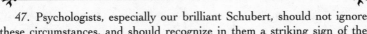

47. Psychologists, especially our brilliant Schubert, should not ignore these circumstances, and should recognize in them a striking sign of the state of Kaspar's mind at the time.

48. Until the time he was able to eat cooked food, he was constantly thirsty, and drank daily from five to six quarts of cold water. He is still a great drinker of water, so much so that our famous water doctor, Professor Oertel, could hold him up to everybody as a model.

49. [Translator's note: This passage is *not* among the pages of Daumer's manuscript that I found in Stuttgart. Where, then, does it come from? The idea is of course found in many places in Daumer, including my manuscript, but not word for word.]

50. [Translator's note: There is an error here. This passage comes from the manuscript Daumer sent Feuerbach. But what Daumer actually said was not a "Turkish" horse, but a *"tückisches"* horse, a stubborn, or willful, horse. See p. 175.]

51. Mr. Merker of Berlin. [Translator's note: See the Introduction, p. 51.]

52. [Translator's note: He was a mathematics teacher in the Gymnasium in Nuremberg who took it upon himself to question Kaspar Hauser about his early life, when he was living in Daumer's house. His manuscript was included in Daumer's 1873 book and is also reproduced in Pies, *Augenzeugenberichte*, pp. 448–55. See also Pies's note on p. 513.]

53. [Translator's note: In the diary by Daumer that I found in Stuttgart, on page 42 is the sentence: "At the beginning of September he began to write down the story of his past fate." Pies notes in the margin: "Important!" See also the Introduction, p. 10.]

54. This refers to an incident when Kaspar was very frightened by the chimney sweep, who was sweeping in the kitchen.

55. [Translator's note: *"Nicht nach Erlangen in Wallfisch."* Erlangen is a city not far from Nuremberg. Could Wallfisch be the name of a restaurant or hotel there? or is it a family name? *Wal* in German means a whale.]

56. [Translator's note: It is not clear to me why Feuerbach would omit this description. When Kaspar Hauser was deposed on October 20, 1829, he provided such a description as best he could. It is printed in Pies, *Augenzeugenberichte*, pp. 471ff. It is interesting that when asked about the man's voice, Kaspar said: "The voice in which he said to me that you must die before you leave the city of Nuremberg, was quiet, but nonetheless I was able to recognize in this quiet voice the man who brought me here to Nuremberg and also the same person who had spoken to me there (in the dungeon) with a quiet or distorted voice."]

57. This is what he always called his foster mother, the mother of Professor Daumer.

58. Every step he reports having made turned out to be true through traces of blood.

59. Traces of blood on the closet could be seen for several days later.

60. How exactly, honestly, and true to nature does Kaspar relate the effects of fear and anxiety. There is no doubt that he did not crawl into the cellar to hide through an already open door. There can be no doubt that he had to have lifted this door on his own, and he did so. But it is just as little open to doubt that Kaspar, the weakling, would have been completely incapable, under any other circumstances, and at any other time, of the Herculean effort needed to lift the cellar trap door.

61. [Translator's note: I do not know what Feuerbach is referring to here. Does he mean that he has found the weapon, or that he knows something about the identity of the perpetrator?]

62. [Translator's note: Full details with transcriptions of the depositions can be found in Pies's *Dokumentation*, chap. 7, "Das Nürnberger Attentat," pp. 57–77.]

63. [Translator's note: In French medieval tales, in Chaucer and Spenser, and in Shakespeare's *A Midsummer Night's Dream*, Oberon is the king of the fairies.]

64. [Translator's note: This is without any doubt a reference to Kaspar's royal birth as the son of the Grand Duke Karl of Baden and Stéphanie. That Feuerbach believed this is clear from the manuscript, where this page contains a genealogical study showing that Feuerbach had already solved the mystery. It is reproduced in Mayer and Tradowsky, *Kaspar Hauser*, p. 409. See my Introduction, p. 29.]

65. [Translator's note:

Doch was verübt' die schwarze Mitternacht
Wird endlich, wenn es tagt, an's Sonnenlicht gebracht.

This sounds like a quote but I have not been able to trace it.]

66. Except for riding, which he still passionately loves. In skill and elegance in riding, as well as in his way of mounting and dismounting, he can hold his own with the most talented riding master. In this respect Kaspar is an object of admiration to several of our best officers.

67. Especially since the attempt on his life.

68. He was finally released from this situation, even as I write this booklet, through the generosity of the honorable Lord Stanhope, who has formally taken him as his foster son. He is living now in Ansbach, where he has been handed over to a competent grade-school teacher, and at the same time living in his house. Later on, accompanied by security, he will follow his beloved foster father to England. [Translator's note: There was nothing competent about his teacher, Meyer, and Stanhope meant Kaspar Hauser nothing good. See the Introduction, pp. 18–26.]

69. [Translator's note: Ernst Wilhelm Hengstenberg, 1802–69, was a Protestant theologian.]

70. He [Kasper] has [recently been] instructed in the religion to which the majority of the inhabitants of Nuremberg, Lutheran Protestants, belong.

APPENDICES

Translation of Mayor Binder's Proclamation

Proclamation

With ref. to a young man raised in unlawful captivity, completely neglected, and then abandoned. 2138 F. 1–4.

From the municipal authorities of the royal Bavarian city of Nuremberg, a case is hereby brought to general public attention that is so unprecedented and in its way scandalous that it is bound to engage the attention of all official institutions, of the police, the judiciary, civil courts, military authorities, but also the empathy of all sensitive people of our fatherland.

On the second day of the Pentecostal holiday, May 26, 1828, in the afternoon between four and five, a young man, unaccompanied, who, to judge by his appearance, was between sixteen and eighteen years old, approached a citizen of this city at the beginning of the Kreuzgasse, near the so-called Unschlittplatz, and asked him where the street called New Tower was. The citizen offered to show the young man the way and accompanied him. On the way the young man produced a sealed letter from his pocket with the following address: To the Honorable Captain of the Cavalry of the Fourth Squadron of the Sixth Regiment of the Light Cavalry in Nuremberg. Whereupon the citizen decided to take him to the Guard Tower in front of the New Gate to inquire there about the matter. On the way the citizen attempted to strike up a conversation with him, but was soon convinced that such would not be possible for lack of understanding. When he reached the New Gate, upon producing the aforementioned letter, the young man was directed toward a nearby house in which lived the addressee, the captain of the cavalry. In his absence his servant tried his best to question the young man, but could not obtain a satisfactory response. Meanwhile the captain of the cavalry had returned and read the letter. He too tried in vain to determine the strange and enigmatic content of the letter by questioning the young man, and so handed the letter and the young man over to the municipal authorities that very evening.

What the letter and the attachments contained is reproduced here in an exact facsimile, numbered one, submitted to the royal court for all the districts of the Upper and Lower Donau [Danube], the Regen and the Isar.

An officer from the municipal authority conducted a first deposition with him, but short, incoherent answers gave rise to no other result but this: that he did not know the place or the surroundings of his birth, or of his residence, or of his origin, and that he had always been with the unknown man until he got to the "big village" (Nuremberg), whereupon the stranger quickly departed.

His behavior during this first deposition provided no reason to assume that it was occasioned by idiocy or dissimulation, but rather led one to believe that this young man, from childhood, had been deprived of all human society and kept prisoner, isolated in an animallike state in the most inhuman manner. The circumstance that primarily justified this conclusion was the fact that he would eat nothing but water and bread. Nevertheless the municipal authority, in order to make certain that there was no deception, ordered the royal forensic physician of the city to observe and examine him, while at the same time the experienced jailer was to observe him carefully in secret as well. But since the physician was not able to discover anything whatsoever that could give rise to suspicions about the young man, after six days the following expert opinion, to quote it exactly, stated: "That this person is neither crazy nor an idiot, but evidently had been raised like a half-wild person, had been forcibly and in the most heinous way removed from all human and societal education, could not be persuaded to consume regular food, but only black bread and water."

The signatory of this proclamation, the head of the municipal authority and of the police senate was able to convince himself of the truth of this judgment in a detailed deposition that he himself conducted with this young man shortly thereafter. What emerged from this deposition was that the young man had no concept of humans or of animals, and that apart from *"Buben"* (boys), by which he meant only himself and the man with whom he had always been, and a *"Roß"* (horse) with which he had played, he knew nothing.

His limited understanding, although it was in the most obvious contrast to his enormous intellectual curiosity and an extraordinary memory, suggesting an excellent hereditary predisposition, soon determined the author of this proclamation to forsake the format of a formal deposition and instead to engage the young man in intimate conversations. Physicians, teachers, educators, psychologists, court officials, police officials, the most astute observers from all social classes, and innumerable people who were deeply moved by his sad past have since been allowed to visit him, and their repeated comments agree with the views of the undersigned police official.

He is now free, as much as is possible under supervision, but remains true to the first account of his fate, apart from the welcome visible daily progress in his mental development. Based on numerous conversations with him, the undersigned can, with confidence, present the following account of his former life in so far as it is clear to himself:

The appearance of Kaspar Hauser—this is how this victim of inhuman treatment is called—is described in the accompanying attachment number 2. (We need only add that he speaks a Bavarian dialect such as is heard in the region of Regensburg, Straubing, Landshut, etc., and perhaps also in Altötting, and Burghausen, and that he is vaccinated on his right arm.) He was always locked up all alone. He heard and saw nobody except the monster who handed him his only nourishment, bread and water. He was permanently confined in a small, narrow, low room at ground level, without a hardwood floor, it would seem, just hard-packed earth, but whose ceiling consisted of two slabs of wood that were pushed and tied together. Two small, oblong windows were shuttered with wooden logs and therefore let in only a few weak rays of hazy light. Never did he see the sun. He sat on the ground dressed in no other clothing except a shirt and short, probably dark-colored pants that were tapered at the knees, held up by suspenders (called *"Halfter"* according to the Bavarian dialect). He played with two white wooden horses, which he called Ross, and a white wooden dog, by hanging various little toys around their necks, and spoke with them as much as his lack of concepts and words permitted. One of these horses was smaller than the other, neither taller than about a foot or a foot and a quarter. The dog was much smaller than either of the two horses—in other words ordinary children's toys. In the ground of his prison there was, so it seems, a hole dug out to form a kind of pot or some similar receptacle, with a cover, in which he could perform his bodily necessities. Not far from that, lying on the ground, was a sack of straw that he at first called his bed. Since on account of his lack of exercise he could barely stand up or walk, but rather when he tried to stand up would fall, he would slide across the floor to his horses and from there to his pot and from there to his sack of straw upon which he slept. This he always did as soon as night fell. Earliest morning would find him once again awake. When he awoke he would find black bread and fresh water in front of his bed and the pot mentioned above would [have been] emptied.

He rightly concluded from this that in place of the food he had eaten the day before, during his sleep he would be brought new food and in the same way the pot would be cleaned. He maintains the same with respect to cutting his fingernails and hair. He changed his shirt rarely, and since he did not know how it happened, he insisted that it must have taken place during his sleep, which was good and sound. The bread he enjoyed was always enough, but there was not always a sufficient supply of water to quench his thirst.

The entrance to his prison was guarded by a small, low door that was locked from the outside. The oven that was inside was white, small, round, looked a bit like a large beehive, and was heated (or as he put it, *"einkenten"*) from the outside. He was in this prison for a long, long, time, but how long he does not know, for he has no concept of divisions of time. He saw nobody in there, no ray of sunlight, no shimmer of the moon, no light, heard no human voice, no sound of a bird, no cry from an animal, no footstep. Then at last the door of the prison opened and the unknown man who took him to Nuremberg entered, barefoot and just about as poorly clothed as he was, and bent over so as not to hit his head, so that although he was only of medium height, he nearly touched the ceiling of the prison and revealed himself to be the one who always brought him bread and water and had given him the horses as a present.

The same man gave him the books listed under attachment number 3, and told him that now he had to learn to read and write and then go to this father, who was a rider, and that he too would become a rider. Thanks to his extraordinary mental gifts, which had not been dulled in spite of a long and terrible incarceration, the efforts of the unknown man were successful. He said that he learned quickly and easily, which can be believed given his current apparent progress, but did not learn much, only barely to read and write his name, since the unknown [man] always returned only after four days, on the fifth day, to instruct him. But he always came in the same clothes, barefoot, and Hauser did not hear him come until he had opened the door.

In order to increase his desire to learn, the man promised him that he would allow him, if he learned well, to ride around the prison with his horses. He still complains bitterly that although he fulfilled that condition and then rode around the prison, the unknown man did not keep his word, but hit him with a stick, and when he cried, punished him (the scars are still visible on his right elbow) and severely forbade him to ride around. He used a pencil for writing, which the unknown man told him was a quill. While the lesson was being administered, the man seriously warned him "never to try to get out the door, because above him was heaven, and in heaven there was a god who would be angry and would beat him if he tried to get out."

In this way a substantial time passed, but in his opinion it was not as long as he had been in Nuremberg, when he was suddenly awakened in the middle of the night. The unknown man stood before him once again and told him that he wanted to take him away at once. He cried over this but soon allowed himself to be calmed down by the cherished fantasy, often presaged and probably also explained, that he would see his father and become, like him, a rider. The unknown man who until now had come to him dressed only in a shirt and short tapered pants and barefoot, had now come dressed in a short jacket (also called a *Jankerl* and a *Kittel*), boots, and a crude, round, black gentleman's hat; and was wearing blue stockings.

He took Hauser on his back, just as he was, dressed only in a shirt and short pants, with a large, broad, black, round peasant's hat, peaked at the top, straight from his prison to the outside and immediately began climbing a long, high mountain until day broke. Hauser had fallen asleep in the meantime and only awakened when he was placed on the ground. The unknown man then taught him to walk, which he found very difficult, since he was barefoot and the soles of his feet were very tender. He had to sit down, but finally he was able to walk better and alternated between walking and resting when the second night came. They lay down in the open air on the ground, and it began to rain hard, or, as he put it earlier, "It poured from heaven." Poor Kaspar was bitterly cold. Nonetheless he fell asleep and at daybreak set out on the voyage in the same way as before, accompanied by the unknown man. Walking had become easier for him, but his legs and back hurt him more and more. The third night they camped out in the fresh air once again, and although it did not rain that night, it was very cold and he once again froze. At the first sign of light of the third day they set forth again in the same way as before, and while they were still far away from here, the unknown man took out of a bundle wrapped in cloth that he had been carrying with him the clothes described below under attachment 2, except for the blue stockings that he removed from his own feet, and dressed Kaspar in them. The man then exchanged his hat, which was a coarse, black man's hat, for the one he had given him when they left the prison, put on his boots again over his bare feet, which were, according to Hauser's opinion, much prettier than the lousy boots that he had to put on, and finally took away the trousers Hauser had worn in the prison. Altered in this manner, they continued on their journey. Their food on the entire trip was the same as that which Hauser had enjoyed in the prison, bread in the form of a large loaf, and water in a bottle, which the unknown man carried in a bag. During the entire trip he taught him to say the Lord's Prayer and one other prayer on a rosary he gave him, and which he saw then for the first time. He had never heard either before, but now he can still recite them. The man entertained him with the story that he was going to see his father and would become a rider, just as he had been, which always made Kaspar happy. On the whole trip they did not go into any house, but passed houses and people, though of course Hauser cannot describe them. The unknown man admonished him to look only at the ground so that he could walk properly, but probably more likely so that he would not be able to form any impression of his surroundings such that he would be in a position to recognize them again. He did strictly as he was told.

When they were finally approaching Nuremberg, which the unknown man called the "big village," he pulled the already mentioned letter out of his pocket and handed it to Kaspar Hauser with the instruction that he was to carry it into the big village and show it and give it to a boy who would then lead him further. It appears that he showed him the way, carefully and over and over, that he was to take on his own, and promised him, when Hauser did not want to separate from him, that he would soon follow him.

Hauser walked, as he had been instructed, straight ahead and so came to the gate, without knowing which one it was, and probably shortly thereafter came to the man who showed him the way.

If this in its own way perhaps unique example of inhuman, heartless behavior, never before recorded, touches everyone with human feelings, so also should even the most inquisitive intellect recognize that this case represents pure truth for the following reasons: The soft hand of our foundling; the simple food that until this very moment he still eats, looking healthy and with a well-nourished body, rejecting with the greatest disgust any other, near or far, that is offered him, or if he tries it with genuine disgust immediately pushes it away; the sensitivity of his sense of smell and taste with respect to the simplest objects, for example, flowers, strawberries, milk, which have no effect on other people; his body, which appears strong, but which experiments showed was weak, not even as strong as that of an eight-year-old child; his gait, which is, in contrast to his appearance, slow, swaying, exhausting for him, more like that of a child of only two years old; his poor nerves, which cause his hands momentarily to tremble and the muscles in his face to twitch at the slightest exertion; his gaze, which is, to be sure, clear and far reaching but not very strong, and which is very sensitive to the influence of daylight; his inclination to look down at the ground as well as his inclination to solitude; a certain discomfort when he is outside in the wonderful realm of nature or when he is among many people; his aversion to loud noises and sounds; his lack of words, ideas, and concepts about all objects, living ones and metaphysical ones, in remarkable contrast to his obvious attempts to make himself understood and to understand, and the manner in which he speaks, in short broken sentences. All these important examples taken together allow one to conclude, quite justly, that he was kept wrongfully imprisoned, excluded from all human company for many, many years.

In contrast is his pure, open, innocent look; his broad, high forehead; the greatest lack of guile in his nature, which still does not distinguish [between] the sexes, cannot fathom that there is a difference, and even now is only able to tell people apart by the different kinds of clothes they wear; his indescribable gentleness; his warmth and kindness, which attract everybody in his presence, as a result of which, initially, he thought even of his oppressor only with tears, and now, with a new sense of freedom, with affection; his attachment to the past, which was initially experienced as a deep nostalgia for his home, his prison, and his jailer, then transformed into a melancholy memory that only now, through loving treatment, he is gradually losing; his devotion, sincere and touching, to all those who often deal with him and show him kindness; but also his trust toward all other people; his protectiveness of the smallest insect; his distaste for anything that could cause even the slightest suffering to a person or an animal; his unconditional obedience and submissiveness to all who wish him well, as well as his freedom from any kind of rudeness or vice, with his sense for what is evil; and finally his extraordinary desire to learn, through which—with the help of a good mind that is quick to understand and remember—his vocabulary, which in the beginning consisted of barely fifty words, now enriched, already includes ideas and concepts of many objects of which, apart from those that were in his prison, he knew nothing, and now encompasses both the idea of time and place; his very special fondness for music and drawing, which were completely unknown to him previously; his desire and skill in learning both of them; and his extraordinary love of order and cleanliness; as well as his childlike being and his pure, unsullied soul—these important phenomena taken all together, in so far as they support and strengthen his claims about his unlawful imprisonment, also promote the fullest conviction that nature has richly provided him with excellent predispositions of mind, temperament, and heart. These circumstances, taken together with a closer examination of the contents of the letters reproduced below as attachment number 1, which reveals them to be improbable and fabricated, justify the urgent suspicion that along with the unlawful confinement, there was a no-less-serious crime connected with deception about his family class, which robbed him of perhaps his parents, and even if they were no longer alive [at the time?], at least his freedom, his fortune, and probably the advantages of noble birth, but in any event along with the innocent pleasures of the joyful world of a child, he was robbed of the greatest treasures (*höchsten Güter*) of life, and his physical and mental development were violently suppressed and held back. The fact that in his prison he was able to speak with his toys, before he had seen the unknown man and had been instructed by him in language, proves that the crime against him goes back to the first years of his childhood, perhaps between his second and fourth year, and therefore had begun in a time when he was able to speak and was perhaps already the object of a noble education, which, like a star in the dark night of his life, shines forth from his entire being.

It is our task to uncover the crime that was without any doubt committed against him, to discover the villain or his helpers who committed it, and in this manner to put him, as far as this is possible, in possession of his lost birthright, not as a means of getting rid of him, since the community that has placed him under its protection loves him and considers him a pawn of love delivered by providence and will not hand over this pawn to anyone until it has full proof of any claim to rights over him. All those officials from the courts, from the police, from the civil and military authorities, and all those who carry in their bosoms a human heart, are urgently requested to communicate to the undersigned police office all, even the most remote, traces, signs, and grounds of suspicion that could lead to the discovery of the crime, so that it will be in a position to hand over the inquiry to the appropriate court for further action. It hardly needs to be reiterated in this context that apart from determining the prison, or at least the probably quiet, isolated area where it is or was to be found, given that the villain who kept Hauser a prisoner there may well have leveled it after our foundling was taken away, and removed all trace of it. The investigation will have to turn to the discovery of a child of two to four years old who has been missing for the last fourteen to eighteen years, and about whose disappearance perhaps dark rumors are circulating.

Every communication, every tip will be gratefully used, and if the informant is named, his name will as far as possible not be revealed. As circumstances warrant, there may be a generous reward.

On the other hand, anonymous information cannot be taken into account.

Nuremberg, July 7, 1828. [Signed:] Binder, First Mayor

Appendix 2

A New Kaspar Hauser Manuscript

The discovery of new material about the mystery of Kaspar Hauser is an extremely rare occurrence. Hence a new manuscript bearing on his life is of considerable significance. This significance is even greater when one takes into account that the manuscript in question is, in fact, the earliest existing document on the life, thought, and words of the "child of Europe." Moreover, it is the source for much of the information in Feuerbach's more famous book. Daumer sent this manuscript to Feuerbach, who used it extensively in writing his 1832 biography of Kaspar Hauser. Daumer, too, published a small book about Kaspar Hauser in 1832. The relation between the two books was never clear. (Daumer's had a small audience and was soon forgotten; Feuerbach's book has hardly ever been out of print since it was first published.) A little-known but important passage in one of the Daumer's later books clarifies the situation and throws some interesting new light on Stanhope as well. Here is the whole passage:

I read with astonishment in a letter from Stanhope [to Feuerbach] of April 25, 1832, which I found in papers in the Feuerbach estate,[1] the following passage: "I found Daumer's book very interesting, because of its subject matter. It is very much to be regretted that I could not talk him out of publishing this book. It was superfluous [given your book] and could even be harmful to the cause because of his presentation. I showed you [Feuerbach] the letter I wrote to him about this, and you were kind enough to agree with me. Since I did not receive any reply from him [Daumer], I thought he had seen my point, and heard nothing more until his book was announced. In this he seems not to have acted openly and generously, in that he led both of us astray." I [Daumer] never received a letter from the count, and certainly not one which advised me against my intention of publishing a book about Kaspar Hauser. I would certainly remember if such a letter had been sent.[2] Even today [in my seventies] I have still not lost my memory. It has never been my practice to allow letters written to me to go unanswered, particularly ones of that nature. Either the letter by Stanhope was lost, which does not seem probable to me, or he, not I, is misleading somebody. Feuerbach was very unhappy that I too was writing a book about Kaspar Hauser, since he did not want to divide the attention of the public which he hoped to win for his book, and see it diverted in a second direction. Moreover, he [Feuerbach] wanted to see to it that what he had extracted from the rich material I sent him, should be found only in his book. He wanted, as one can see from the passage I quoted, to use Stanhope to encourage me to take no further action and leave everything to him. Stanhope wrote a letter to that effect and showed it to Feuerbach, but deceived him, it would seem, in that he never sent the letter [to me]. One can imagine why he did this. He was not really on Feuerbach's side, nor on that of his cause [Kaspar Hauser's welfare], and did not want to help. It was fine with him for things to take a bad turn. As one can see from the letter, Feuerbach had expressed the same concern, namely that I would reveal more than the careful selection he thought prudent to publish. It is in fact true that I am very unsophisticated in such matters, and considered it my duty to say everything I knew and thought to be true [about Kaspar Hauser], even if such things appeared unbelievable to others. Stanhope, however, did not want to allow himself to be used to prevent this [namely, my publishing my book]; but here too Stanhope played foul, and pretended that he had done what he could in this matter [when in fact he had done nothing]. Now I understand the grudge that Feuerbach bore me. "The matter," wrote Stanhope, "took exactly the course you expected; the facts will appear unbelievable to many people. . . . The true authentic picture, the one you published, should have appeared on its own." Stanhope himself seized the opportunity immediately to dig up a whole host of doubts about Hauser's story, not only about those parts of his story that were obscure, extraordinary or strange, but also other matters, to which he raised the most trivial objections which were in part unjustified by the standards of normal reasoning. After Feuerbach's death he attacked Feuerbach's account, which in the letter [to Feuerbach himself], he characterized as being "the true and authentic account," calling it "dishonest," "absurd," and "fabricated." He was particularly critical because so much of the account was based on my notes. Stanhope thus reveals himself to be a paragon of falsehood and dishonesty, and no sensible, honest person could fail to be repulsed. The noble Lord could never have imagined in his wildest dreams that his letters would one day fall into my hands. Marvelous are the ways of fate! After all this time, I find myself in a position to see through and expose the entire intrigue.[3]

The new manuscript consists of 170 typed pages, a copy of handwritten notes made by Kaspar Hauser's first teacher, Georg Friedrich Daumer, during the years (1828–30) that Kaspar Hauser lived in his house in Nuremberg.

That such notes had ever been taken was known from only a single source, a note that Daumer made in a late-published book about Kaspar Hauser.[4] He said there that he had sent a *handwritten* copy of his original notes to the great judge, Paul Johann Anselm Ritter von Feuerbach, for use in writing his Kaspar Hauser book.[5] Here is the passage:

> I sent my observations on Hauser to Feuerbach[6] in the form of a handwritten copy, made by somebody else. Because of eye-strain, I was not myself able to read through it and correct any errors in it. The copyist did in fact make errors, which were unfortunately not caught, precisely in the notes in question and that is how they got into Feuerbach's book. I had spoken of an "unruly" (*tückisches*) horse; this was turned into a Turkish (*türkisches*) horse. So naturally when the horse trainer read this he must have wondered about it. I had written: "Hauser never felt anything in his seat, only a little bit in his thighs." Instead of "only" the copyist read "or" and so Feuerbach writes: "He rode for hours without getting sore, or maybe just a little pain in his thighs or seat."[7]

In fact, we do find the first passage reproduced in our manuscript, which is a further indication that the text is genuine. However, the second passage is not found in the present manuscript, a puzzling omission. The only explanation I can think of is that the passages were all separately written out on cards, and this particular one was missing. I am surprised, though, that Pies did not notice this and comment on it somewhere in the manuscript.

This is the *only* reference that might have alerted scholars to the fact that these notes, and a handwritten copy, had at least at one time existed and had been used by Feuerbach in writing his book.

Material concerning Kaspar Hauser has been assiduously collected in Germany for the last 165 years. No document answering the description given by Daumer has ever been found, or indeed even referred to.

Among the many authors of books about Kaspar Hauser, one scholar stands head and shoulders above all the rest, the one truly great Kaspar Hauser researcher, Hermann Pies (1888–1983). Pies began writing the first serious historical works on Kaspar Hauser in the 1920s. He visited every open archive, and it was thanks to his early work in the State Library in Munich that we possess most of the documents that we do on Kaspar Hauser. The vast majority of the originals were destroyed during World War II. We only have Pies's copies. These were, however, so carefully made that his books on the basis of these documents are models of their kind.

Pies worked on Kaspar Hauser for more than sixty years. When he died, in 1981, Johannes Mayer of Stuttgart inherited his library, correspondence, and archive. Dr. Mayer graciously allowed me to work for some time in this archive.

It was there that I found the notebook in question. What I found was a typed and bound work of 170 pages, with Pies's handwritten annotations. At first it was not clear to me what, exactly, this manuscript was. Pies had written on the spine of the volume: *Daumer and Feuerbach on Kaspar Hauser.* Perhaps, I thought, Feuerbach had interleaved his own observations.[8] But a detailed reading showed that all the notes were by Daumer alone. At first I assumed that these were copies of original notes for Daumer's many subsequent volumes on

Kaspar Hauser. But a closer reading showed me that there were passages that were not *anywhere* in the published record.

Only, it would seem, Daumer, Feuerbach, and Pies had seen this manuscript. But was it authentic? The age of the paper seemed to be about sixty years old. Could it possibly be a forgery? What would be the point? Who would or could have done such a thing, and to what end? The material is certainly important, but it does not alter our basic view of Kaspar Hauser, it merely adds to it. I could not imagine how an unauthentic manuscript would have made its way into Pies's library. On the other hand, we could not explain the fact that Pies had let such a discovery go unrecorded: Nowhere in Pies's voluminous writings is this manuscript even hinted at.

The only way to authenticate the manuscript would be to find a reference to it in one of the vast number of letters to and from Pies.

I was lucky.

One envelope of correspondence contains letters to and from the German jurist and historian of law, Professor Gustav Radbruch.[9] In the 1930s Radbruch was writing his much-admired biography of Anselm von Feuerbach. Only one small part of that book dealt with Feuerbach's relation to Kaspar Hauser, but it was only natural that Radbruch would turn to the leading scholar on the topic, Hermann Pies, before he published. Naturally Radbruch was in touch with Feuerbach's descendants, who lived in South Germany, in Lindau on the Lac de Constance (Bodensee). While there he saw a handwritten copy of Daumer's original notes, and told Pies about it in a letter reproduced below. He told him also that Feuerbach was willing to send it to him. He said he would send Pies that section of the manuscript of his book that dealt with Kaspar Hauser. Pies did not reply for several months, but when he did, it was to be one of those great letters that one is privileged to see only very rarely, in which the stature of the man and a feel for the time is revealed. It also, greatly to our fortune, describes the manuscript in question, and details its unique importance. The letter itself is long, and somewhat complicated for a reader completely unfamiliar with Kaspar Hauser research. But if ever it could be said that a letter was worth quoting in full, this is that case. I have attempted to elucidate all the references in notes to the letter. Much of the subject matter is dealt with in my introduction to this volume, and wherever this is the case I give the page number.

First the letter from Professor Radbruch to Dr. Pies, dated December 7, 1933:

> Many thanks for your kind letter. I am greatly looking forward to receiving your manuscript. In the meantime I was in Lindau (Bodensee) at the Feuerbachs. There I saw a sizable Kaspar Hauser manuscript, namely Daumer's notes on his observations on Kaspar Hauser, in a copy that Feuerbach used as the foundation of his book on Kaspar Hauser. Mr. Feuerbach is prepared to send it to you. With best wishes, I remain, Radbruch.

Pies replied on April 24, 1934:

> Dear Professor:
> First I must ask your forgiveness for not having sent long ago the article I promised you on Feuerbach and Kaspar Hauser. But, especially before Easter, and still to this day, my days were so taken up with official work that I had to put everything else on hold. I want to thank you further for kindly sending me your Feuerbach manuscript, at least that portion of it which concerns Feuerbach's relation to Hauser. I am sure I do not need to tell you how much your writing interested me. The introduction about the "myth" of Kaspar Hauser I consider to be the best thing I have read until now on this aspect of this many faceted topic. (I wrote on the same topic in the *Fränk[ische]. Zeit.*, in their special tribute on the one hundredth anniversary of the death of Kaspar Hauser.) Similarly, I think that Henriette Feuerbach's "honor-saving" of Feuerbach, this great proof of her deep love, pious reverence, and

powerful commitment to the truth, was the most appropriate way to end your Feuerbach/Hauser chapter. But the portion falling between this introduction and the ending I liked less. The style is brilliant. In particular, the way you used quotes betrayed the sharp eye and sure taste of an expert. But—allow me to be honest—I have the feeling that you wished to "protect" Feuerbach, as if you could not quite rid yourself of a slight suspicion that Feuerbach in the case of Kaspar Hauser had been "taken in." Instead of going into details, I would like, partly as a replacement for my essay, which is not yet finished, briefly to lay out for you my thoughts on the relation between Feuerbach and Kaspar Hauser. First as to the external facts: Feuerbach hears about the Nuremberg Moritat [a kind of puppet theater about Kaspar Hauser]. He acquaints himself in person with the situation [by paying a visit to Kaspar Hauser in Nuremberg].[10] In his letters to von der Recke,[11] he gives his impression of what he saw there. Meanwhile: There is a struggle for venue between the Mayor, Binder, and the Court of Appeals.[12] (Also involved is the local government, siding against Binder, with von Mieg as the president—he is the predecessor of Stichaner—But these arguments between the government and the Court of Appeals are not so important. They are mainly just turf battles of the different officials involved.)

Naturally the "Binder Novel"[13] is impeachable. (By the way, the collection by Meyer, called *Authentic Observations*,[14] is not complete: Usually the signature of the Court of Appeals is von Griner, Counsel to the Court of Appeals.) Feuerbach seems to have been involved primarily as the presiding judge of the Court of Appeals. His view of Kaspar Hauser is clear: Naturally, at that time, he could still have regarded the hypothesis that Kaspar Hauser was really the prince of Baden as a "romantic legend."[15] Before October 1829 interest was beginning to fade. Then an attempt is made on Kaspar Hauser's life, and he becomes a European sensation. Feuerbach once again visits Kaspar Hauser and acquaints himself with the situation. (His impressions, in his own handwriting, were printed in Bartning's book).[16] At that time, I believe, he was "morally convinced" of the identity between Kaspar Hauser and the prince of Baden, for what possible reason could there be for an attempt on his life if the victim was not "of high birth"—and what other "high birth" if not from Baden?[17] After 1829, but before he published his book at the end of 1831, Feuerbach received the copy of Daumer's notes on Kaspar Hauser. The last of these several hundred sheets of paper with notes on them is dated 1830. These notes are far more convincing than the later *Observations on Kaspar Hauser* (vol. 2, 1832),[18] which Daumer reworked [on the basis of these original notes?]. (I received this copy from Mr. Feuerbach in Lindau.[19]) Some of the pieces, to judge from their content, could not have been invented, all of them carry the unmistakable stamp of truth. (*Here,* at least, Daumer does not appear as the notorious "Fantasist" that he has been [in the later books], and I believe that it was these "notes" that finally strengthened Feuerbach's conviction of the "truth" of Kaspar Hauser.[20] At this point a controversy began in the professional literature. *For* Kaspar Hauser is Hitzig, in the *Annalen*.[21] *Against* Kaspar Hauser is Merker in the competing journal: *Beiträge*.[22]

Merker was from the very beginning angry that his application to see the official documents on the case were sent to Binder, the mayor, who sent them on to the local court. This was in 1829. The local court ruled against Merker having the documents (since the case was still pending). Hitzig, on the other hand, got everything. (The whole thing got so out of hand that Merker was, at the demand of the Nuremberg authorities, officially deposed in Berlin and was unable, at that time, to bring any concrete complaint against Hitzig.) Feuerbach's *Aktenstücke*[23] provided the *Annalen* with decisive material against the competition, and Merker was for the moment defeated. It was at this time [the end of 1831],[24] that Feuerbach's exhaustive brochure appeared, which finally made the case clear for all time to any *disinterested* and objective party. For Feuerbach it was naturally clear that the case is a "mystery," and that it is precisely in the nature of a mystery to remain mysterious. For the policeman Merker, who had a "sixth sense," on the other hand, understandably, it was no "mystery." Even today [in 1934], for the enraged[?][25] policeman, there are only two sorts of people: criminals and those who cannot be proven to be criminals. At the same time, of course, there were also some "errors" in Feuerbach's book, as, for example, the story of Kaspar Hauser's native ability to ride a horse, and some others, which provided the skeptic sufficient ground for attack.[26] (To close the case of Merker: after Feuerbach's death, Stanhope sent Merker his and Kaspar Hauser's teacher Meyer's *"Materialien,"* and there Merker was able, in tones of loud triumph, to declare to the astonished world that "the case of Kaspar Hauser is now, at last, finally explained in my favor.") Unfortunately the dead man, Feuerbach, was no longer able to lash back.[27] Feuerbach's final act on behalf of Kaspar Hauser was the *Mémoire*.[28] Naturally, concrete proofs for such a "political crime" [that is, a crime by the ruling royal house] can only be found with difficulty or perhaps not at all. (Moreover Feuerbach knew about the "story of the message in the bottle."[29]) He was equally convinced of the "danger" of his mission [to show that Kaspar Hauser was the prince of Baden.] (Even earlier he was afraid of "poison and daggers," as I read somewhere in the biographical *Nachlasswerk* of Ludwig Feuerbach.) A retraction of the content of the *Mémoire* [Memorandum] never took place. In short: Feuerbach had, to the end of his life, a well-rounded and well-grounded picture of Kaspar Hauser's life and fate.

Now, what has Feuerbach been accused of? Here we have carefully to distinguish the theory of Hauser as "foundling," and Hauser as "prince." I: Stanhope reproached Feuerbach for having written a novel.[30] For a number of reasons, which I have explained in several places in my books on Kaspar Hauser, I only believe assertions of Stanhope when they are also otherwise documented. At the end of his life Feuerbach was continuously sick, even mentally unbalanced. All the letters collected by his son [the philosopher Ludwig Feuerbach], prove that Feuerbach was plagued by illness throughout his entire life. I have collected dozens of passages that prove this. However, the best proof that the contrary was true is his work itself. Merker himself says of precisely Feuerbach's Kaspar Hauser book (I am citing from memory here): "Feuerbach has always written enchantingly, but in this book, he has written convincingly!"[31] Feuerbach himself belittles his small book! But this is a widely distributed virtue, or vice, of authors. On the one hand, I have found a passage in one of his letters where, on the contrary, he greatly praises his opus. So there is nothing to this self-description. After all, Feuerbach himself spoke of Kaspar Hauser disparagingly. Yes, and who has never so spoken about his fellow human beings? It certainly casts no doubt on Kaspar Hauser's "authenticity." That Kaspar Hauser sometimes was troublesome (as he was to both Daumer and Tucher) is clear. II: In regard to the prince theory. Yes, that was a dangerous story, at least Feuerbach considered it dangerous, which is crystal clear from the letter he wrote to Schmidt,[32] accompanying the memorandum. He certainly had no desire to betray his secret thoughts to just any stranger he happened to meet. This is how the correspondence between Feuerbach and Eberhard (Gotha) is to be explained.[33] On purely official grounds, it was incumbent on Feuerbach to research anything of importance that was brought to his attention. Naturally this included Eberhard's accusations. He could hardly write him: "My Dear Sir: You are on a false trail." A defender of Feuerbach has already shown that the whole style of the letter betrays Feuerbach's irony. This is especially true where Feuerbach speaks [of Kaspar Hauser] being "only a canon in miniature — one hardly misses the tonsure."[34] This is perfectly clear to me. The following counter-argument appears even more conclusive to me: Had Feuerbach taken the matter seriously, he would have waited for the results of the research (which were, in any case, negative) before so clearly betraying what he thought in that rather pompous passage in his book where he speaks of: "high and mighty Colossuses who stand guard in front of golden gates," etc.[35] It is characteristic that whenever a new objection to Feuerbach is brought forth it is always presented as a brand new "fact"! Thanks to the quiet and not-so-quiet help of Stanhope, Merker had already used all these counterarguments in his battle against Feuerbach. (He did not know anything about the Memorandum but he polemicized against those passages in the *"Seelenleben"* [Feuerbach's Kaspar Hauser book] that repeat the prince theory.) At that time the memory of the great man, who had recently died, was still too revered for these arguments to have sullied his reputation. They were completely forgotten. And Julius Meyer, who wrote in what was then a still very measured manner (otherwise he would have been immediately annihilated), did not have much success. Mittelstädt[36] hauled out, without knowing anything about them, the same arguments as Merker, but he had more success, thanks to the ballast of documents that in the eyes of the uninformed seemed to lend credibility to his arguments. Von der Linde[37] was belaboring the same point. To say nothing of Engel,[38] the angel who didn't have a clue, the most uninformed among the uninformed.

And so it was that in the writings about Feuerbach, in university speeches on the occasion of the hundredth anniversary of his birth, or the hundredth anniversary of his death, etc., there could slip in the version that: "But he really was wrong with respect to Kaspar Hauser! And he admitted he was wrong!" And more of the same. No! I want to make it clear: Feuerbach may have made a mistake. Everybody can make a mistake. He may have made mistakes in the case of Kaspar Hauser just as he did in writing up other cases during the course of a life rich in thoughts and events. But he did not make any *more* mistakes in the case of Kaspar Hauser [than in the others—that is, he made only minor errors]. Above all, nowhere is there to be found a retraction of his views on Kaspar Hauser. It is clear that there are ever-renewed attempts by more or less interested parties to throw mud on Feuerbach's views on Kaspar Hauser. The deeper psychological reason for this is also clear to me: There are two kinds of people in the world. There are those who, like Feuerbach, are for the abolition of torture. (And they do abolish it, just as Feuerbach did, if they are powerful enough and capable of acting.) The other kind of people are in favor of using torture, like Mittelstädt in the characteristic quote in Kolb (1883, p. 38, note[39]). The first love "myth" (to call it this, just this once), as did Feuerbach, Daumer, and others. The others see in everything only lies and deception. My dear Professor, please excuse this long letter. . . . I will be very interested in the complete text of your book, which I hope will appear soon and enjoy the great success due you and the memory of a great man, now dead. With kindest wishes, I remain, Yours truly, Pies.

Radbruch replied immediately, in a gracious letter dated April 27, 1934:

Dear Dr. Pies:

I am very grateful that you wrote back so quickly and in such detail. Your criticism, quite apart from all the single facts, touches on a point that is important to me. I really wanted to know what an informed and clever reader would be able to discern about my own point of view regarding Kaspar Hauser from my comments. Your remarks show me that the skeptical tone I have used toward Kaspar Hauser is too sharp. Actually I tend rather to believe in him. You are completely right: All the reactions to Kaspar Hauser can be divided into two types of people, and I consider myself, when the question is put in this way, very definitely on one side. But as a scholar I do not feel myself qualified to decide on a question that requires special study. Moreover, all arguments for one alternative over the *non liquet* [undecided] have not yet fully come out. As a biographer of Feuerbach I have to be careful that the interest in my book be not fully swallowed up by interest in Kaspar Hauser himself, which would without doubt be the case should I take a position pro or contra. So my comments had to leave the main question in the balance, and only attempt to make Feuerbach's position understandable even in case he should have made a mistake. As I reread my piece, it became clear that one could all too easily form the impression that I believed Feuerbach really did make a mistake, and precisely your remarks showed me that some passages will have to be presented differently. I hope when you read the finished book you will be able to notice the influence of your comments on the final version. In any event I am deeply grateful to you. With kindest regards, I remain, yours truly, Radbruch.

Thus the authenticity of this new document is beyond dispute. When we put all our documents together, then, this is what we get:

Daumer kept handwritten notes about Kaspar Hauser. They were almost illegible (he was nearly blind) and he had them copied by hand and sent to Feuerbach. Feuerbach used them in his book about Kaspar Hauser. The manuscript stayed in the Feuerbach family until 1933, when Radbruch saw it. It was sent to Pies. I believe that what Pies was sent consisted of several hundred handwritten single sheets. Pies had these typed and made handwritten marginal notes indicating anything not obvious from the typed copy. Pies then returned the manuscript. When the French took control of Lindau at the end of World War II, many manuscripts, books, and papers were burned. I presume that this was the fate of that manuscript, since it has not been preserved by the family.

Pies, however, had his copy. The occasion to refer to it never came, for Pies's first major book, containing Daumer's writings, had already been published in 1925. The subsequent volumes were concerned with later developments in the Kaspar Hauser case. Pies *may* have felt that there was no appropriate way to call attention to its existence. Perhaps he hoped to publish it separately. In any event, 164 years after it was written, it has again surfaced.

The present document is fresh in ways that no other surviving document from the time of Kaspar Hauser is. Feuerbach's book, by contrast, though it is a wonderful text in its own right, is contrived. The three later works by Daumer himself about Kaspar Hauser are clumsy and lack the spontaneity of this text. It is probably fortunate for us that this document was not conceived as a work for publication. Of course this document, too, like all the other records dealing with Kaspar Hauser, is limited by the narrowness of Daumer's own interests. It would seem that nobody ever thought to ask Kaspar Hauser for the record: What do you actually *remember* about your cage? Have you *any memories at all* about anything preceding? Do you remember what you *felt* while you were there?

This is perhaps the single most valuable and authentic document that has come down to us. Only one other document could surpass it in historical significance: Kaspar Hauser's original diary. Presumably he burned it, though this has never been established, since everybody around him wished to read it for the wrong reasons. Perhaps it is even now lying in some unknown attic.

The discovery of this new manuscript sheds new light on the Kaspar Hauser story because it allows us more direct access to the living Kaspar Hauser, because it gives us his actual voice. It does this better than the few pages of his own writings that were preserved, because those were "exercises" written with great deliberation, not spontaneous comments in the way some of these quotations are.

I am pleased to note that the entire manuscript has just

been published by Eichborn Verlag (Frankfurt am Main, September 1995) in the series *Die andere Bibliothek* (The other library), edited by Hans Magnus Enzensberger. The text is edited by Johannes Mayer, and I contribute an essay about the discovery of the text. The volume, by Georg Friedrich Daumer, is entitled *Anselm von Feuerbach: Kaspar Hauser.*

Appendix 3

Translation of Kaspar Hauser's Autobiography

Three versions of Kaspar Hauser's autobiography exist. All were written in 1828, during the time he was living in Daumer's house. I have translated the earliest of these versions, as given in Pies, *Augenzeugenberichte* (p. 439). It is dated "Beginning of November 1828," so some five months after Kaspar Hauser appeared in Nuremberg. Pies calls it "the oldest long fragment of the autobiography" and he says that he took it from Antonius von der Linde, who published it in 1888[1] and who had inherited the handwritten manuscript from Daumer. Why Linde, an enemy of Kaspar Hauser and Daumer, should have had access to the latter's papers is not clear. But Linde carefully preserves the original text, with all the errors in spelling and punctuation. Naturally it is difficult to convey this in the translation. I have not attempted to maintain the spelling errors, nor have I kept Kaspar Hauser's exact punctuation, although it probably indicates something of the rhythm of his thinking, or at least the mental pauses he was making.

———

To show how the original looked, here is a typical sentence from the first page (439) of the text along with a literal translation: "*Ich habe zwey* [misspelled] *spill* [misspelled] *Pferd* [singular rather than plural], *und Ein* [spelling mistake] *Hund gehabt, und so Rothe bänder* [misspelled] *wo ich die Pferd* [grammatical error] *Butz* [grammatical error] *habe;* "I had twe pley horse, and an dog, and such redd ribons where I horse dicorate did." In spite of the errors, it is clear what he meant to say.

Daumer's 1832 book, *Mitteilungen über Kaspar Hauser,* has a section with writings by Kaspar Hauser. Daumer writes (p. 55):

> I encouraged him as early as 1828 to write down the story of his fate. As he was accustomed endlessly to rewrite his essays, there are several beginnings extant. The first reads as follows: "Kaspar Hauser I want to describe it myself, how hard it was for me. There where I was always locked up in this prison I thought all was well, since I did not know anything about the world and for as long as I was locked up and I never saw another person. I had two wooden horses and a dog, with these I always played, but I cannot say, whether I played the whole day or not since I did not know what a day was or a week, and I want to describe what the prison was like there was straw in there" and so on.

"Another beginning is the following [Daumer then gives the first sentence of the text I translate below]. From a third attempt, done in February 1829, I give below a fragment. We can already see in this version a more educated, though still a very natural and naive style." Daumer then provides several pages of this "third version" (I translate a portion of it in my Introduction). Daumer goes on to say that Kaspar Hauser continued to rework his autobiography, and provides the first two sentences: "Life story of Kaspar Hauser in Nuremberg. What adult could fail to feel deeply touched at my guiltless imprisonment during my young years, where I spent the most tender years of my life. While other young people enjoyed life living enchanted golden dreams and pleasures, I had not yet been awakened to life." Daumer comments: "He considered this beginning very beautiful and took it badly when I said that it was worthless." The only puzzle here is that what Daumer calls the first beginning, of which only the first three sentences have been preserved, is slightly more sophisticated than the supposedly later version, the one translated here, which is very primitive. Of course we are probably speaking of only a matter of days or weeks between them. The original handwritten versions have long been lost. Pies (*Augenzeugenberichte*, p. 448) also provides the essay by Dr. Hermann, the friend of Daumer, who had questioned Kaspar Hauser about his life while he was living in Daumer's house, and the official depositions taken of Kaspar Hauser by the police, about his early life in the prison. All versions agree by and large, and make the idea of a hoax seem highly improbable if not impossible.

Here follows my translation of the complete preserved fragment:

I will write the story of Kaspar Hauser myself! I will tell how I lived in the prison, and describe what it looked like, and everything that was there. The length of the prison was 6 to 7 feet, and 4 feet in width. There were two small windows which were 8 to 9 inches in height and were [the same] width; they were in the ceiling as in a cellar. But there was nothing in it but the straw where I lay and sat, and the two horses, a dog, and a woolen blanket. And in the ground next to me was a round hole where I could relieve myself, and a pitcher of water; other than that there was nothing, not even a stove. I will tell you what I always did, and what I always had to eat, and how I spent the long period, and what I did. I had two toy horses, and a [toy] dog, and such red ribbons with which I decorated the horses. And the clothes that I wore it was short pants, and black suspenders, and a shirt, but the pants and suspenders were on my bare body, and the shirt was worn on top, and the pants were torn open in back, so I could relieve myself. I could not take off the pants, because nobody showed me how. I will give a picture of how I spent the day, and how my day went.

When I woke up I found water and bread next to me. The first thing I did, I drank the water, then ate a little bread until I was no longer hungry, then I gave bread and water to the horses, and the dog, then I drank it all up. Now I start to play, I remove the ribbons. It took me a long time until I had decorated a horse, and when one was decorated, then I again ate a little bread, and then there was still a little water left; this I finished, then I decorated the second one, which also took a long time, as did the first, then I felt hungry again, then I ate a little bread, and would have liked to drink water but I no longer had any with which I could quench my thirst. So I picked up the pitcher probably ten times, wanting to drink, but never found any water in it because I assumed the water came by itself. Then I spent time decorating the dog. When the thirst was too terrible, I always went to sleep because I was too thirsty to play. I can imagine I must have slept a long time, because whenever I awakened, there was water, and bread. But I always ate the bread from one sleep to another. I always had enough bread but not enough water, because the pitcher was not large, it did not hold enough water, perhaps the man could not, give me more water; because I [*sic*, mistake for "he"?] could not obtain a bigger pitcher. And how long I had been playing I cannot describe because I did not know what was an hour, or a day, or a week. I was always in a good mood and content, because nothing ever hurt me. And this is how I spent the entire period of my life until the man came, and taught me to draw. But I did not know what I was writing. So now came the man for the first time to me, but I didn't hear him come. All of a sudden he put a small chair in front of me, and brought paper, and pencil and placed [them] on the chair. I always stare a little at the paper. All of a sudden the man takes my hand, puts the pencil in my hand, and said I should pay close attention, then I will get beautiful horses, and pointed to my horse, you will get more, if I pay close attention, and do well, he meant my writing. Then he showed me, and guided my hand. The man was behind me, and then I did it all by myself and I spent a long time writing by myself, and on like this, and remembered what he told me, and from this time on I knew what a horse was called, and then I always said when I played horse, no, away, run, you stay, and the man was gone again. I didn't know anything, where he went, but the chair, and the paper, he left, this is the first time I noticed him, see him I did not, because he was behind me, and where the man placed the chair I left it. I was not clever enough to have removed it. When I lay down and when I woke up again I again drank the water, and ate the bread, and the first thing I did, was start to write, and when I finished writing, I took the horse, and decorated it, as always and if I hit my hand a little I always said, horse, don't run away, you stay here; but before I had always said, don't run away, you stay here because I didn't know it what they were [that is, didn't know what a horse was called]. Then surely I slept, two or three more times, I describe it, I think, it must have been two or three days, until that man came, and when he came the second time, it was exactly the same. I did not hear him come, like the first time. And when he came the second time, he brought a small book; he placed it on the chair, like the paper, and the pencil, then he took my hand, and placed a finger on the little book, and read it out to me, three or four times then I knew it. Then he said I should remember well, then he took a horse and rolled it, and I liked that, and remembered everything, and I kept on learning, and the man was behind me, and when I couldn't remember a word very well, he told it to me again; then I said it perhaps only two more times, and the man was gone, and I took my horse and did the same with it, because the man had said if I pay careful attention, I may also do so. And when I remembered the words well then I did the same thing with the horse that he showed me, and I rolled it so vigorously that I hurt myself. And then that man came and beat me with a cane, and hurt me so much that I silently wept, so that my tears rolled down; and he hurt my right elbow, and I didn't know where the blow came from all of a sudden; since I never heard the man, when he arrived. When he beat me I kept very still, because it hurt me very much, and I decorated my horses, and I put the ribbons down so silently that the horse itself did not know how silently I did it;[2] and when I relieved myself, I removed the cover very quietly. And the straw upon which I would lie and sit I was not able to leave, first because I did not know how to walk and second because I could not get away. It was as though I was restrained and never thought that I would want to get away, or that I was locked up. And after he beat me enough time passed that I certainly woke up twenty more times, [that is, it lasted for twenty days?] and played with the horses until he came and carried me out of my prison. Then he came again, and again brought paper, and said I should do the same thing, he meant writing. Now I had to write my name again and I had not forgotten what he taught me initially and I had to repeat this again, and I knew everything he had taught me. Then he was gone. When he was gone, I again played with my horse; and the water and bread remained the same as when the man came for the first time. The water and bread, always come, when I woke up, the bread and water were there as they had been before the man came to see me.

On the same day, on which he had me write my name again.

Then he carried me off. Then this man came, and picked me up from my sleep and took off my short pants and put on another pair of short pants and a large hat and boots and jacket, and when he dressed me, he placed me against the wall, and put my two hands around his neck. When he carried me out, of the prison, he had to bend down, and carried me up a small mountain [stairs], and already I started to cry. And then the man said I should stop or I would get no horse but when I came to the top of the small mountain I was so cold because I had never had that air, and such a terrible odor overtook me that it hurt me and then we went up the second mountain, and I fell asleep. But I cannot say whether the mountain lasted a long time or a short one [how long we went uphill] and how far he carried me. I also cannot say, and when I woke up, I was lying on the ground, and I was lying on my face, and there was a terrible odor and everything hurt me so much. When I woke up I turned my head. The man must have seen that. He came and picked me up, and taught me to walk, and pushed my feet with his feet, because at the beginning he held my two arms, because I could not walk a step. And then the man said I should always watch the ground and pay careful attention so that I could walk alone. The first thing that always happened was that I cried. Kaspar don't cry or you won't get a horse. I cried a lot, because it was so difficult to walk, and everything hurt me, but when he said that I would not get a horse I immediately stopped crying. And I walked barely eight steps. Then the man placed me on the ground, and again with my face toward the ground, I rested for a little but I could not lie there very long because I found the odor too strong. Then I lifted my head and he picked me up again and continued dragging me along. The second time I went a few steps further than the first time, and my feet then hurt me more than I can say. Then he gave me bread and water. Then I sat down on the ground, and he was behind me, and as I finished the bread and water, he again dragged me on and for the first time led me by one arm, and I could not say how everything hurt me, and we went on several steps further than the second time, and it turned dark, and I was very tired, and my feet hurt a lot, then I lay down on the ground and slept, and how long I slept I cannot say. When I woke up it was daylight, and I was rested, but the pain did not go away, it always stayed the same, and I went on another eight steps which was probably the furthest I walked. When the first night was over, but I cannot say with certainty whether it was really night, it is possible that my eyes were closed from pain because the pain was too great, then he again gave me bread and water, and then this man taught me to pray. He must have said it three times, and told me I should pay attention so that you will get a beautiful horse. In the large village lives your father; he has pretty horses, and you can become a horseman like your father has been. And now it turned night for the second time, and the terrible pain came as on the previous night, so I lay down on the ground, and fell asleep, but I cannot say how long I always slept. But when I woke up, it was always light; when I woke up the man moved me on, I walked on a bit, and I started to cry, and said, horse, horse, because my, feet hurt so much. Then the man said I should stop crying, or I would get no more horses, and I again stopped crying, even if my feet hurt a lot. I may have rested only ten times, and this man always sat behind me, and I again got bread and water, but when I ate the bread, and drank the water, he moved me on again, and then I probably rested only eight or nine times, and I again started to cry, and said horse, horse, horse, and thereby I meant to say, he should take me home to my horses, where I was locked up; but I couldn't say that. Then the man said: stop crying. You will soon have a horse. Then I rested only twice, then he again took off my short pants and put on long pants, and another hat, and when he put on the clothes he was always behind me, but when I had on those clothes, I may have rested twenty or thirty times until we reached the large village. When we were in the city, he put a letter in my hand, and said I should remain standing there until such a one as you are will come, then you tell him he should take you to where this letter belongs. So I stood there a long time, until a boy came along, but my feet hurt me so much, as did the arm with which I held the letter. Finally somebody came, who took me to the house; and when I got there, I was so tired, and my feet hurt so much that I cannot say it [more than I can say], and then I started to cry, then they brought me something on a plate, I did not know what it was supposed to be, because I had never seen a plate or a bowl, and then in a little glass, they also brought me something else, and I also didn't know what it was supposed to be, and the odor alone hurt me, then they gave me bread, and water, that I recognized right away, that I ate immediately, and the water that they gave me was my best, and they put me in a horse stable, and when I got there the odor was so strong and I had many headaches, and I didn't know what all this was. Then they led me away from this house, and took me to another house, and they removed me from that house, and my feet hurt so much, that I didn't know how to walk. And when I arrived in the second house there were many boys and they bothered me so much and they always talked with me and I couldn't understand what they said. Then they led me to another house, and I could barely walk anymore, because I had so much pain, and it wasn't until the third house that I could sleep, but I was very happy when I could sit down, and immediately fell asleep, with all the pain I had.

The first day when I awakened I sat up, and it was so bright I didn't know where I was, and everything hurt me, and my eyes hurt a lot, and I kept looking for my horses and saw none, thereupon I started to cry. There was somebody else [in the room], he came over and said something to me, but I did not understand what he was saying, but I said to him *Ross, Ross, ham* [horse, horse, home]. Then he returned to his bed, and lay down again, and I cried again, then he still stayed on his bed for a while, then he got up, and he took the water and I thought he wanted to drink but drink he did not he put it in his mouth and washed, and when I saw that, I didn't know what he was doing, and then he came over to me again and he again said many things to me but I understood nothing of what he said, and then somebody else came and brought me bread, and water, and that one spoke so loudly that he really hurt me. Then many tears flowed from my eyes, then I was able to say everything that the man had told me, that I should become a horseman like my father, and would get beautiful horses, and that I said to the man, I could not call Hildel [Hiltel] anything else but the man because I did not yet know how to speak to the jailer because I do not know how to talk, but when he brought water and bread he spoke very loudly and for a long time, then he left, then I said to Hildel *Heim weissen* [take home], then he told me I should tell him where I came from, I did not understand this when he asked me this then he again left, then I started to cry so that the tears fell from my eyes, then the man who was locked up with me came over to me again and told me to stop crying, and said a lot more to me, but I did not understand anything else he said to me, but this I did understand, when he told me I had to stop crying, then I stopped, and said to him horse, rider like father is then he said something else, but I did not understand what he said, and when he said this he again went back to his bed, and then I remained sitting until the jailer came, and when he came, he brought the meal to me in a bowl, and to the other [man] and as he put down the bowl, I was so overcome by odors that I cannot even describe it, and felt a lot more pain, and as he placed it in front of me, I [didn't] know what this was supposed to be I have never seen a bowl and a spoon, and the man who was with me also got something in a bowl, he ate everything, and when he ate up his, he took my bowl and the spoon and held it for me and said I should eat and that I also did not understand when he said this, then I said I don't know, then he ate it up, but I did eat the bread which Hildel had brought, and when he put the food down he always said I should say where I'm from and because I did not understand him, I always said don't know, horse, rider like my father is, then Hildel said, if I don't tell where I'm from, I cannot become a rider, but I understood nothing of all this and then I always said, don't know, then he left again then I again cried for a long time, then this man came over again and said I stop crying, and I did and he said even more but I did not understand all that he said, then it was evening and Hildel again brought bread, and water, then I started to cry and said want to go home, white horse, then Hildel spoke to me always quite sharply and that always hurt me [physically] a lot in the head then I ate the bread and drank the water, then it was night, then I slept again, now it became day for the second time, and I sat up again and again started crying, and again cried until Hildel came, and brought the bread, then I said again home horse and rider want to be like my father, then Hildel said what he always said, and always so sharply that it hurt me, and because I never understood Hildel what he said I always said don't know and cried again then he left again, then again the man who was locked up with me came over and said I should stop crying then I stopped again, and then he said more, but I did not understand what he said. Toward 9 o'clock he left and then I was alone, and when he was gone I again started to cry until Hildel came at noon and brought the food and bread—[manuscript ends abruptly].

Kaspar Hauser's Dreams

Kaspar's dreams are strange, disturbing experiences halfway between visions, hallucinations, and dreams. In 1831, in a deposition, the thirty-two-year-old Tucher tells about taking Kaspar on a visit to the Veste Castle in Nuremberg on September 14, 1828 (so five months after arriving in Nuremberg), the first Kaspar made. They were walking up the steps when the large French doors to one of the palace rooms became visible. Kaspar stopped and looked troubled. Asked what was the matter, he told Tucher that the doors reminded him suddenly of a dream he had had on the night of August thirtieth, some two weeks earlier (he had mentioned the dream to Tucher, but the latter had not paid much attention). He stared at the doors for a long time. Then they proceeded up the stairs, and Kaspar said that these stairs were like the ones in that dream, only the ones in the dream were more beautiful. When they reached a great hall with paintings, Kaspar stopped, stared, and then went into convulsions, "as he always did when he was thinking deeply about something." His dream was coming back to him in greater detail, and in full color. He began recounting the dream, then stopped and said "with deep emotion": 'It feels like I had such a house, I don't know what this means.'" At the end of the dream, he saw himself lying in a bed, and a woman came to the door, with a yellow hat with thick white feathers in it. After her, a man walked into the room, dressed all in black, a tall hat on his head, a sword on his hip, and on his chest a cross on a blue ribbon. The woman came to Hauser's bed and stood still, the man stood behind the woman. Hauser asked the woman what she wanted. She did not answer. He repeated his question. She still did not answer. She held in her hand a white kerchief, which she held out to him and which he only noticed after he asked her for the second time what she wanted. Then the man went out the door, and the woman followed him. That was the end of the dream.

Tucher then said that on November 11, less than a month later, Kaspar told him about another dream: that his mother came and stood in front of his bed, wept profusely, and called him Gottfried over and over, a name he did not recognize. This was not, said Kaspar, the same woman as the one in the earlier dream. Tucher said that he got the feeling that deeply buried memories were attempting to make their way into consciousness.[1]

This same dream is related in our manuscript by Daumer:

1828. During the night of November 10, Kaspar Hauser dreamt that his mother came to his bed and called his name. He believed he awakened when he heard her call. The lady placed her blue wrap next to him and covered his face with hot tears. She talked about many things, but he had forgotten them. But he remembers that she called him Gottfried, a name he had not heard since he had been in Nuremberg. He wept much in his dream, so that a tear-soaked spot could be seen on his pillow. His eyes were red and swollen. He wept while talking about his dream and felt very sick and much affected all day. The woman, who in an earlier dream came to his bed in a castle, had a different face than his mother, one that was unknown to him. The latter [his mother] he recognized instantly.[2]

The question that arises, then, is whether Kaspar Hauser told this same dream to both Daumer and Tucher or whether Tucher merely heard it from Daumer. It would seem that Kaspar Hauser told *both* dreams directly to Tucher. We know for certain that he told him the first one, since Tucher says so explicitly: "Kaspar Hauser told me about a dream that he had during the night of August 30 to 31, 1828, that is, three months after he arrived here. I immediately wrote down what he told me and am now repeating it exactly."[3] What we don't know, however, and what Tucher does not tell us, is when did Kaspar Hauser tell him this? At the time or months later? There are some more clues: Tucher goes on to say that "the memory of this dream came to him clearly for the first time when he visited the local palace for the first time on September 14, 1828. I well remember him speaking about it, but I do not know how it came about that his account was not immediately given full attention, for normally nothing, not even the most minor detail, was left unnoticed."[4] What seems to follow from this is that this dream was not the product of Kaspar thinking others wanted such a dream. Nor did anybody jump upon it as a means of solving the puzzle of his identity. Its authenticity seems vouched for. Tucher says about the first dream (and it would probably be true of the second one as well): "I can therefore give expression to my conviction that old memories which had disappeared from his waking consciousness but were dormant in his soul, may well form the basis of this dream."[5] I would have to agree. The question is: What dreams are found "interesting" enough to recount to more than one person? Was the dream "memorable" to Kaspar Hauser because it dealt with his noble origins, or was the dream in and of itself of interest to him because of its vividness, or perhaps its emotional content?

It is impossible to say, at this time, whether Daumer encouraged Kaspar Hauser to believe that these dreams were genuine memories of a life led before he was imprisoned. It does not seem impossible. Certainly Daumer took them to be actual reminiscences and continued to show an interest, as we see from a later entry in the same manuscript:

> In the spring of 1830 he said to me: "I dimly feel as though I had had a teacher at one time." He said that it seemed to him, as a result of a dream-state (upon awakening, still half asleep), that, as a fourteen-year-old child[6] he had been taken by his father to a room on the lower floor of the castle that he had dreamed about earlier, to meet with a teacher. His father warned me to study be-

cause some day he would have to take his place and threatened punishment if he became inattentive. (p. 153)[7]

Daumer then asked Kaspar more details about the first dream. (These were reported by him in a book he published in 1873). Did he, asked Daumer, remember anything about a coat of arms? Kaspar did not know what this term meant. Daumer presumably explained (it is unclear whether he actually did). Kaspar said he knew neither the word nor the object. However, in the dream there was a picture he remembered seeing, inside the door, on the wall. He then drew for Daumer what he remembered seeing in the dream. This drawing has been preserved. What it shows is indeed a coat of arms: an animal of uncertain origin (lion), a scepter (a word and object he did not know), crossed swords, a cross, and so on. Daumer had to content himself with wondering whether any castle contained such a coat of arms. The question remained unanswered until many years later, in 1929, when the historian Fritz Klee found an almost identical coat of arms in a castle at Beuggen, which had always been the subject of rumors: This, said the inhabitants, was the place where Kaspar Hauser was incarcerated.

It is fascinating to speculate that whoever was responsible for the crime had not counted on Kaspar dreaming something from a real past that could alert somebody to the secret. Nor had anyone reckoned with the idea that Kaspar would learn to draw. It was only as he made this sketch that he began to recognize that he had a talent for drawing. One of the first, if not the very first, tempera drawings he made, on April 22, 1829, was of a plant. There was always something a little bit mysterious about it, since it did not seem, like almost all the other drawings of plants Kaspar made, to be based on a model. Only very recently, in 1987, did it occur to anybody that this drawing bore a striking resemblance to the window in the dungeon of a castle in Pilsach (owned during Kaspar Hauser's life by Karl Ernst Freiherr von Griessenbeck, 1787–1863). In fact, a few years ago, the current owner of this very same castle, while doing renovations, found a white toy wooden horse of precisely the dimensions described by Kaspar Hauser.

It is difficult to say if these dreams are entirely authentic. Freud was once asked: "Can a man be held responsible for his own dreams?" His terse answer was, "Whom else would you hold responsible?" This wonderful witticism is immediately convincing—until one thinks about it. Then it is hard to avoid the recognition that somebody else is *always* responsible for one's dreams. Kaspar Hauser, like the rest of us, was undoubtedly set to dreaming by experiences imposed on him from without. Can another person, though, be held responsible for one's own memories? We should bear in mind that we do not know what Kaspar Hauser actually dreamed, since there are a number of restrictions: Evidently he told Daumer only what he thought his teacher would be interested in (no free association reigns here). Moreover, we do not know how much of what he actually told Daumer was preserved. We are restricted by what Daumer remembered, and then further by what he chose to write about in his diary. And even in that writing there were bound to be distortions and falsifications, because Daumer was keeping the diary for a specific purpose. *He* was not the dreamer. And his own ability to express himself was imperfect to say the least. Nonetheless we cannot rewrite history and demand different texts. Kaspar Hauser was happy and eager to recount his dreams, and they seemed to flow from him. But these were only dreams he had *after* he was in Daumer's house. It seems not to have occurred to anybody to ask him if he ever dreamed while in prison. Or whether he dreamed now *about* his time in prison. The dreams he did have and remember and retell are nevertheless of genuine importance and cannot simply be dismissed as having been dreamed *sur commande,* as it were. For one thing, we have Daumer's assurance, in his later book[8] (responding to criticisms of his earlier work), which I am inclined to believe:

> I never caused, influenced, or led Hauser to his remarks about his dreams, visions, apparent memories from his unknown former life. In no way can they be regarded as my production. Actually, part of the time I paid too *little* attention to such remarks. An example would be the castle he dreamed about, which he considered to be a recollection. Friends have correctly criticized me for this.

Here Daumer has an important footnote that reads:

> On page 30 of my book *Enthüllungen* I remarked: In the beginning I gave the matter no importance whatever, and thought that Hauser was just indulging in fantasies, until, with the help of my friend, professor and former councillor of state von Hermann, who saw into these things more deeply than I did, I came to believe that Hauser could not possibly have imagined something of the kind, and that this castle must surely exist somewhere. President Feuerbach very definitely realized this to be true and said so.

The last sentence is particularly important, since presumably Daumer is speaking from firsthand experience. Does he mean that Feuerbach told him so directly, or told others, or is he only referring to the published *Mémoire* (Memorandum, see pp. 29ff.), which does indeed use one of Kaspar Hauser's dreams as a proof of his memory of having lived in a castle?

In any event Kaspar Hauser's dreams are a rich resource for the historian and the psychologist. I believe they are genuine and that they point to early memories of a life very different from the one he was forced to lead in this dungeon.

Appendix 5

Wolf Children

According to legend the founders of Rome, Romulus and Remus, were wild, or feral, or wolf children. Why is the legend of wolf children such an old one, and so persistent? What is the essential power of this story, and what is the appeal of the myth that lies behind it? The issues go deep, and although the answer may not tell us much about the real nature of wolves, it certainly reveals something of human fantasies about wolves and the fascination with a figure such as Kaspar Hauser.

Arnold Gesell, in a review written during World War II of the Singh-Zingg book (to be discussed in this appendix), said that in thinking about the topic of wolf children, "Profound prejudices are stirred if not awakened. We shun instinctively too close identification with *lupus* or even *canis familiaris*. Nevertheless, in these days of inhuman warfare, we may have reason to temper with a trace of humility, our sense of superiority over the wolf species."

In the 1940s the American public was startled to read about the one case of a wolf child reported in the literature that was assumed to be entirely authentic, and the only firsthand account by one of the major players.

The Reverend J. A. L. Singh lived in India, in a village some seventy-five miles southwest of Calcutta, where he and his wife ran an orphanage. One day in October 1920 he was out hunting with friends, when he heard from some villagers that they were terrified of two ghosts that lived in the woods near the village. They lived inside an enormous termite mound—I have seen such mounds in India as high as eight feet—and came out in the evening. Singh built a platform in some trees nearby and waited. Here is what happened in his own words:

The same Saturday, October 9, 1920, evening, long before dusk, at about 4:30 or 5:00 P.M., we stealthily boarded the machan [platform] and anxiously waited there for an hour or so. All of a sudden, a grown-up wolf came out from one of the holes [it was a white-ant mound as high as a two-storied building, rising from the ground in the shape of a Hindu temple. Round about, there were seven holes, afterwards found to be seven tunnels leading to the main hollow at the bottom of the mound], which was very smooth on account of their constant egress and ingress. This animal was followed by another one of the same size and kind. The second one was followed by a third, closely followed by two cubs one after the other. The holes did not permit two together.

Close after the cubs came the ghost—a hideous-looking being—hand, foot, and body like a human being; but the head was a big ball of something covering the shoulders and the upper portion of the bust, leaving only a sharp contour of the face visible, and it was a human. Close at its heels there came another awful creature exactly like the first, but smaller in size. Their eyes were bright and piercing, unlike human eyes. I at once came to the conclusion that these were human beings.

The first ghost appeared on the ground up to its bust, and placing its elbows on the edge of the hole looked this side and that side, and jumped out. It looked all round the place from the mouth of the hole before it leaped out to follow the cubs. It was followed by another tiny ghost of the same kind, behaving in the same manner. Both of them ran on all fours. . . . The white-ant mount in the jungle was about seven miles away from the village Godamuri. We brought the men straight to the spot; half of us boarded the machan, but I remained with them to instruct them to cut out a door in the particular white-ant mound on the seventeenth of October, 1920, Sunday, at about 9:00 A.M. . . .

October 17, 1920. After a few strokes of the spade and shovel, one of the wolves came out hurriedly and ran for his life into the jungle. The second appeared quickly, frightened for his life, and followed the footsteps of the former. A third appeared. It shot out like lightning on the surface of the plain and made for the diggers. It flew in again. Out it came instantly to chase the diggers—howling, racing about restlessly, scratching the ground furiously, and gnashing its teeth. It would not budge out of the place.

I had a great mind to capture it, because I guessed from its whole bearing on the spot that it must have been the mother wolf, whose nature was so ferocious and affection so sublime. It struck me with wonder. I was simply amazed to think that an animal had such a noble feeling surpassing even that of mankind—the highest form of creation—to bestow all the love and affection of a fond and ideal mother on these peculiar beings, which surely once had been brought in by her (or by the other two grown-up wolves who appeared before her) as food for the cubs. Whoever these peculiar beings, and whatever they might be, certainly they were not their cubs. To permit them to live and be nurtured by them (wolves) in this fashion is divine. I failed to realize the import of the circumstances and became dumb and inert. In the meantime, the men pierced her through with arrows, and she fell dead. A terrible sight!

After the mother wolf was killed, it was an easy job. When the door was cut out, the whole temple fell all round, very fortunately leaving the central cave open to the sky, without disturbing the hollow inside. The cave was a hollow in the shape of the bottom of a kettle. It was plain and smooth, as if cemented. The place was so neat that not even a piece of bone was visible anywhere, much less any evidence of their droppings and other uncleanliness. The cave had a peculiar smell, peculiar to the wolves—that was all. There had lived the wolf family. The two cubs and the other two hideous beings were there in one corner, all four clutching together in a monkey-ball. It was really a task to separate them from one another. The ghosts were more ferocious than the cubs, making faces, showing teeth, making for us when too much disturbed, and running back to reform the monkey-ball.

Singh called the two girls, one of whom he estimated to be only about a year and a half and the other about eight, Amala and Kamala. He took them back to his orphanage in order to reclaim them for "humanity and for Christianity." He failed. Amala died a year later, and Kamala lived until she was about seventeen. Amala never spoke. Kamala, barely. Singh kept a diary of his attempts to deferalize the children, and it was this book that was published in the United States by Harper in 1942, as *Wolf Children and Feral Man* by J. A. L. Singh and R. M. Zingg.[1] The case had already been written about in 1941 by no less an authority on child development than Arnold Gesell, professor of pediatrics at Yale University, in his book *Wolf Child and Human Child* (also published by Harper).

Nevertheless, many scientists expressed extreme skepticism about the authenticity of the story, or at least of the story of the children's capture. After all, there was only the Reverend Singh's word for it. No other witnesses ever surfaced, and attempts to trace his companions on the hunt were in vain.

The case for skepticism was put most forcefully, but also charmingly, by Ashley Montagu, who wrote: "With all the good will in the world . . . we cannot accept the story of the discovery of the wolf-children and their presumed rearing by wolves as true." He went on to say that even though "emotionally I am in favor of the Singh-Zingg and Co. story, as a scientist, I cannot accept it."

An American professor of sociology, William F. Ogburn, and the renowned Indian scholar Nirmal K. Bose (who had once been Gandhi's secretary), wrote a long account of their attempts in India to verify the account, calling it "On the Trail of the Wolf-Children."[2] Ogburn and Bose wrote their account because "if their most precise and detailed account was disproved, then less credence would be placed in other stories of wolf-children and the probability of their being fantasies and myths would be great; and much less attention would need to be given to them. Great gains in science have resulted from destroying error as well as by adding knowledge" (ibid., p. 127).

But it does not follow that we should pay no attention to the underlying fascination. Myth, or fantasy, the story is an important one.

What they discovered is that "the police and census records of 1920 showed no village of the name of Godamuri. . . . Thus the net result of our joint enquiry was that the village of Godamuri could not be traced anywhere, and that none of the people interviewed, had ever heard of any event of this kind" (ibid., p. 173). They were skeptical, too, of Singh's motives: "The effect of his story of the rescue of the children from wolves and of his success in humanizing Kamala appears to have brought him recognition as a missionary and possibly to have brought in some money" (ibid., p. 191).

Nevertheless, in 1977 Charles Maclean, an English novelist and historian, went on a similar mission, and at the end of a book that essentially merely retells Singh's story in different words, claims (on the last page) that

> we eventually succeeded in finding Godamuri, which had changed its name—as Indian villages sometimes do—to Ghorabandha. . . . From Ghorabandha we then drove south-east for six or seven miles (in accordance with Singh's sketch map) to the Santal village of Denganalia, where the older people well remembered how the wolf children were captured in the forest near-by a long time ago. One old man, Las Marandi, had actually taken part in the hunt as a boy of sixteen and testified that the Reverend Singh, whom he was able to describe quite clearly, along with two Europeans . . . and Dibakar Bhanj Deo, had been present on the *machan* at the time of the rescue.

In support of the authenticity of this discovery, he notes that "the Santals appeared uninterested in the information they passed on; there was no question of their having read about the wolf children; and the story was far from being a widespread folk tale in the jungle areas we visited."[3]

If Singh's book is the most famous example of a claim for the authenticity of wolf children, Rudyard Kipling's *Jungle* books, written in 1894 and 1895, are the most famous works of imaginative fiction on this theme. Singh, of course, knew the *Jungle* books, as did most literate Indians. Kipling himself was by no means the first person in India to imagine stories of wolves raising children. Such accounts were common in

India, and the author of a book (published in 1884) that Kipling knew, Robert A. Sterndal, wrote in his scholarly and charming *Natural History of the Mammalia of India and Ceylon:*

> Hundreds of children are carried off annually, especially in Central Indian and the North-west provinces. Stories have been related of wolves sparing suckling young infants so carried off, which, if properly authenticated, will bring the history of Romulus and Remus within the bounds of probability. I have not by me just now the details of the case of the "Boy-Wolf" of Lucknow, which was, I believe, a case vouched for by credible witnesses. It was that of a boy found in a wolf's lair, who had no power of speech, crawled about on his hands and knees, ate raw flesh, and who showed great wildness in captivity. I think he died soon after being caught. The story of the nursing is not improbable, for well-known instances have been recorded of the *ferae*, when deprived of their young, adopting young animals, even of those on whom they usually prey.[4]

Kipling's father wrote: "India is probably the cradle of wolf-child stories, which are here universally believed and supported by a cloud of testimony, including in the famous Lucknow case of a wolf boy the evidence of European witnesses [*sic*]."[5] No doubt Kipling heard these stories from his father.

Perhaps if we understand why the theme recommended itself to Kipling we will come closer to understanding humanity's constant preoccupation with wolves and feral children. For obvious reasons this theme had deep emotional resonances for Kipling. Randall Jarrell has written: "To Kipling the world was a dark forest full of families: so that when your father and mother leave you in the forest to die, the wolves that come to eat you are always Father Wolf and Mother Wolf, your real father and real mother, and you are—as not even the little wolves ever quite are—their real son."[6] Kipling spent the first six years of his life in India, primarily Bombay, and regarded these years as edenic. He was exquisitely sensitive to the atmosphere around him: "I have always felt," wrote Kipling in old age, "the menacing darkness of tropical eventide, as I have loved the voices of night-winds through palm and banana leaves, and the song of the tree-frogs."[7]

For mysterious reasons Kipling's parents took him and his sister to Southsea in England, and left them both for six years in a dreary boarding-house, with complete strangers who were committed to destroying the creativity of these unusually vivacious and open youngsters. Kipling, in his never-completed autobiography *Something of Myself*, was to describe it as sheer hell.

The curious thing is that the life *actually* led by Amala and Kamala, as described by the Reverend Singh, was infinitely sad and depressing. It is not possible to read about it without thinking that they would both have been better off left with the wolves. What had Reverend Singh accomplished? He had deprived those two children of their only source of happiness. They both died, one shortly after being captured, the other some years later. The Reverend Singh thought he was saving their souls. But perhaps he had, in his arrogance, ignored the wolf souls they may have had.

What is the desire that fuels these stories? It is not just the desire to be accepted by an alien species but the wish to be connected, on some deeper level, with another species—to be understood, and to understand. There is some fascination with the warmth, the darkness, and security of the den, with a mother and a father and siblings, living in harmony, protected, playing, out of the elements. We can measure this by the thrill almost everybody experiences upon seeing the few photographs that exist of the inside of a real wolf den (such as those accompanying the book *White Wolf*).[8] The desire to be part of that den, or to imagine that it would be at least possible to be part of such a world, is immense.

NOTES

Introduction

1. Defined by John Money (*The Kaspar Hauser Syndrome of "Psychosocial Dwarfism": Deficient Statural, Intellectual, and Social Growth Induced by Child Abuse* [Buffalo, New York: Prometheus Books, 1992], p. 19) as "the mystery of how isolation, abuse, and neglect in childhood might induce a syndrome of overall physical and mental growth retardation, following which catchup growth would be at best only partial and incomplete." See also E. Nau and D. Cabanis, "Kaspar-Hauser-Syndrom," *Münchener Medizinische Wochenschrift* 108, no. 17 (1966), pp. 929–31. The term was first used by Alexander Mitscherlich in his 1950 article "Ödipus und Kaspar Hauser," *Der Monat* 3 (1950), pp. 11–18.

2. It appeared on her 1987 album *Solitude Standing*.

3. See Hans Peitler and Hans Ley, *Kaspar Hauser: Über tausend bibliographische Nachweise* (Ansbach: C. Brügel & Sohn, 1927). A great deal has been written *since* 1927, of course. During Kaspar Hauser's lifetime some seventy books and articles were published about him. It is certain that he did not know of all of them, and may perhaps have seen only the book by Feuerbach and the attack by Merker (see p. 51).

4. Quoted in Richard Bernheim, *Wild Men in the Middle Ages: A Study in Art, Sentiment, and Demonology* (Cambridge, Mass.: Harvard University Press, 1952), p. 11.

5. I have taken the text from Hermann Pies, *Kaspar Hauser, Eine Dokumentation*, Ansbach: C. Brügel & Sohn, 1965, pp. 24–34. The text itself was first printed in two newspapers, the *Friedens und Kriegskurier* and the *Nürn-*

211

berger Intelligenzblatt, on July 14. The dates here are important. Binder was among the first to see Kaspar Hauser, either on the very day of his arrest or the next day. He wrote his proclamation on July 7. On July 11 Feuerbach visited Kaspar Hauser (which means that he heard about him through means *other* than the proclamation). On July 14 the proclamation was published, but after Feuerbach's official complaint the document was withdrawn from circulation. Kaspar Hauser was then, obviously at Feuerbach's request, handed over to his first teacher, Georg Friedrich Daumer (four days later, on July 18).

6. The appendices consist of three documents. The first is a copy of the two letters that Kaspar Hauser had with him. After producing them Binder says:

> There is a great similarity in the handwriting of both letters. Also, both are clearly written in one and the same ink, and it therefore follows that the second letter [meant to be taken as written by Kaspar's mother] was not written 16 years ago, but only recently, and is therefore fabricated. For if the second letter is 16 years older than the accompanying letter, the ink would have taken on a completely different color than the one found in the first letter. This seems however not to have been taken into account by the otherwise shrewd, malicious evil imposter.

The second is a description of the appearance of Kaspar Hauser. It corresponds fairly closely to that given by Feuerbach (see pp. 79ff.). But, curiously, Feuerbach writes in his note that he took his description from his own observations, since the police files he obtained did not contain it. This means that the document Feuerbach had in front of him, whether published in the newspaper or from some other source, did not contain this appendix, nor did the papers he received later. In the version published by Pies (*Dokumentation,* p. 33), unfortunately reproduced without any indication of where he took it from, there is a final sentence that gives information not available elsewhere: "Kaspar says, *'Er kümmt ʃcho, wenn i a Reiter were, wie mei Voter aner gween i,'* instead of *'Er kommt ʃchon, wenn ich ein Reiter werde, wie mein Vater einer geweʃen iʃt'* [He will surely come, if I become a rider as my father was] etc. etc. But now through lessons his dialect is improving from day to day." The third appendix is a description of the objects and books that Kaspar Hauser had with him when he arrived. These are the same as those given by Feuerbach.

7. It was typical that the widely read paper in German-speaking countries, published in Vienna, the *Allgemeine Theaterzeitung für Kunʃt, Literatur und geʃellʃchaftliches Leben,* in the following year had no less than twenty-five reports about Kaspar Hauser (Johannes Mayer, *Philip Henry Lord Stanhope: Der Gegenʃpieler Kaʃpar Hauʃers* [Caspar Hauser's adversary] [Stuttgart: Urachhaus, 1988], p. 271).

8. He was the father of the philosopher Ludwig Feuerbach (whose ideas provoked Marx to write his *Theses Against Feuerbach*), himself a friend of Daumer and Kaspar Hauser. The older Feuerbach wrote the Bavarian Criminal Code of 1813, which served as a model for the rest of Germany for the entire nineteenth century. "His personality was dramatic and passionate," says the authoritative *Neue Deutsche Biographie*. There are several biographies, the best being the one by Gustav Radbruch: *Paul Johann Anselm Feuerbach: Ein Juristenleben* (Vienna: Springer, 1934).

9. This is from Feuerbach's book on Kaspar Hauser.

10. See my book *A Dark Science: Women, Sexuality and Psychiatry in the Nineteenth Century* (New York: Farrar, Straus & Giroux, 1986).

11. In 1834 an English translation of this book appeared: *Caspar Hauser: An Account of an Individual Kept in a Dungeon, Separated from All Communication with the World, from Early Childhood to about the Age of Seventeen, Drawn up from Legal Documents by Anselm von Feuerbach, President of one of the Bavarian Courts of Appeal, etc.* This work, published by Simpkin and Marshall in London, had a short introduction by Francis Lieber, dated Boston, November 1832, and was translated by one Henning Gottfried Linberg. However, either the translator or the "editor" decided that certain passages were best omitted from the work, for reasons not entirely clear (sometimes it seems to have been out of inadvertence; at others somebody thought the language was too "rough"), and so there has actually never existed a complete English translation. The Linberg translation is long out of print, and very hard to find even secondhand.

12. The only "companions" that Kaspar Hauser had in his prison were two wooden horses and a wooden dog. He clearly thought they were alive, and missed them when he was separated from them. He did not understand that they were not real until many months after his appearance in Nuremberg. We read, in a passage in Daumer's unpublished diary, the following:

> In September he said that there were three things that were the most joyous occasions in his life since arriving in Nuremberg. The first was when he was once again given toy horses. The second was the first loving treatment he experienced in the house of Mayor Binder. The third was when he by chance discovered the kind of bread he had enjoyed in his prison. He wept from joy at the first and third. (p. 79)

13. Johannes Mayer and Peter Tradowsky, *Kaspar Hauser: Das Kind von Europa* (Stuttgart: Urachhaus, 1984), p. 57.

14. His poems have been set to music by Brahms, and Thomas Mann · said that one of them, at least, ranks as one of the great poems in the German language. He also translated a number of Persian and Arabic poems into German, and was something of a mystic, with odd religious views for his time.

15. Daumer was among the first to visit Kaspar Hauser. Kaspar arrived on May 26. On July 18 he moved to Daumer's house. Daumer writes, in his chronology of the story (Georg Friedrich Daumer, *Kaspar Hauser: Sein Wesen, seine Unschuld, seine Erduldungen und sein Ursprung* [Kaspar Hauser: his nature, his innocence, his suffering, and his origins] [Regensburg: A. Coppenrath, 1873], p. 74) that he met Kaspar Hauser "approximately three weeks before he moved to my house," which would place his first meeting with Kaspar on June 26, one month after his arrival. It is not clear whether Daumer knew about the weeping from firsthand observation by his friend Freiherr von Tucher, who introduced him to Kaspar, or whether he heard it directly from Kaspar himself. The information was not reproduced anywhere else, nor was it known that Kaspar Hauser wept for eight days and eight nights. That is a long time, and provides a very different picture of Kaspar Hauser's first week "out of captivity."

16. Pies writes in the margin of the last sentence: *"Wichtig!"* (important!).

17. I have taken the text from Hermann Pies, *Kaspar Hauser: Augenzeugenberichte und Selbstzeugnisse* (Stuttgart: Robert Lutz Verlag, 1925), pp. 419ff. All the fragments of Kaspar Hauser's autobiography have been collected in this volume, and occupy some thirty pages. I have translated the full text of this first version in appendix 3.

18. The question has often been asked whether any child could survive on a diet of bread and water without life-threatening problems. It should be noted that the bread was rye bread, probably made with molasses, and contained four herbs: cumin, anise, fennel and coriander, which no doubt provided some vitamins. I have asked several pediatricians whether survival would be possible, but have not had any definitive answer. The general medical view, however, seems to be that it would be unlikely.

19. Georg Friedrich Daumer (*Mitteilungen über Kaspar Hauser* [Information about Kaspar Hauser] [Nuremberg: Heinrich Haubenstricher, 1832], vol. 1, p. 8) introduces this version as follows: "The following is a part of a third attempt from February, 1829, in which can be seen a more educated but nonetheless still natural and naive writing style." This would seem to indicate that Daumer had a more complete version, but it has never been recovered and must now be considered lost. The version I translated from is taken by Pies from Philip Henry Stanhope's *Materialien zur Geschichte Kaspar Hausers* (Material on the case of Kaspar Hauser) (Heidelberg: J. Mohr, 1835), but he notes the variants between this version and the one published by Daumer. This means, as Pies notes, that there must have existed two very similar but nonetheless not identical versions (p. 508).

20. Daumer notes in his manuscript: "It can be assumed that during his imprisonment he was rarely awake. He himself estimates that he was awake for only three or four hours" (p. 74). This information is not repeated anywhere else. It would seem that Daumer asked Kaspar Hauser a direct ques-

tion, and this was his response. If he was in a kind of twilight state, and perhaps drugged with opium a good part of the time, it is not surprising that there would be an enormous change once he was outside the prison.

21. Pp. 150–51. Since this is such an important passage, and never previously published, here is an alternative translation:

In September and October he frequently stated that he could no longer imagine his erstwhile mental state. He would like to see himself as he had been when he whiled away his time playing. Frequently, while alone, he was trying to understand his condition at that time. It was beyond understanding, he said, that during his imprisonment he never thought about himself—had not reflected whether there were other beings beside him or whether anything else existed outside his cage, nor where the bread and water came from that he found daily and consumed. The entire period before he began to learn to read existed in his memory only in hazy and vague form.

It seems clear to me that this narrative contains the actual words that Kaspar Hauser used to Daumer—when one thinks about it, an extraordinary event. It is fortunate that this document was somehow miraculously preserved. Daumer, in his first book, *Mitteilungen*, is clearly writing with this passage in mind when he begins his second volume (p. 113). He even quotes a part of the passage I have just translated from the manuscript.

22. Actually our knowledge is now immensely greater, thanks to the diligent scholarship of Johannes Mayer in his seven-hundred-page *Philip Henry Lord Stanhope*, which contains many letters and previously unpublished documents that Mayer found in the Stanhope family archives in Chevening. Mayer is able to establish beyond doubt that Stanhope was intimately connected to the house of Baden and received money from the royal family. Right from the beginning, his interest in Kaspar Hauser was tied to the political fortunes of princely families in Austria and Germany. Whatever the reality was, these families perceived in Kaspar Hauser a potential ally or enemy, and Stanhope was ideally situated to exploit this perception, which he did with a guile, cunning, and ruthlessness that was to lead to the undoing of Kaspar Hauser—who neither knew nor suspected his own importance to the ruling houses of Europe.

23. On the very day that Kaspar Hauser was attacked, October 22, 1829, Stanhope wrote his banker (Merkel) in Nuremberg, asking him to send him a picture of Kaspar Hauser, and all information from the police and other authorities regarding the attempt on Kaspar's life. His banker answered, saying that the "investigations into his [Kaspar Hauser's] origins are being seriously pursued but kept secret by the court." These important facts were only recently uncovered by Mayer in the Stanhope archives, and published in his book *Stanhope*, p. 282.

24. It is found in the notes of Mayer's *Stanhope,* p. 613. Mayer points out that Caroline, countess of Albersdorf, writes in her book about being an eyewitness to Stanhope's visit to Nuremberg, and that he was staying at an inn with two suspicious-looking characters. The book is called *Kaspar Hauser oder Andeutungen zur Enthüllung mancher Geheimnisse über Hausers Herkunft, die Ursache seiner Gefangenhaltung und Ermordung* (Kaspar Hauser or allusions to the revelation of a number of secrets about Kaspar Hauser's origins, the reason for his imprisonment and murder) (Regensburg, 1837). We know from elsewhere in Mayer's book that Stanhope met with Hennenhofer, the presumed murderer of Kaspar Hauser.

25. Feuerbach, *Kaspar Hauser,* page 182 of the edition included in the useful collection edited by Jochen Hörisch, *Ich möchte ein solcher werden wie... Materialien zur Sprachlosigkeit des Kaspar Hauser* (I would like to be like... Material about the lack of speech of Kaspar Hauser) (Frankfurt am Main: Suhrkamp, 1979).

26. Pies, *Dokumentation,* p. 67.

27. Ibid., p. 69.

28. Ibid., p. 97.

29. Text of the letter in Mayer and Tradowsky, *Kaspar Hauser,* p. 545.

30. Tucher said that Stanhope had told the boy that "he was a Hungarian magnate... and it was expected that he treat his subjects (*Untertanen*) with care and love." See Mayer, *Stanhope,* p. 384.

31. *Sein Wesen,* p. 288. Daumer refers to a similar passage on page 233 of his *Enthüllungen über Kaspar Hauser* (Revelations about Kaspar Hauser) (Frankfurt am Main: Weidinger Sohn, 1859): "I can, should it be requested, name a witness who observed the public embraces of the lord with great astonishment." This is the only reference that I have been able to find to a possible homoerotic attachment on the part of Stanhope for Kaspar Hauser. In Peter Sehr's fine film, this theme is made explicit. Daumer also refers to a letter from Meyer's wife, in which she speaks of how Stanhope allowed (encouraged?) Kaspar to kiss and stroke him (p. 288).

32. Mayer, *Stanhope,* p. 401.

33. Examples of Meyer's endless picking on Kaspar can be found in Pies, *Dokumentation,* p. 126ff.

34. He had the great good fortune, however, to be taught by Johann Heinrich Fuhrmann, thirty-six years old in 1833, a gentle, kindly priest, who delivered the burial address and also wrote a charming essay on Kaspar Hauser, published a year later, in 1834, and reproduced in Pies, *Augenzeugenberichte und Selbstzeugnisse.* Both were also reprinted in Tradowsky, *Johann Simon Heinrich Fuhrmann: Kaspar Hauser* (Dornach: Rudolf Geering Verlag, 1983).

35. He had said many times that the man had done nothing bad to him and he did not want him punished if he should ever be caught. It was only when for the first time in his life he looked at the star-studded night sky that

he said he realized what he had been robbed of by his incarceration in the dungeon, and asked if his jailer realized what he was depriving him of. It was an actual question, not a criticism. For examples, see pp. 42ff.

36. Pies, *Dokumentation*, p. 132.

37. Kaspar Hauser managed, from time to time, to escape his teacher. On January 22, 1833, for example, he was taken to meet the twenty-year-old Richard Wagner in Bamberg. No text has come down to us of what the two young men said to each other.

38. Pies, *Dokumentation*, p. 207.

39. Daumer, *Sein Wesen*, p. 501. Johann Ludwig von Klüber (1762–1837) is one of the most mysterious players in the Kaspar Hauser drama. He is reputed to have been the lover of Countess Hochberg, who arranged for the murder of Kaspar Hauser. His son Friedrich Adolf (1791–1858) was the personal secretary of Leopold, the son of the countess, who came to the throne instead of Hauser. Feuerbach died under mysterious circumstances on a visit to Klüber to discuss Kaspar Hauser. (There has never been any suggestion that Klüber was involved in what looks like a case of poisoning, but one can't help wondering.) Meyer informs us that after Feuerbach's death, Klüber became Kaspar Hauser's guardian (he had taken over from Tucher), a strange and rather remarkable circumstance that seems not to have been noted earlier (*Stanhope*, p. 214). Letters from and to Klüber can be found in von der Linde's two-volume *Kaspar Hauser: Eine neugeschichtliche Legende* (A contemporary legend) (Wiesbaden: Verlag von C. Limbarth, 1887) and in Mayer's volume on Stanhope.

40. Reproduced in Pies, *Kaspar Hauser: Fälschungen, Falschmeldungen und Tendenzberichte* (Forgeries, perjuries and biased reports) (Ansbach: Ansbacher Museums Verlag, 1973), p. 103.

41. Ibid., p. 104.

42. Reprinted in Hörisch, *Ich möchte ein solcher werden wie*, p. 256.

43. Pies, *Dokumentation*, p. 225. Hermann Pies published the full medical reports, *Die amtlichen Aktenstücke über Kaspar Hausers Verwundung und Tod* (Official documents relating to Kaspar Hauser's mortal wound and death) (Bonn: Kulturhistorischer Verlag, 1928). They have been reprinted by Peter Tradowsky, *Kaspar Hauser: Arztberichte* (Kaspar Hauser: doctors' reports) (Dornach: Rudolf Geering Verlag, 1985.) Dr. Friedrich Wilhelm Heidenreich, thirty-four years old at the time, who actually performed the autopsy, published his report in 1834. In it, reprinted by Pies, *Augenzeugenberichte*, p. 399, he notes that "in the first days after he was wounded, the mood of the public was very much against Kaspar Hauser." He goes on to say that "once the corpse was autopsied, the size of the wound showed that he could hardly have brought it about himself, and the majority of people were once again inclined to believe in an assassination." (See, too, his deposition, quoted by Pies, *Dokumentation*, p. 158.)

44. Ibid., p. 205.

45. Pathetically Kaspar answered that he did not think his life was in danger since he now had a fosterfather (*Pflegevater*) who would take care of him. This was a reference to Stanhope, the very man who was probably directly or indirectly collaborating with Kaspar Hauser's murderer.

46. Pies, *Dokumentation,* p. 204.

47. Ibid., p. 154.

48. Ibid.

49. Reproduced in Pies, *Kaspar Hauser,* pp. 62ff.

50. He wrote two excellent books about Kaspar Hauser that are still worth reading today (see the bibliography).

51. Pies, *Augenzeugenberichte,* vol. 2, p. 315.

52. Pies is certain he learned about it on the trip from Vienna to Munich (*Kaspar Hauser,* p. 63).

53. Daumer, *Enthüllungen,* p. 170.

54. Daumer, *Sein Wesen,* p. 293.

55. She published two books, *Kaspar Hauser oder Andeutung zur Enthüllung mancher Geheimnisse über Hausers Herkunft, die Ursache seiner Gefangenhaltung und Ermordung* (Regensburg, 1837), and the two-volume *Kaspar Hauser oder die richtige Enthüllung der bisher unbekannten Geheimnisse* (Kaspar Hauser or the correct revelation of previously unknown secrets) (Munich, 1839). See Mayer, *Stanhope,* p. 352.

56. Actually, it was not "many" at all, but primarily Meyer and Stanhope, both of whom had good reasons to make this claim.

57. One can fairly feel the indignation of the anonymous writer at the suggestion that an English lord could even be imagined guilty of such a heinous deed.

58. Andrew Lang: *Historical Mysteries* (London: Smith, Elder & Co., 1904), chap. 6, "The Mystery of Kaspar Hauser: The Child of Europe," pp. 118–42. Lang's *Blue Fairy Book* is still a much-loved children's classic.

59. As early as July 1828, mayor Binder had received a letter asking: "Is not Kaspar Hauser the son of the Grand Duchess Stéphanie?" And Feuerbach had a letter with the same content in 1829. See Mayer, *Stanhope,* p. 271.

60. "Rumors of poisoning [in this case of the crown prince, Alexander, who was born in 1816 and died a year later], which were already quietly whispered about in the earlier case [Kaspar Hauser], came up again and became louder and bolder." Cited by Pies, *Dokumentation,* p. 252. These notebooks and diaries are a valuable source, see Karl August Varnhagen von Ense, *Denkwürdigkeiten und Vermischte Schriften,* 9 vols. (Leipzig, 1843–46 and 1859), as well as *Tagebücher* (diaries), 14 vols. (Hamburg and Zurich, 1861–70). Pies gives all the important passages.

61. From a letter found in the Stanhope family archives, Kent, Chevening, by Mayer (*Stanhope,* p. 395).

62. In the *Mémoire* (memorandum), of which more follows, Feuerbach says that "it is not insignificant that not long after Kaspar Hauser appeared

in Nuremberg, a rumor was circulated, and one that came from Baden: Kaspar is the prince of the house of Baden, who was claimed to be dead, the son of the Grand Duchess Stéphanie. This rumor would from time to time surface, and has done so especially in recent times" (Pies, *Dokumentation*, p. 242).

63. Pies, *Dokumentation*, p. 78.

64. That it was so understood by many readers is clear from the response of Karoline, queen of Bavaria, to whom Feuerbach had sent a copy of the book. She asked him, then, about his proof of a *Majestätsverbrechen* (a crime against royalty), and it was this question that impelled Feuerbach to write his famous *Mémoire* to the queen, attempting to prove his hint (see *Kaspar Hauser*, by Mayer and Tradowsky, p. 552). As early as February 6, 1832, the *Augsburger Tageblatt* spoke of Kaspar Hauser as the "mutmassliche[r] Prätendent [. . .] von Baden" that is, the heir apparent (ibid., p. 550).

65. Mayer and Tradowsky, *Kaspar Hauser*, p. 409.

66. Karoline, queen mother of Bavaria (1776–1841), princess of Baden, the sister of Karl von Baden, hence Kaspar Hauser's aunt. She was the stepmother of King Ludwig I of Bavaria. Her husband Maximilian I, king of Bavaria, had died in 1825.

67. The document was published by Ludwig Feuerbach in a two-volume work entitled *Anselm Ritter von Feuerbachs Leben und Werken, aus seinen ungedruckten Briefen und Tagebüchern, Vorträgen und Druckschriften* (Leipzig: Verlag von Otto Wigand, 1852). It was published under a pseudonym in 1859, 1889, and 1892 (see Mayer and Tradowsky, *Kaspar Hauser*, p. 180). Often called the secret "Mémoire" (Memorandum), it begins with the words *"Wer möchte wohl Kaspar Hauser sein?"* (Who might Kaspar Hauser be?), sometimes given as its title. It has been reprinted in Pies, *Dokumentation*, pp. 327ff. Pies discusses the reaction in his *Kaspar Hauser: Die Wahrheit über sein Auftauchen und erste Nürnberger Zeit* (Kaspar Hauser: The truth about his appearance in Nuremberg and his early time there) (Saarbrücken, 1956). (See reprint in bibliography.) New and important documents pertaining to the *Mémoire* can be found in Mayer, *Stanhope*, pp. 412ff.

68. Quoted in Mayer and Tradowsky, *Kaspar Hauser*, p. 179.

69. When the king heard about Kaspar Hauser's death, he wrote in his diary: "Very sorry over the death of the rightful Grand Duke of Baden, if he was Kaspar Hauser, which is probable." Quoted by Prinz Adalbert von Bayern in *Der Zwiebelturm* 5 (1951), p. 125, and also in Mayer and Tradowsky, ibid., p. 214.

70. Sophie (1805–72), archduchess of Austria, mother of Kaiser Franz Joseph I. Austrian politics was intimately involved in the affairs of Baden and Bavaria, as Mayer details in his book on Stanhope.

71. Elisabeth (1801–73), queen of Prussia.

72. Letter quoted in Mayer, *Stanhope*, p. 415.

73. Ibid., p. 415.

74. Joseph Hickel was thirty-eight years old in 1833. He was a police officer (*Gendarmerieoberleutnant*) assigned early on to the Kaspar Hauser case, presumably by Feuerbach, who trusted him. He accompanied Kaspar Hauser on several trips, as far away as Hungary, in search of clues for his identity. He became friendly with Stanhope, and after Feuerbach's death seems to have allowed himself to be manipulated by Stanhope against the interests of Kaspar Hauser. The two books by Julius Meyer, the son of Kaspar Hauser's teacher in Ansbach (the first and most influential, *Authentische Mittheilungen über Kaspar Hauser* [Authentic observations on Kaspar Hauser], a cynical misnomer if ever there was one, was published in Ansbach in 1872), contain letters from Hickel that Pies was able to demonstrate are forgeries. Stanhope probably wrote them. But whether Stanhope or Hickel was the author of these letters, they contradict the actual evidence of other documents that are indisputably by Hickel. For more information on this topic, see Pies, *Fälschungen*.

75. See his 1951 article, "Königin Caroline von Bayern und Kaspar Hauser."

76. To Hungary.

77. Schmidt.

78. This is a reference to a letter that Stanhope wrote Feuerbach on January 23, 1832, in which he writes: "I was told that the grand duchess when she read your book wept bitter tears and had red eyes for a long time afterwards" (Mayer, *Stanhope*, p. 403).

79. A reference to Luise von Hochberg, her son Leopold (1790–1852), who became grand duke of Baden in 1830, and his wife, Sophie of Baden (1801–65).

80. The text is given by Mayer, *Stanhope*, pp. 416–17. He found the letter in the Stanhope family archive, Chevening, Kent.

81. Pies (*Fälschungen*) vouches for Hickel and was able to show that the letters by Hickel published in 1872 and 1881 by Julius Meyer, the son of Kaspar Hauser's Ansbach teacher, were fabrications. (Hickel died in 1862.) On the other hand, Hickel seems to have gone along with the plan, first formulated by Stanhope and Meyer as early as 1834, of fabricating the letters. This information is new, and was found by Mayer (see *Stanhope*, pp. 503ff).

82. In his unpublished manuscript on the Kaspar Hauser question, written in 1908, pp. 73–74. (Anselm von Feuerbach thought his grandfather was systematically poisoned by arsenic starting in 1829.) Daumer wrote that Eduard von Feuerbach "died, if I remember correctly, suddenly and unexpectedly with symptoms of having been poisoned" (*Sein Wesen*, p. 82). Eduard Feuerbach (1803–43), did die, suddenly, on April 25, 1843. His uncle, Joseph Anselm von Feuerbach (1798–1851), professor of archeology in Freiburg, one of the great judge's sons, husband of Henriette von Feuerbach (herself a noted cultural figure whose brother, the physician Wilhelm

Heydenreich, 1798–1857, first recognized that Kaspar Hauser's wound was fatal), and father of the painter Anselm von Feuerbach, was apparently also poisoned. On the words Feuerbach supposedly wrote on the piece of paper, see also Pies, *In Memoriam Adolf Bartning* (Ansbach: C. Brügel and Sohn, 1930), p. 167. See too Mayer, *Kaspar Hauser*, pp. 206–8. The great grandson of Feuerbach told Bartning that "My father held the piece of paper in his own hands on the occasion of a visit to his aunts in Nuremberg and copied down the exact quotation. It contained the words: Somebody gave me something." Mayer, *Kaspar Hauser*, p. 206.

83. I could be wrong about this. In a letter that Johannes Mayer found in the Kent Archive from Feuerbach to Stanhope, dated May 12, 1832 (op.cit., p. 416), Feuerbach writes: *"K[lüber] war stets im Interesse der jenigen Familie, welche durch Tötung oder sonstige Entfernung Kaspars gewinnen konnte und wirklich gewonnen hat. Er war und ist immer noch für dieselbe eingenommen: doch ich fürchte, schon durch dieses wenige zu viel gesagt zu haben."* (Klüber was always [operating] in the interest of that family [namely Hochberg] who stood to gain from Kaspar's death or removal by other means, and did in fact gain. He was and is still prejudiced on their behalf. But I fear that even by saying this little, I have said too much.)

84. Mayer, *Stanhope*, p. 409.

85. There is a letter from Klüber dated May 30, 1833, reporting the death of Feuerbach after a two-hour visit with him the day before. He reports in it that an autopsy was performed and nothing was found, so the "illness was declared to be nervous" *(die Krankheit wurde für nervös erklärt)*. Daumer, *Sein Wesen*, p. 461. Also in Mayer and Tradowsky, p. 204.

86. Mayer, *Stanhope*, p. 451.

87. Mayer, *Stanhope*, p. 406.

88. Marie Amalie Elisabeth Caroline Markgräfin von Baden was born on October 11, 1817. She married William Alexander Anton Archibald, duke of Hamilton, marquis of Douglas and Clychester, in 1843.

89. Mayer and Tradowsky, *Kaspar Hauser*, p. 281.

90. Nothing certain is known. But the fact that Kaspar Hauser was able to learn to speak fluently in so short a time suggests that he had already acquired the basics of language. This was the view of Daumer *(Sein Wesen*, p. 422) and others.

91. Mayer, *Kaspar Hauser*, p. 780.

92. According to Daumer *(Sein Wesen*, p. 133), it was widely suspected that Karl was poisoned at the time of the Congress of Vienna, in 1815. He died in 1818, only thirty-two years old. He is said to have spoken these words on his deathbed: "My two sons and I have all been poisoned."

93. *"Man hat mich umgebracht und meine Söhne"* he said to several of his courtiers. See Mayer, *Stanhope*, p. 209. Varnhagen gives a blistering account of Karl's last days: *"Die Umgebung war trostlos ... dem Kranken durfte man nicht sagen, wie schlecht es um ihn stand; aber dass er nicht lange Leben könne, dass er Gift*

bekommen habe, wiederholte er selbst öfters unter jammervollen Ausrufen. . . . Er saß tagelang niedergeschlagen und gelangweilt da." (The surroundings were bleak . . . one could not tell the sick man how things stood with him; but that he could not live long, that he had been given poison, he himself repeated many times with miserable cries. . . . He sat there the whole day depressed and bored.) (Quoted in Mayer, *Stanhope*, p. 205, from the twelve volumes of memoirs of K. A. Varnhagen von Ense, published in Leipzig in 1871, *Denkwürdigkeiten des eigenen Lebens*.) Writing in a lively and direct style, Varnhagen was a particularly valuable eyewitness to these events. The relevant passages can be found in Pies, *Dokumentation*, pp. 246ff. His death of course widowed Stéphanie and allowed the son of Countess Hochberg to ascend the throne.

94. One of the most important articles (because the author had family access to previously unpublished letters and other documents) about this case is "Königin Caroline von Bayern und Kaspar Hauser," by Prince Adalbert von Bayern (1886–1970). From one of these letters (quoted on page 107) we learn that "King Ludwig I of Bavaria remarked on December 23, 1833, that his external minister, Freiherr von Gise, 'told him in confidence what my deceased brother-in-law, Count Eugen von Leuchtenberg, told him, but that he did not want to reveal: namely that his cousin, the widowed grand duchess of Baden [Stéphanie, Kaspar Hauser's mother] was of the opinion that her eldest son, whose corpse she never saw, had not died but was kidnapped!'" Caroline of Bavaria wrote to her daughter on Monday, March 12, 1832 (thus while Kaspar Hauser was still alive), in response to the question of who Kaspar Hauser was: The general consensus is that Hauser is one of the sons of my poor brother. Although I am convinced that at least one [of his sons] did not die a natural death, I have, unfortunately, no doubt that the crime has been successfully committed." (The German original says precisely this: *Obschon ich überzeugt bin, dass wenigstens der Eine keines natürlichen Todes gestorben ist, so habe ich unglücklicher Weise trotzdem keinerlei Zweifel, dass das Verbrechen voll ausgeführt worden ist"* [p. 123].) What this article proves conclusively is that both royal houses were hardly indifferent to the question of who Kaspar Hauser really was, both during and after his lifetime. For some members of the royal households it was, and remained, an obsession. Kaspar's aunt, Marie von Hamilton, who was born in 1812, was visited in 1875 by Bogdan Graf von Hutten-Czapski (1851–1936), who reported that she showed him a picture of Kaspar Hauser and then said: "This is Kaspar Hauser, my unfortunate brother. My mother and I were always convinced that he was my brother." In 1875 Louise Baronin Belli di Pino, a lady-in-waiting to her mother, visited the countess of Hamilton and "told the noble lady that I was convinced that Kaspar Hauser was the son of her mother. She answered me: *Maman est morte avec cette conviction! Et je crois qu'il était mon frère"* (Mother died believing this, and I believe that he was my brother). Both quotations are in Mayer, *Stanhope*, p. 319. He took the for-

mer from *Sechzig Jahre Politik und Gesellschaft,* vol. 1 (Berlin, Bogdan, Graf von Hutten-Czapski, 1936), and the second from the Tucher archives.

95. See his *Neue Beiträge zur Kaspar-Hauser-Forschung* (Nuremberg: J. L. Schrag Verlag, 1929).

96. According to Pies, *Dokumentation,* p. 294, it was the belief of both doctors, Preu and Osterhausen, Kaspar Hauser's first two physicians, that he lived in freedom for the first three or four years of his life. This agrees with Klee's research as well.

97. Feuerbach, *The Kaspar Hauser Question,* p. 88. This manuscript, which has been edited by Johannes Mayer, was just published in Hans Magnus Enzensberger's series *Die andere Bibliothek,* along with our edition of Daumer's manuscript. I was able to see it and cite it through the kindness of Mr. Mayer. The full title of the new book is: *Anselm von Feuerbach, Georg Friedrich Daumer, Eduard Feuerbach: Kaspar Hauser,* Ediert und mit Hintergrundberichten versehen von Johannes Mayer und Jeffrey M. Masson. (Frankfurt am Main: Eichborn Verlag, 1995).

98. Cases like that of Kaspar Hauser are not entirely unknown even in modern times. One, cited by Lane (p. 179; see note 100 for full reference), which he took from Lucien Malson's book about the Wild Child of Aveyron, bears a striking resemblance to that of Kaspar Hauser. It reports: "Yves Chenau was discovered in 1963 at Saint-Brévin, in Loire-Atlantique, by his uncle and some gendarmes; he had been living in a cellar for eighteen months, imprisoned there by his wicked stepmother. 'When he came out,' his uncle recounts, 'he took a long time to get accustomed to the light. He was shown a cat and a cow and asked what they were. He no longer knew.' Didier Leroux—sent to cover the story by a major Paris newspaper—and who saw the child at the Nantes hospital, states 'His gaze wanders apathetically over things and people. He does not speak; he no longer knows how to speak.'"

99. Jean-Jacques Rousseau, *Discours sur l'origine de l'inégalité parmi les hommes* (Paris, 1754; reprint, Paris: Garnier, 1962), pp. 94–96: "These children walk on all fours and require careful instruction before they can walk upright.... [The child from Hesse] had been taken care of by wolves.... He walked so like an animal that pieces of wood had to be tied to his legs for him to hold himself erect ... on his two feet.... The same was true of the child discovered in the forests of Lithuania who had lived among bears. According to Abbé Condillac he did not reveal the slightest sign of reason. He walked on all fours, lacked the power of speech and uttered sounds quite unlike anything human. The young savage from Hanover who was taken to the English court some years ago had the greatest difficulty in learning to walk on two feet.... Two other savages were discovered in the Pyrenees running up and down the mountainside like quadrupeds." Lucien Malson, *Wolf Children and the Problem of Human Nature: The Wild Boy of Aveyron by Jean Itard* (New York: Monthly Review Press, 1972; originally

published as *Les enfants sauvages* [Paris: Union Générale d'Editions, 1964]), p. 38.

100. The material that follows comes from the excellent book by Harlan Lane, *The Wild Boy of Aveyron* (Cambridge, Mass.: Harvard University Press, 1979).

101. Lane, *The Wild Boy*, p. 56. Claude Lévi-Strauss also believes this, and claims that "most of these [abandoned] children were congenitally abnormal and it is imbecility, which they nearly all seem to have suffered, that is the original cause of their abandonment and not, as some contend, its result." Cited in Lane, *The Wild Boy*, p. 172. The reference to Lévi-Strauss is to his book, *Les structures élémentaires de la parenté* (Paris: Presses Universitaires de France, 1949), pp. 3–4. Lane says that Maria Montessori shares this view.

102. Lane, *The Wild Boy*, pp. 62–63.

103. Octave Mannoni, in "Itard et son sauvage," *Les Temps Modernes* 233 (October 1965), pp. 647–63, regrets that Itard was no Freud. The literature on the Wild Boy of Aveyron is nearly as extensive as that about Kaspar Hauser (see the bibliography in Lane). I recommend Lane, *The Wild Boy*, and Malson, *Wolf Children and the Problem of Human Nature*, mentioned in notes 99 and 100.

104. It is clear from the Daumer manuscript, which Feuerbach had in front of him when writing his own account, that both men were fascinated by Kaspar Hauser's unusual sensory apparatus, the fact that he was so sensitive to taste, smells, sounds, and sights. In this he resembled an infant. For Feuerbach and Daumer, it was as if Kaspar Hauser's development had completely frozen at this early stage, and part of their task was to set his natural growth back into motion. At the same time they worried about "spoiling" the natural purity of the infant in him.

105. Daumer, *Mitteilungen*. See the reprint by Peter Tradowsky (Dornach: Rudolf Geering Verlag, 1983), p. 119.

106. This important letter was published by Pies, *Die Wahrheit*, pp. 69–73.

107. Perhaps Feuerbach meant by this word that he was a genius.

108. On Hahnemann, see Richard Haehl: *Samuel Hahnemann, His Life and Work* (London: Homeopathic Publishing Co., 1922). See also Harris L. Coulter, *Divided Legacy: A History of the Schisms in Medical Thought*, vol. 2 (Berkeley, Calif.: North Atlantic Books, 1988). Chapter 6 is devoted to Hahnemann. Hahnemann wrote that he, like Kaspar Hauser, knew no childhood.

109. *Sein Wesen*, p. 175.

110. *Sein Wesen*, p. 276.

111. From Ernst Kantorowicz, *Frederick the Second 1194–1250*, translated into English by E. O. Lorimer (London: Constable & Co., 1931). See also Thomas Curtis van Cleve, *The Emperor Frederick II of Hohenstaufen: Immutator Mundi* (Oxford: Clarendon Press, 1972), pp. 31–32:

It is related also that, in an effort to discover what language men would naturally speak if reared in complete seclusion and denied the hearing of all spoken words, he caused new-born infants to be reared by foster-mothers who were "to suckle and bathe them but in no wise to speak to them." For as Salimbene relates, "he desired to know whether or not they would speak Hebrew, which is the original language, or Greek, Latin, or Arabic, or the language of the parents from whom they were born. . . . But the infants died."

The author writes that "one can only conclude that, if excessive cruelty accompanied Frederick's efforts in experimentation, it was because he lived in an age when cruelty was not uncommon, appearing at times as an attribute of piety. The significant feature of all this is that Frederick II had the will to seek for truth by means of experimentation in those realms of thought where passive acceptance was the established order of the day" (p. 318).

112. Quoted from John Edwards, *Multilingualism* (London: Routledge, 1994), p. 16.

113. Herodotus, *The History*, translated by David Grene (Chicago: University of Chicago Press, 1987), pp. 131–32.

114. In this book Rousseau cites examples of feral children, or *homo ferus*.

115. An idea echoed, no doubt deliberately and consciously, by Daumer in the foreword to his 1873 book about Kaspar Hauser (*Sein Wesen*): "*Hauser bewies in jener Periode, dass der Mensch edel geschaffen ist und dass die Bestialität nicht die Grundlage seiner Natur bildet*" (Hauser demonstrated, during that period, that man is created noble and that bestiality does not constitute the essence of his nature), p. 17.

116. A. F. Bance, "The Kaspar Hauser Legend and Its Literary Survival," *German Life and Letters* 28 (1975), pp. 199–210.

117. Perhaps it was with this remark in mind that Daumer notes in the manuscript that "lost children living in the wilderness present a very different picture from that of Kaspar Hauser" (p. 120).

118. Malson, *Wolf Children and the Problem of Human Nature*, p. 39.

119. *Caspar Hauser, nicht unwahrscheinlich ein Betrüger* (Berlin: August Rücker).

120. *Vier populäre Vorlesungen über Kaspar Hauser* (Berlin: Verlag der königlichen geheimen Oberhofbuchdruckerei, 1857).

121. Ibid., p. 170; cited by Daumer, *Enthüllungen*, p. 35. One cannot say that this tendency has entirely disappeared. Dieter Zimmer's "Tarzans arme Vettern: Über Wilde Kinder und Wolfskinder," in his book *Experimente des Lebens: was uns die Wissenschaft über wilde Kinder, Zwillinge und unser eigenes Verhalten lehrt* (Munich: Wilhelm Heyne Verlag, 1993), is a contemporary example.

122. "Der schönste Krimi aller Zeiten," in his Afterword to Jakob Wassermann's *Caspar Hauser oder die Trägheit des Herzens*, 10th ed. (Munich: Deutscher Taschenbach Verlag, 1992, first published in the *Frankfurter Allgemeine Zeitung*, Jan. 9, 1980).

123. Stefan George's (1868–1933) beautiful German translation of this stanza reads:

> *Kam ich zu spät, zu frühe?*
> *Ich weiss nicht wie mirs ergeht.*
> *O ihr all! schwer ist meine Mühe —*
> *Sprecht für mich ein Gebet!*

Very different is the version by the contemporary German songwriter Wolf Biermann:

> *Zu früh kam ich zu spät auf diese Erde.*
> *Auf diesem Kahlkopf steh ich als ein Haar.*
> *Mein Elend schreit, doch du, ich bitt' dich: Bete*
> *Für mich, den armen Hauser, den Kaspar.*

(Too early I came too late into this world. / On this bald head I stand like a single hair. / My suffering screams, but you—I beg you: Pray / For me, poor Hauser, Kaspar.)

124. Herman Melville, *Billy Budd, Sailor and Other Stories*. Selected and Edited with an Introduction by Harold Beaver (New York: Penguin Books, 1967), p. 331. In his notes, the editor says that "in 1833 Hauser was stabbed and died of the knife wounds—probably self-inflicted in a psychopathic fit. For Melville, however, this youth reared in apparent isolation had long been a romantic hero, the symbolic outsider unspoiled by civilization." Melville was still revising the unfinished *Billy Budd* when he died in 1891.

125. See Ursula Sampath, *Kaspar Hauser: A Modern Metaphor*, Studies in German Literature, Linguistics, and Culture, vol. 67 (Columbia, S.C.: Camden House, 1991). See also Ulrich Struve, *Der Findling: Kaspar Hauser in der Literatur* (Stuttgart: J. B. Metzler, 1992). This theme had already been tackled in 1935 in Otto Jungmann, *Kaspar Hauser: Stoff und Problem in ihrer literarischen Gestaltung* (Würzburg).

126. See note 125.

127. A somewhat more balanced view, with many historical examples, especially from nineteenth-century French psychologists (and a valuable bibliography) can be found in Ian Hacking's *Rewriting the Soul: Multiple Personality and the Sciences of Memory*. (Princeton: Princeton University Press, 1995).

128. See, in particular, Lawrence Wright, *Remembering Satan: A Case of Recovered Memory and the Shattering of an American Family* (New York: Alfred A. Knopf, 1994); Richard Ofshe and Ethan Watters, *Making Monsters: False Memories, Psychotherapy, and Sexual Hysteria* (New York: Charles Scribner's

Sons, 1994); Elizabeth Loftus and Katherine Ketcham, *The Myth of Repressed Memory: False Memories and Allegations of Sexual Abuse* (New York: St. Martin's Press, 1994); Michael D. Yapko, *Suggestions of Abuse: True and False Memories of Childhood Sexual Traumas* (New York: Simon & Schuster, 1994); Richard Wexler, *Wounded Innocents: The Real Victims of the War Against Child Abuse* (Buffalo, N.Y.: Prometheus Books, 1995). There is, unfortunately, no comparable list of books maintaining the integrity of the reality of memories of sexual abuse in childhood. The politics of memory has yet to be written. For some of the background, see Louise Armstrong: *Rocking the Cradle of Sexual Politics: What Happened When Women Said Incest* (New York: Addison-Wesley, 1994).

129. Mark Pendergrast: *Victims of Memory: Incest Accusations and Shattered Lives* (Hinesburg Vt.: Upper Access, Inc., 1995), p. 48: "Masson's work provided an important scholarly cornerstone for the nascent Incest Survivor Movement and its renewed search for repressed memories. Soon modern therapists would once again encourage 'abreactions.'"

130. See, in particular, my *The Assault on Truth: Freud's Suppression of the Seduction Theory* (New York: Farrar, Straus & Giroux, 1984), which gives most of the new documents. For a more narrative account see my *Final Analysis: The Making and Unmaking of a Psychoanalyst* (New York: Addison-Wesley, 1990). For the background on which Freud, too, depended, see my *A Dark Science.*

131. *The Complete Letters from Sigmund Freud to Wilhelm Fliess, 1887–1904,* edited and translated by Jeffrey Moussaieff Masson (Cambridge, Mass.: Harvard University Press [The Belknap Press], 1995).

132. I call this a loss of moral courage, because nobody at the time was willing to vindicate the "stories" Freud heard from his women patients, or show solidarity with these women who were clearly telling Freud the truth. Freud's 1896 paper, "The Etiology of Hysteria," was universally rejected when it was published. In rejecting my views, scholars have claimed that it took even more courage for Freud to attribute these "stories" to a young girl's imagination, and that Freud's shift to the reality of childhood sexuality, in his book *Three Essays on the Theory of Sexuality,* was more profoundly upsetting to Victorian society than was the thought of men abusing children. But this is simply not true, as I discovered when I looked at the reviews of this book in the 1905 German medical periodicals. Some did indeed reject Freud's views, but many of the reviews were positive. Evidently men did not find the idea that children imagine rather than experience sexual abuse at their hands all that threatening.

133. Not a trivial matter when we consider that women were simply not permitted until very recently to write firsthand accounts of sexual violence at the hands of men. I know of no autobiographical published account in the nineteenth century of childhood sexual abuse, though undoubtedly they happened and were written about.

134. See W. G. Niederland, "Schreber's Father," *Journal of the American Psychoanalytic Association* 8 (1960), pp. 492–99; Morton Schatzman, *Soul-Murder: Persecution in the Family* (New York: Random House, 1973).

135. As just one example, the father invented a device to force children to sit straight, an iron crossbar fastened to the table at which the child sat to read or write. The bar pressed against the collarbones and the front of the shoulders to prevent forward movements. The child could not lean for long against the bar "because of the *pressure* of the hard object against the bones and the consequent *discomfort*. . . . I had one manufactured which proved its worth time and again with my own children." In Schreber's *Memoirs* he reports on a "delusion": "One of the most horrifying miracles was the so-called *compression-of-the-chest-miracle* . . . it consisted in the *whole chest wall being compressed*, so that the state of oppression caused by the lack of breath was transmitted to my whole body."

136. See M. D. Everson and B. W. Boat, "False Allegations of Sexual Abuse by Children and Adolescents," *Journal of the American Academy of Child and Adolescent Psychiatry* (1989), 28, pp. 230–35. According to this article, the fabrication rate is 4 percent to 8 percent.

137. It has become fashionable in the last few years to claim that Freud actually suggested memories of abuse to his patients, rather than their remembering them. See Russell A. Powell and Douglas P. Boer, "Did Freud Mislead Patients to Confabulate Memories of Abuse?" *Psychological Reports* 74 (1994), pp. 1283–98. See also Frederick Crews, "The Revenge of the Repressed," *New York Review of Books*, Dec. 1, 1994, pp. 49–58. In fact we have almost no knowledge of what Freud actually did with his patients. The only real source is the Freud/Fliess letters that I edited for Harvard University Press (*The Complete Letters of Sigmund Freud to Wilhelm Fliess, 1887–1904*), which provide very little material on which to base any conclusion.

138. Judith Herman and Emily Schatzow found that fifteen of fifty-three women, or 28 percent, had delayed memories of sexual abuse. See their article "Recovery and Verification of Memories of Childhood Sexual Trauma," *Psychoanalytic Psychology* 4 (1987), pp. 1–14. John Briere and Jon Conte found that when asked if they had ever forgotten an experience of sexual abuse before the age of eighteen, fifty-nine percent of 450 people said yes. For other, similar studies, see Charles L. Whitfield, *Memory and Abuse: Remembering and Healing the Effects of Trauma* (Deerfield Beach, Fla.: Health Communications, 1995).

139. Children who have been abused are often targeted later in life by older men who recognize the symptoms and take advantage of the vulnerability that is the legacy of sexual abuse. Stanhope's questionable wish to kiss Kaspar Hauser could be interpreted in this light. See the passages I quote on p. 17.

140. Linda Meyer Williams, "Recall of Childhood Trauma: A Prospective Study of Women's Memories of Child Sexual Abuse," *Journal of Con-*

sulting and Clinical Psychology 62, no. 6 (1994), pp. 1167–76. The passages I quote are from p. 1170.

141. See her book *The Secret Trauma: Incest in the Lives of Girls and Women* (New York: Basic Books, 1988).

142. It does seem astonishing and inexplicable that in May 1828 Kaspar Hauser could say but a few stereotypical phrases, for example *heimweissa* ("show me the way home?"), without knowing what they meant, and a few months later could provide a coherent if sketchy narrative account of his life. It is as if he were remembering speech, not learning it, somewhat like a person who forgets a foreign language and then, on returning to the country, begins quickly to regain it.

143. See Leonard Shengold, *Soul Murder: The Effects of Childhood Abuse and Deprivation* (New Haven: Yale University Press, 1989). On the literature preceding Feuerbach, and on his influence on the later literature from a juridical perspective, see Wilfried Küper's thorough book *Das Verbrechen am Seelenleben: Feuerbach und der Fall Kaspar Hauser in strafrechtsgeschichtlicher Betrachtung* (Heidelberg: Manutius Verlag, 1991).

144. It seems that we go through cycles of recognition and denial when it comes to child abuse, whether physical or sexual. There was a period in France in the 1880s when both were acknowledged and written about, but the books that were published then are sadly long out of print and even completely forgotten. See my *Assault on Truth* for details of this French literature.

145. See the article, first published in 1888, "Sudden Death of a Girl about Thirteen Years Old as a Result of Intense Emotion," which I translated from the German and published in *A Dark Science*.

146. See D. James Henderson, "Incest," in *Comprehensive Textbook of Psychiatry*, edited by A. M. Freedman, H. I. Kaplan, and B. J. Sadock, 2nd ed. (Baltimore: Williams and Wilkins, 1975), p. 1536. For a critique, see two excellent books: Judith Lewis Herman, *Father-Daughter Incest* (Cambridge, Mass.: Harvard University Press, 1981), and Russell, *The Secret Trauma*.

147. Meyer complained that he could not convince Kaspar Hauser of the truth of the saying "All good is rewarded, and all evil punished." This passage and the one quoted in the text are found in *Notizen über Kaspar Hauser* by J. G. Meyer, reprinted in Pies, *Augenzeugenberichte*, p. 305.

148. Tucher was asked in a deposition on January 31, 1834, whether Kaspar Hauser knew the existence and contents of the several works that appeared during his lifetime which accused him of being a charlatan. Tucher responded that he definitely knew about Merker's booklet and had probably read it (Pies, *Dokumentation*, p. 120). He had purchased (!) a copy of Feuerbach's book, which he wanted to give as a gift to Mayor Binder's sister. The second book by Merker, also directed against Kaspar Hauser, "lay open in the living room of the Meyer household." It is interesting (and

in character) that Meyer would have left this piece of hate literature against his houseguest lying open to be seen.

149. The play is about the tyranny of language—about how Kaspar Hauser's socialization into language was a form of torture and personal destruction. If Feuerbach felt that Kaspar's soul was murdered as a result of his imprisonment, when he was removed *from* society, Handke believed that his soul was murdered when he was accepted *into* society. Werner Herzog, in his wonderful film *Jeder für sich und Gott gegen Alle* (Every man for himself and God against all), which came out in 1974, conveyed something of the same tragedy. Both Handke's play and Herzog's film, as he himself told me, were based on Feuerbach's book. Mechthild Blanke compares Handke's play with Feuerbach's book in "Zu Handke's *Kaspar*," in *Über Peter Handke*, edited by Michael Scharang (Frankfurt: Suhrkamp, 1972), pp. 27ff.

Appendix 2. A New Kaspar Hauser Manuscript

1. Feuerbach's papers were hardly well preserved after his death. But it is interesting to learn that Daumer was friendly enough with the family (he remained a good friend of the son Ludwig Feuerbach) to be able to see them and quote from them as in this passage. We learn more about the fate of the Feuerbach literary estate from page 461 of Daumer's *Sein Wesen* book. In this passage he tells of an unnamed friend who visited (date unspecified) one of the daughters of Feuerbach (the letter the friend sent Daumer was dated February 23, 1872). She told the friend that

> Eduard [a son of Feuerbach, who, according to Daumer, was poisoned!] took possession of these documents and other writings that were part of the estate. After his death they presumably came into Ludwig's possession. He was still living, though damaged by a stroke. He lives in this area on the Rechenberg. I went there. But what a shock was produced by the sight of that man! I found him in a state of complete dementia, incapable of stringing two words together. His memory was almost totally gone. I tried to explain the reason for my visit in the simplest words, spoken clearly and succinctly. I soon became aware that he had not understood me. His wife, sitting next to him, confirmed this. Finally, my efforts and hers succeeded in getting him to understand that the matter in question was the papers concerning Kaspar Hauser in his father's estate. There seemed to be a flicker of understanding on his part. With great difficulty he let us know that he had collected all of those papers after his father's death. However, he could not recollect what had happened to them. He only said: "It's all here." He was not aware that his brother Eduard presumably had taken charge of them. Thereupon he went to another room and after a while returned with a three-inch-thick bundle of papers. The bundle consisted

only of papers in great disarray, dealing with literary and legislative matters. I then asked permission to search myself with the help of his wife and in the presence of the incapacitated man. Permission was granted immediately. I found huge stacks of old Feuerbach's writings, twenty times as many papers as Ludwig had collected. They testified to the vast erudition of the president in fields other than law; but everything was in total disorder without any trace of papers having to do with Hauser. Nothing of the documents I sought, nor any correspondence dealing with Hauser. The room where this took place was a vast rock-lined hall. There was a large desk in the center, and bookshelves and cupboards lining the walls. . . . The documents were passed on after the president's death to his two sons; then they were lost in the night. There is but a faint gleam left by them, which perhaps is but a will o' the wisp. At least it is certain that the attack of the *"negative Kritik"* [presumably Hauser's enemies] on the man they hated so deeply and who was supposed to have destroyed the papers, failed.

2. Actually this is one of the few places where Daumer seems to be mistaken. Mayer is in possession of a letter from Stanhope to Daumer written on December 9, 1831, attempting to discourage him from publishing his book on Kaspar Hauser.

3. Daumer, *Sein Wesen*, p. 490.

4. Von der Linde, *Kaspar Hauser: Eine neugeschichtliche Legende*, vol. 2, p. 21, has a footnote in which he calls these notes a "fraudulent reconstruction" (*Rekonstruktionsschwindel*) on the part of Daumer, since he let forty years pass before he referred to it in 1873 (*die er 40 Jahre hingehen liess*). However, Feuerbach makes no attempt to hide the fact that he had received many communications from Daumer, although he never states explicitly how much of these communications he had used for his own work.

5. *Kaspar Hauser: Sein Wesen*, pp. 257–8.

6. A letter from Tucher to Feuerbach of July 20, 1830 (in the private possession of Mayer), announces that he is including Daumer's notes with his letter (*lege ich hiermit die abgeschriebenen Notizen über Kaspar Hauser vor*). Hence we now know the exact time they were sent to Feuerbach.

7. Because of the importance of this passage, here is the original German:

Ich schickte meine Bemerkungen über Hauser an Feuerbach mittelst einer von fremder Hand gefertigten Abschrift, welche ich, meiner leidenden Augen wegen, nicht selbst durchsehen und von Fehlern reinigen konnte; der Abschreiber machte solche, die nicht geändert wurden, unglücklicher Weise, gerade bei den in Rede stehenden Notizen und so kamen sie auch in Feuerbachs Buch. Ich hatte von einem tückischen *Pferde gesprochen, daraus wurde ein* türkisches, *worüber sich nun der Stallmeister, als er es las, freilich gar sehr verwundern musste. Ich hatte geschrieben: "H. verspürte nie etwas an dem Gesässe, sondern nur etwas Weniges an den Schenkeln." Aus "sondern" wurden in der Abschrift wahrscheinlich "oder," und so steht bei F.: "Er ritt stunden-lang ohne sich wund zu reiten, oder nur in den Schenkeln oder im Gesässe Schmerzen zu empfinden.*

8. Pies had bound in with the Daumer notes a manuscript by Feuer-bach's grandchild, an unpublished book about Kaspar Hauser. This explains the "von Feuerbach" on the spine.

9. Gustav Radbruch (1878–1949) was the minister of justice in 1922–23 in Germany, during which time he fought for the right of women to be made judges. He was the first professor to lose his chair in Nazi Germany in 1933. His book on Feuerbach, *Paul Johann Anselm Feuerbach: Ein Juristenleben,* a small masterpiece, appeared in 1934.

10. On July 11, 1828.

11. The letter was written by Feuerbach to Elise von der Recke on September 20, 1828, and was published by Pies in his book *Augenzeugenberichte,* pp. 98–105. I translate extracts from the letter in the Introduction on p. 43.

12. This is a reference to an argument between the different seats of government with respect to who had jurisdiction over the Kaspar Hauser affair. The documents have all been collected in Pies, *Die Wahrheit über sein Auftauchen,* pp. 85ff. I discuss this in the Introduction on p. 6.

13. This is a reference to Binder's *Bekanntmachung,* the proclamation, which was published on July 14, 1828, and is the "germ cell" of all later accounts concerning Kaspar Hauser. I have translated the entire document in appendix 1.

14. This is a reference to a book by Julius Meyer, *Authentische Mit-theilungen über Caspar Hauser* (Ansbach: Verlag von Fr. Seybold, 1872). Julius Meyer was the son of the teacher with whom Kaspar Hauser lived in Ansbach (see Introduction, p. 18). This book contains letters from Lieu-tenant Hickel that Pies was able to show were forgeries.

15. Feuerbach wrote a letter on April 8, 1830, to King Ludwig of Bavaria:

Among the many rumors and charges spread about Kaspar's origins, some of them silly, some proved to be untrue, some beyond the bounds of any possible judicial investigation, there is one which goes as follows: Our mysterious foundling is the prince of Grand Duke Carl of Baden and Stéphanie, who was exchanged, put in somebody else's place, and then caused to disappear. He is, therefore, no less a person than the actual gen-uine grand duke of Baden himself!

See Pies, *Dokumentation,* p. 78.

16. See Hermann Pies, *In Memoriam Adolf Bartning: Altes und Neues zur Kaspar-Hauser-Frage aus dem literarischen Nachlass des Verstorbenen* (Ansbach: C. Brügel & Sohn, 1930). Also Adolf Bartning, *Neues über Kaspar Hauser: Vortrag gehalten am 22. April 1927 von Rechtsanwalt Bartning (Hamburg) in der*

Hamburgischen Forensisch-Psychologischen Gesellschaft (Ansbach: C. Brügel & Sohn, 1927). These are among the more serious works written about Kaspar Hauser, and Pies himself helped to edit the work when Bartning unexpectedly died in the middle of his important research.

17. This is a reference to Feuerbach's *Mémoire* (Memorandum) to the queen mother of Bavaria (who was the sister of Kaspar Hauser's father, Karl of Baden), which was given to her in February 1832. In this document Feuerbach comes to the conclusion that Kaspar Hauser was the legitimate heir to the throne of Baden. He states his conclusion in the words Pies puts into quotation marks. See the Introduction, pp. 28ff.

18. This is a reference to Daumer's two short booklets on Kaspar Hauser, entitled *Mittheilungen über Kaspar Hauser,* that were both published in 1832 in Nuremberg by Heinrich Hubenstricher. The book has been reprinted by Peter Tradowksy (Dornach: Rudolf Geering Verlag, 1983). Feuerbach and others thought they were poorly written and would do Kaspar Hauser no good. See pp. 173ff.

19. The Feuerbach family lived in Lindau, and it was a direct descendant who handed over the manuscript to Pies, as Radbruch, of course knew, since he was the one who suggested it in the first place. It almost sounds as if Pies does not want to admit that he did not already know of the existence of this manuscript, whereas in fact it was Radbruch who first learned about the manuscript and brought it to Pies's attention.

20. Daumer wrote three volumes about Kaspar Hauser, the first (a small work in two short booklets) published in 1832, and then two much larger volumes, one in 1859 and the last one in 1872. Daumer was much criticized for his credulity and for believing in Kaspar Hauser's "magic powers." It is true, however, that the diary is a much more factual account, hence more valuable both to Feuerbach and to us.

21. Hitzig, criminal director im Berlin, *Caspar Hauser,* in *Annalen der deutschen und ausländischen Criminal-Rechts-Pflege* 7 (1830), pp. 434–58.

22. Johann Fr. Merker, *Caspar Hauser, nicht unwahrscheinlich ein Betrüger* (Berlin: August Rücker, 1830).

23. *Einige wichtige Actenstücke den unglücklichen Findling Caspar Hauser betreffend. Zur Berichtigung des Urtheils des Publicums über denselben mitgetheilt von Herrn Staatsrath und Appellationsgerichts-Präsidenten von Feuerbach in Ansbach für Hitzigs Annalen der deutschen und ausländischen Criminalpflege und daraus besonders abgedruckt* (Berlin: 1831).

24. Feuerbach, *Kaspar Hauser.* The book actually appeared in bookstores a few weeks before the end of 1831.

25. The German word is *"enragierten,"* which means, literally, "enraged," but it is probably a typo for *"engagierten,"* which means somebody who is much involved in the subject matter, which makes more sense here.

26. This is a reference to a mistake Feuerbach made in reading the manuscript that Daumer sent him. It is discussed in this appendix on pp. 175ff.

27. Feuerbach died on May 29, 1832, under mysterious circumstances. See my Introduction, pp. 33ff.

28. This refers to a document, mentioned earlier, that Feuerbach wrote, entitled: *Mémoire: Wer möchte wohl Kaspar Hauser sein?* (Memorandum: Who might Kaspar Hauser be?) that was sent to Queen Karoline of Bavaria in 1832, but was not published until 1852, edited by his son Ludwig Feuerbach, the philosopher, in *Anselm Ritter von Feuerbachs Leben und Wirken, aus seinen ungedruckten Briefen und Tagebüchern, Vorträgen und Druckschriften* (Leipzig: Verlag von Otto Wigand, 1852, vol. 2), pp. 319ff. The text has been reprinted in Pies, *Dokumentation*, pp. 237–42.

29. This refers to the *Flaschenpostgeschichte*, which I tell about in the Introduction, pp. 36ff. The documents have been assembled by Pies, *Dokumentation*, pp. 281ff.

30. Stanhope says this in his *Materialien zur Geschichte Kaspar Hausers gesammelt und herausgegeben von dem Grafen Stanhope* (Heidelberg: Akademischen Buchhandlung von J. Mohr, 1835). But as Pies has shown in several places (*Die Wahrheit*, and *Fälschungen* in particular), Stanhope fabricated many passages. This is just such an example. Stanhope is referring to a passage in Feuerbach's Kaspar Hauser book in which the Binder proclamation is referred to as "novelistic." But this is a completely other matter, which I have explained in the Introduction, pp. 6ff. There is absolutely no evidence to bolster Stanhope's claim that Feuerbach said, of his book on Kaspar Hauser, "I have written a novel," though one can easily imagine that many people thought it read like a novel, which it does, without, thereby, losing any of its authenticity. See Pies, *Die Wahrheit*, p. 269, for documents. Stanhope (p. 47 of his *Materialien*) writes: "He himself (Feuerbach), began, in the last period of his life, to doubt the truth of the story, and, as I have learned from a completely trustworthy witness, he said: 'Perhaps Feuerbach in his old age has written a novel'" (Pies, *Die Wahrheit*, p. 265).

31. This is, in fact, not an exact quotation from Merker (*Beiträge* [1832], p. 60), which actually reads: *"Feuerbach konnte ausgezeichnet schreiben, hier schrieb er hinreissend!"*

32. Feuerbach's Memorandum, mentioned above, was brought to the queen by Lieutenant Hickel, for whom an audience was arranged by Friedrich Ludwig von Schmidt (1764–1857), a confidant of the queen, and somebody whom Feuerbach knew and trusted. Schmidt was also present at the birth of the prince in 1812.

33. Friedrich Eberhardt was the chief of police in the city of Gotha. A woman there claimed at the end of 1832 that Kaspar Hauser was her long-lost son. Feuerbach wrote Eberhard a series of letters, the matter was investigated, and it turned out that her son had died in 1811. See Mayer and Tradowsky, *Kaspar Hauser*, p. 195, and Hermann Pies, *Die Wahrheit*, pp. 265ff.

34. This is a reference to a letter that Feuerbach wrote to N. N. Eberhardt on December 29, 1832, in which he says of Kaspar Hauser that he is *"nur ein Kanonikus oder Domprobst en miniature, an dem man kaum die Tonsur vermisst."* Quoted in Pies, *Die Wahrheit,* p. 269.

35. This is a reference to a passage in his Kaspar Hauser book in which Feuerbach obscurely but unmistakably refers to Kaspar Hauser's royal birth. See my Introduction, p. 29, for a discussion of this passage. There is difficulty in the text of this letter. Possibly it has been mistranscribed. The German reads: *"ehe er seine so pompös in seinem Buch ausgesprochene Meinung von 'den hochgewaltigen Kolossen, die vor goldenen Toren Wache stehen,' usw., aufgab."* The last word, *aufgab,* normally means "gave up." But Feuerbach did *not* give this view up. The sense of the passage must be as I have translated it.

36. Otto Mittelstädt, 1834–99, was a conservative German judge who wrote a vicious book against Kaspar Hauser, *Kaspar Hauser und sein badisches Prinzenthum,* in 1876, trying to prove that he was no prince. It has been largely discredited, since it subsequently came to light that Mittelstädt was in the pay of the house of Baden.

37. Linde, *Kaspar Hauser: Eine neugeschichtliche Legende, Vol. 1: 1828–1833; Vol. 2: 1834–1884* (Wiesbaden: Verlag von Chr. Limbarth, 1887).

38. Engel wrote a series of poorly researched and poorly written books about Kaspar Hauser, attempting to prove that he was a fraud. They were so bad that after reading them I did not write down the details.

39. The footnote in question quotes from an article that Mittelstädt wrote in the June issue of a newspaper called *Vom Fels zum Meer* (From mountains to the sea), in which he does indeed justify torture, at least if the quotation given by Kolb is correct.

Appendix 3. Translation of Kaspar Hauser's Autobiography

1. Antonius von der Linde: *Zum Kaspar-Hauser-Schwindel.* 1. Die älteste (noch ungedruckte) "Selbstbiographie." Kaspar Hausers erste Selbstbiographie. (Kaspar Hauser as fraud. The previously unpublished, oldest autobiography. Kaspar Hauser's first autobiography) Nach dem Original herausgegeben (Wiesbaden, 1888). I have not succeeded in obtaining a copy of this rare book. I have used Pies's reprint for the text.

2. The sentence could also mean: "I myself did not know how quietly I did it."

Appendix 4. Kaspar Hauser's Dreams

1. All these passages are given in Pies, *Dokumentation,* pp. 53ff.
2. Daumer manuscript, p. 151.
3. Pies, *Dokumentation,* p. 53.
4. Ibid., p. 53.
5. Ibid., p. 54.
6. One can't help wondering if this is not a misprint for *"vierjähriges Kind"* ("a four-year-old"). At fourteen, of course, Kaspar Hauser was in the dungeon. Dreams, on the other hand, are not bound by any chronology from the real world!
7. The last sentence could also be translated as: "His father had admonished him to study because some day he (Hauser) would have to take his place and he threatened punishment if he became inattentive."
8. *Sein Wesen,* p. 475.

Appendix 5. Wolf Children

1. In 1940 R. M. Zingg, a professor of psychology at the University of Denver, published a paper entitled "Feral Man and Extreme Cases of Isolation" in the *American Journal of Psychology* 53: 487–515, in which he discussed all known cases of feral children. The article was expanded in his book. Rousseau, in his *Discours sur l'origine de l'inégalité parmi les hommes* (Paris: 1754; reprint, Paris: Garnier, 1962), pp. 94–96, discusses several of these cases. The best known was the wolf child of Hesse, who was found in 1344 running wild in the woods. According to the story, a hole had been dug for him by wolves. They had carpeted it with leaves and at night would encircle him with their bodies in order to protect him from the cold. See Malson, *Wolf Children and the Problem of Human Nature,* p. 39.
2. *Genetic Psychology Monographs* 60 (1959), pp. 117–93. The quotation from Ashley Montagu is found on p. 124.
3. Charles Maclean, *The Wolf Children* (New York: Hill & Wang, 1978), p. 300.
4. Reprint, New Delhi: Himalayan Books, 1982), p. 233. Many cases of children raised by wolves were reported by William Henry Sleeman, *A Journey Through the Kingdom of Oudh,* 2 vols. (London, 1858). He was in Oudh between 1849 and 1850, and reports seven cases in all. (For more on wolf children in India, see Malson, *Wolf Children,* p. 45). See also E. B. Tylor, "Wild Men and Beast Children," *Anthropological Review* 1 (1863), pp. 21–32, the first specialist on cases of isolation, who discusses the cases cited by Sleeman. It would be interesting to know whether Kipling had seen any

of this literature. I would imagine he had. Certainly his father would have. Of even greater interest: Did they know about Kaspar Hauser?

5. John Lockwood Kipling, *Beast and Man in India: A Popular Sketch of Indian Animals in their Relations with the People* (London: Macmillan & Co., 1904; reprint, New Delhi: Inter-India Publications, 1984), p. 281.

6. Randall Jarrell, "On Beginning to Read Kipling," in *Rudyard Kipling*, ed. Harold Bloom (New York: Chelsea House, 1987), p. 21. The essay was originally published in 1961.

7. Charles Carrington, *Rudyard Kipling: His Life and Work* (London: Macmillan, 1957), p. 44.

8. Jim Brandenburg, *White Wolf* (Minoqua, Wisc.: Northword, 1988).

BIBLIOGRAPHY

Albersdorf, Gräfin Caroline von. *Kaspar Hauser oder Andeutungen zur Enthüllung mancher Geheimnisse über Hausers Herkunft, die Ursache seiner Gefangenhaltung und Ermordung* (Kaspar Hauser or allusions to the revelation of a number of secrets about Kaspar Hauser's origins, the reason for his imprisonment and murder). Regensburg, 1837.

Allgemeine Deutsche Biographie. Vol. 6. Leipzig: Dunder & Humbolt, 1877, pp. 731–45: S.V. J. P. A. Feuerbach.

Baier, Hermann. *"Die Wiener Reise des Staatsminister Freiherrn von Reitzenstein und der Fall Kaspar Hauser." Badischer Beobachter* 89, March 31, 1932.

Bapst, Edmond (ambassadeur de France). *À la conquête du trône de Bade: La comtesse de Hochberg, la grande-duchesse Stéphanie, Gaspard Hauser.* Paris: A. Lahure, 1930.

———. *Une mère et son fils: La Grande-Duchesse Stéphanie et Gaspard Hauser.* Paris: A. Lahure, 1933.

Bartning, Adolf. *Neues über Kaspar Hauser: Vortrag gehalten am 22. April 1927 von Rechtsanwalt Bartning (Hamburg) in der Hamburgischen Forensisch-Psychologischen Gesellschaft.* Ansbach: C. Brügel & Sohn, 1927.

Bayern, Prinz Adalbert von. "Königin Caroline von Bayern und Kaspar Hauser." *Der Zwiebelturm: Monatsschrift für das bayerische Volk und seine Freunde* 5 (1951), pp. 102–28.

de Bernardy, Françoise. *Stéphanie de Beauharnais (1789–1860): Fille adoptive de Napoléon Grande-duchesse de Bade.* Paris: Librairie Académique Perrin, 1977.

Bock, Friedrich. "Ein neuer Brief des Präsidenten Anselm v. Feuerbach." *Fränkische Monatshefte* 7, no. 5 (1928), pp. 193–97.

Braun, J. "Kaspar-Hauser-Litteratur." *Börsenblatt für den deutschen Buchhandel und die verwandten Geschäftszweige.* Leipzig 280, 1901, pp. 10718–20, 10750–52.

Brunner, E. "Kaspar Hauser? Graphologische, mikroskopische und mikrophotographische Handschriften-Untersuchung und Gutachten." *Zeitschrift für Menschenkunde: Blätter für Charakterologie und angewandte Psychologie* 5, no. 6 (1930), pp. 343–408.

Conradt, Marcus. *Fünfeinhalb Jahre unter Menschen: Armer Kaspar Hauser.* Stuttgart: Klett, 1983.

Daumer, Georg Friedrich. *Mitteilungen über Kaspar Hauser* (Information about Kaspar Hauser). Nuremberg: Heinrich Haubenstricher, 1832. (Reprint, with introduction by Peter Tradowsky, Dornach: Rudolf Geering, 1983.

————. *Enthüllungen über Kaspar Hauser* (Revelations about Kaspar Hauser). (The long subtitle reads: *Mit Hinzufügung neuer Belege und Documente und Mittheilung noch ganz unbekannter Thatsachen, namentlich zu dem Zwecke, die Heimath und Herkunft des Findlings zu bestimmen und die vom Grafen Stanhope gespielte Rolle zu beleuchten. Eine wider Eschricht und Stanhope gerichtete historische, psychologische und physiologische Beweisführung.*) Frankfurt am Main: Verlag von Weidinger Sohn, 1859.

————. *Kaspar Hauser: Sein Wesen, seine Unschuld, seine Erduldungen und sein Ursprung in neuer, gründlicher Erörterung und Nachweisung. Mit einer Anzahl bisher noch unveröffentlichten Aufsätze, Nachrichten und Erklärungen gewichtvoller Beobachter, Zeugen und Sachkenner, namentlich auch zur Ergänzung des theils an sich mangelhaften, theils noch ungenügend und mit Weglassung relevanter Bestandtheile mitgetheilten Actenmaterials* (Kaspar Hauser: his nature, his innocence, his suffering, and his origins). Regensburg: A. Coppenrath, 1873.

Eulenberg, Herbert. *Die Familie Feuerbach in Bildnissen.* Stuttgart, J. Engelhorns Nachf., 1924.

Ende, Clara von. "Introduction à une bibliographie raisonnée de Gaspard Hauser suivie d'un aperçu chronologique de la question." *Revue germanique* 5, no. 2 (March-April, 1909), pp. 202–17.

Eschricht, Daniel Friedrich. *Unverstand und schlechte Erziehung: Vier populäre Vorlesungen.* Berlin: Verlag der königlichen geheimen Oberhofbuchdruckerei, 1857.

Evans, Elizabeth E. *The Story of Kaspar Hauser from Authentic Records.* London: Swan Sonnenschein & Co. 1892.

Ferrari, Oreste. *Il Mistero di Kaspar Hauser (1828–1833).* Verona: A. Mondadori, 1933.

Feuerbach, Paul Johann Anselm Ritter von. *Einige wichtige Actenstücke den unglücklichen Findling Caspar Hauser betreffend. Zur Berichtigung des Urtheils des Publicums über denselben mitgetheilt von Herrn Staatsrath und Appellations-*

gerichts-Präsidenten von Feuerbach in Ansbach für Hitzigs Annalen der deutschen und ausländischen Criminalpflege und daraus besonders abgedruckt. Berlin, 1831.

———. *Kaspar Hauser. Beispiel eines Verbrechens am Seelenleben des Menschen.* Ansbach: J.F. Dollfuss, 1832.

———. *Kaspar Hauser. An account of an individual kept in a dungeon, separated from all communication with the world, from early childhood to about the age of seventeen,* translated by Henning Gottfried Linberg. Boston: Allen & Ticknor, 1833; London: Simpkin and Marshall, 1833.

———. *Caspar Hauser: An Account of an Individual Kept in a Dungeon, Separated from All Communication with the World, from Early Childhood to about the Age of Seventeen, Drawn up from Legal Documents by Anselm von Feuerbach, President of one of the Bavarian Courts of Appeal, etc. Third Edition, with a memoir of the author. To which are added, Further interesting details by G. F. Daumer, and Schmidt von Lübec.* London: Simpkin and Marshall, 1834.

———. *Leben und Wirken: Aus seinen ungedruckten Briefen und Tagebüchern, Vorträgen und Denkschriften, veröffentlicht von seinem Sohne Ludwig Feuerbach.* 2 vols. Leipzig: Verlag von Otto Wigand, 1852.

———. *Anselm Ritter von Feuerbachs biographischer Nachlass.* 2 vols. Leipzig: Verlagsbuchhandlung von J.J. Weber, 1853. Reprint, Scientia Verlag Aalen, 1973.

———. *Merkwürdige Verbrechen.* Edited by Cay Brockdorff. Berlin: Buchverlag der Morgen, 1973.

———. *Kaspar Hauser: Beispiel eines Verbrechens am Seelenleben des Menschen.* Edited by Helmut Bender. Waldkirch: Waldkircher Verlagsgesellschaft, 1981.

———. *Erkentnisse über Kaspar Hauser. Mit Nachwort und Auswahl-Bibliographie von Armin Forker.* Leipzig: Zentralantiquariat der deutschen Demokratischen Republik, 1983.

———. *Merkwürdige Verbrechen.* Frankfurt am Main: Eichborn Verlag, 1993.

Flake, Otto. *Kaspar Hauser.* Mannheim: Kessler Verlag, 1950. Reprint, Fischer, Frankfurt am Main, 1990.

Fuhrmann, Johann Simon Heinrich. *Trauerrede bei der am 20. Dezember 1833 erfolgten Beerdigung des am 14. desselben Monats meuchlings ermordeten Kaspar Hauser, gehalten und nur auf vielseitiges Verlangen herausgegeben von H. Fuhrmann, königl. III Pfarrer bei St. Sumbert in Ansbach.* Bamberg: J.E. Dresch, 1833.

———. *Kaspar Hauser. Beobachtet und dargestellt in der letzten Zeit seines Lebens von seinem Religionslehrer und Beichtvater.* Ansbach: J.W. Dollfuss, 1834.

———. *Kaspar Hauser.* Edited by Peter Tradowsky. Dornach: Rudolf Geering Verlag, 1983.

Haas, Rudolf. *Stéphanie Napoleon: Grossherzogin von Baden: Ein Leben zwischen Frankreich und Deutschland 1789–1860.* Mannheim: Südwestdeutsche Verlagsanstalt, 1976.

Heidenreich, F. W. "Kaspar Hausers Verwundung, Krankheit und Leichen-öffnung." *Journal der Chirurgie und Augen-Heilkunde* 21 (1834), pp. 91–123.

Hesse, Günter. "Die Krankheit Kaspar Hausers." *Münch. med. Wschf.* 109, no. 3 (1967), pp. 156–63.

Heyer, Karl. *Kaspar Hauser und das Schicksal Mitteleuropas im 19. Jahrhundert: Studienmaterialien zur Geschichte des Abendlandes.* Stuttgart: Verlag des freien Geistesleben, 1983.

Hitzig, Criminal-Director in Berlin. "Caspar Hauser." *Annalen der deutschen und ausländischen Criminal-Rechts-Pflege* 7 (1830), pp. 434–58.

———. "Erinnerung an Feuerbach." *Hitzig Annalen* 2 (1830), pp. 434ff.

Hofer, Klara. *Das Schicksal einer Seele, Die Geschichte von Kaspar Hauser, unter Berücksichtigung der neuesten Feststellungen.* Nuremberg, 1924.

Hörische, Jochen, ed. *Ich möchte ein solcher werden wie . . . Materialien zur Sprachlosigkeit des Kaspar Hauser* (I would like to be like . . . Material about the lack of spech of Kaspar Hauser). Frankfurt am Main: Suhrkamp, 1979.

Kaspar Hauser. Seine mysteriöse Ermordung, sein hartnäckiges Weiterleben. Freiburg: Dreisan-Verlag, 1983. Contains Baron Alexander von Artin, *Kaspar Hauser. Des Rätsels Lösung!* First printed in Zurich, 1892.

Kaspar Hauser: Arztberichte. Preu, Osterhausen, Albert, Heidenreich. Edited by Peter Tradowsky. Dornach: Rudolf Geering Verlag, 1985.

Klee, Fritz. *Neue Beiträge zur Kaspar Hauser-Forschung.* Nuremberg: J.L. Schrag Verlag, 1929.

Kluncker, Karlhans. *Georg Friedrich Daumer. Leben und Werk 1800–1875.* 1984: Bonn, Abhandlungen zur Kunst, Musik und Literaturwissenschaft, Bd. 349.

Kolb, Georg Friedrich (Under the pseudonym F. K. Broch). *Kaspar Hauser. Kurze Schilderung seines Erscheinens und seines Todes. Zusammenstellung und Prüfung des bis jetzt vorliegenden Materials über seine Abstammung; Mittheilung seither noch nicht veröffentlichter Thatsachen, und kritische Würdigung der Angaben von Feuerbach, Eschricht und der neuesten von Daumer.* Zurich, 1859.

———. *Kaspar Hauser. Ältere und neuere Beiträge zur Aufhellung der Geschichte des Unglücklichen.* Regensburg: Verlag von Alfred Coppenrath, 1883.

Kramer, Kurt. *Kaspar Hauser: Kein Rätsel unserer Zeit: Historischer Report über ein Schicksal zwischen den Mahlsteinen der Politik.* Ansbach: Verlagsgesellschaft, 1978.

Küper, Wilfried. *Das Verbrechen am Seelenleben: Feuerbach und der Fall Kaspar Hauser in strafrechtsgeschichtlicher Betrachtung.* Heidelberg: Manutius Verlag, 1990.

———. *Reflexionen—Maximen—Erfahrungen von Paul Johann Anselm Feuerbach.* Heidelberg: Manutius Verlag, 1992.

Lang, Heinrich Ritter von. "Caspar Hauser'sche Literatur." *Jenaische Allgemeine Literatur-Zeitung* 101–105 (1834), pp. 322–70.

Lakies, Holger, and Gisela Lakies-Wild. *Das Phänomen: Entwicklungspsychologisch bedeutsame Fakten des Hauser-Mysteriums.* Ansbach: Verlagsgesellschaft, 1978.

Leonhard, K. "Kaspar Hauser und die moderne Kenntnis des Hospitalismus." *Confin. psychiat.* 13 (1970), pp. 213–29.

Leonhardt, Ulrike. *Prinz von Baden genannt Kaspar Hauser. Eine Biographie.* Reinbek: Rowohlt, 1987.

Lieb, Adolf Anton. "Kaspar Hauser und der Kampf des Königs Ludwig I. von Bayern um den badischen Kurpfalzanteil." *Nachrichtenblatt für die Mitglieder und Freunde des Bayerischen Volksbundes "Treu-Bayern"* 2, no. 10/11 (Aug. 1951), n.p.

von der Linde, Antonius. *Kaspar Hauser: Eine neugeschichtliche Legende. Vol. 1: 1828–1833, Vol. 2: 1834–1884.* Wiesbaden: Verlag von Chr. Limbarth, 1887.

Mann, Golo. "Romane von gestern—heute gelesen: Jakob Wassermann, Caspar Hauser." *Frankfurter Allgemeine Zeitung,* Jan. 9, 1980. In *Caspar Hauser oder die Trägheit des Herzens. Roman,* by Jakob Wassermann: Deutscher Taschenbuch Verlag, 1992.

Mayer, Johannes. *Philip Henry Lord Stanhope: Der Gegenspieler Kaspar Hausers* (Caspar Hauser's adversary). Stuttgart, Urachhaus, 1988.

———. "Noch einmal: Der Fall Kaspar Hauser—Nachtrag zur "Prinzen-Theorie." *Neue juristische Wochenschrift* 44 (June 23, 1991), pp. 1462–65.

———. *Hauser: Das Kind von Europa: In Wort und Bild dargestellt von Johannes Mayer und Peter Tradowsky.* Stuttgart: Urachhaus, 1984.

Mayer, Johannes, and Jeffrey M. Masson, Eds. A. V. Feuerbach, G. F. Daumer: *Kaspar Hauser.* Frankfurt am Main: Eichborn Verlag, 1995.

Merkenschlager, F., and K. Saller. *Kaspar Hauser: Ein zeitloses Problem.* Nuremberg: Lorenz Spindler Verlag, 1966.

Merker, Johann Fr. *Caspar Hauser, nicht unwahrscheinlich ein Betrüger* (Caspar Hauser, most likely a fraud). Berlin: August Rücker, 1830.

Meyer, Julius. *Authentische Mittheilungen über Kaspar Hauser* (Authentic observations on Kaspar Hauser). *Mit Genehmigung der k. bayer. Staatsministerien der Justiz und des Innern zum erstenmale aus den Gerichts- und Administrativ-Acten zusammengestellt und mit Anmerkungen versehen.* Ansbach: Verlag von Fr. Senhold, 1872.

———. "Ansbach Beziehungen zu den Feuerbachs." In Julius Meyer, *Onoldina.* Ansbach, 1908, pp. 63ff.

Mistler, Jean. *Gaspard Hauser: Un drame de la personalité.* Paris, 1971.

Mitscherlich, Alexander. "Ödipus und Kaspar Hauser. Tiefenpsychologische Probleme der Gegenwart." *Der Monat* 3 (1950), pp. 11–18.

Mittelstädt, Otto. *Kaspar Hauser und sein badisches Prinzenthum.* Heidelberg: Verlagsbuchhandlung von Fr. Wassermann, 1876.

Nau, E., and D. Cabanis. "Kaspar-Hauser-Syndrom." *Münchener Medizinische Wochenschrift* 108, no. 17 (1966), pp. 929–31.

Ogburn, William F., and Nirmal K. Bose. "On the Trail of the Wolf-Children." *Genetic Psychology Monographs* 60 (1959), pp. 117–93.

Petzholdt, J. "Bibliographisch-kritische Übersicht der Kaspar-Hauser-Literatur." *Neue Anzeiger für Bibliographie und Bibliothekwissenschaft* (January 1859), pp. 1–5, 36–41; *Nachtrag zur Kaspar-Hauser-Literatur* (1864) 141–42; *Neuester Nachtrag zur Kaspar-Hauser-Literatur* (April 1872) 129–33; *Neuestes aus der Kaspar-Hauser-Frage* (1873) 302–4; *Daumer & die Kaspar-Hauser-Literatur* (February 1876) 49–51; *Neuester Nachtrag zur Kaspar-Hauser-Literatur* (1878) 271–73; *Hauseriana*, 198–200; *Neuester Nachtrag zur Kaspar-Hauser-Literatur* (1881) 200–202; *Noch mehr zur Kaspar-Hauser-Literatur* (1882) 381–83; *Zum Kaspar-Hauser-Schwindel* (January 1883), 268–69. 1884: 198

Peitler, Hans, and Hans Ley. *Kaspar Hauser: Über tausend bibliographische Nachweise.* Ansbach: C. Brügel & Sohn, 1927.

Pierson, W. "Geschichte Kaspar Hausers unparteiisch dargestellt." *Deutsche Warte: Umschau über das Leben und Schaffen der Gegenwart* 2, no. 9 (1872), pp. 531–50.

Pies, Hermann. *Kaspar Hauser Augenzeugenberichte und Selbstzeugnisse.* 2 vols. Stuttgart: Robert Lutz Verlag, 1925.

———. *Fälschungen und Tendenzberichte einer "offiziellen" Hauserliteratur: Aktenmässige Feststellungen.* Nuremberg: J.L. Schrag, 1926.

———. *Die amtlichen Aktenstücke über Kaspar Hausers Verwundung und Tod* (Official documents relating to Kaspar Hauser's mortal wound and death). Bonn: Kulturhistorischer Verlag, 1928.

———. *In Memoriam Adolf Bartning: Altes und Neues zur Kaspar-Hauser-Frage aus dem literarischen Nachlass des Verstorbenen.* Ansbach: C. Brügel & Sohn, 1930.

———. *Die Wahrheit über Kaspar Hausers Auftauchen und erste Nürnberger Zeit.* Saarbrücken, 1956.

———. *Kaspar Hauser: Eine Dokumentation.* Ansbach: C. Brügel & Sohn, 1966.

———. *Kaspar Hauser: Fälschungen, Falschmeldungen und Tendenzberichte* (Forgeries, perjuries and biased reports). Ansbach: Ansbacher Museumsverlag, 1973.

———. *Kaspar Hauser: Augenzeugenberichte und Selbstzeugnisse.* Edited by Johannes Mayer Vol. 1. Stuttgart, Urachhaus, 1985.

———. *Kaspar Hauser: Die Wahrheit über sein Auftauchen und erste Nürnberger Zeit: Augenzeugenberichte, Selbstzeugnisse, amtliche Aktenstücke, Fälschungen und Tendenzberichte.* Vol. 2. Stuttgart: Urachhaus, 1987.

Radbruch, Gustav. *Paul Johann Anselm Feuerbach: Ein Juristenleben.* Vienna: Springer, 1934.

Rauber, A. *Homo sapiens ferus oder die Zustände der Verwilderten und ihre Bedeutung für Wissenschaft, Politik und Schule.* Leipzig: Denicke's Verlag, 1885.

Schanberg, Joseph. *Aktenmässige Darstellung der über die Ermordung des Studenten Ludwig Lessing aus Freienwalde in Preussen bei dem Kriminalgerichte des Kantons Zürich geführten Untersuchung von Dr. Joseph Schanberg. Zweites Beilagenheft. Beiträge zur Geschichte Kaspar Hausers.* Zürich: Friedrich Schulthess, 1837.

Schmidt von Lübeck, Georg Philipp. *Über Caspar Hauser.* Vol. 2. Altona: Karl Aue, 1831–32.

Scholz, Hans. *Der Prinz Kaspar Hauser: Protokoll einer modernen Sage.* Hamburg: Hoffmann & Campe, 1964.

Schreibmüller, Walter. "Bilanz einer 150jährigen Kaspar Hauser-Forschung. *Jahrbuch des historischen Vereins für Mittelfranken.* Vol. 91, pp. 129–72. Ansbach: Selbstverlag des historischen Vereins f. Mittelfranken, 1982–83.

———. "Neues zur Identität Kaspar Hausers?" *Jahrbuch für fränkische Landesforschung* 48 (1988), pp. 221–25.

Seifert, Fedor. "Schöne Literatur und Feuerbach: Die Anfänge der Kriminalpsychologie." *Neue juristische Wochenschrift* 38, no. 28 (1985), pp. 1591–95.

Shengold, Leonard. "Kaspar Hauser and Soul Murder: A Study of Deprivation." *International Review of Psycho-Analysis* 5 (1978), pp. 457–76.

Simon, Nicole. "Kaspar Hauser's Recovery and Autopsy: A Perspective on Neurological and Sociological Requirements for Language Development." *Journal of Autism and Childhood Schizophrenia* 8, no. 2 (1978), pp. 209–17.

Singer, Georg Friedrich. *Leben Kaspar Hausers oder Beschreibung seines Wandels von seinem Beginn bis zu seinem Grabe.* Regensburg: E. Auernheimer, 1834.

Singh, J. A. L., and R. M. Zingg. *Wolf-Children and Feral Man.* Denver: University of Denver, 1942.

Skizze der bis jetzt bekannten Lebensmomente des merkwürdigen Findlings Caspar Hauser in Nürnberg mit der naturgetreuen Abbildung desselben, auf Stein gezeichnet von Fr. Hans Stengel, Zeichnungslehrer in München. Kempten: Druck und Verlag bei Daunheimer, 1830.

Spoerri, Theod. *Genie und Krankheit: Eine psychopathologische Untersuchung der Familie Feuerbach.* Foreword by E. Kretschmer. Basel/New York: S. Karger, 1952.

Stanhope, Philip Henry. *Über Kaspar Hausers Leben. Von ihm selbst geschrieben. Dem Grafen Stanhope mitgetheilt von dem Herrn Präsidenten von Feuerbach. Getreu nach der Urschrift abgedruckt. Als Manuscript gedruckt.* Karlsruhe: Wilhelm Hasper, 1834.

———. *Materialien zur Geschichte Kaspar Hausers gesammelt und herausgegeben von dem Grafen Stanhope* (Material on the case of Kaspar Hauser). Heidelberg: Akademischen Buchhandlung von J. Mohr, 1835.

————. *Tracts Relating to Caspar Hauser by Earl Stanhope, Translated from the Original German.* London: James S. Hodson, 1836.

Striedinger, Ivo. "Wer war Kaspar Hauser?" In *Die Einkehr* 6, no. 24 (1925), pp. 93–98.

————. "Hauser, Kaspar, der rätselhafte Findling, 1828–1833." In *Lebensläufe aus Franken.* Ed. by Anton Chroust, Vol. 3, pp. 199–215. Würzburg: Rabitssch & Mönnich, Univ. Verlagsbuchhandlung, 1927.

————. "Neues Schrifttum über Kaspar Hauser: Zur 100. Wiederkehr seines Todestages (17. Dezember 1833) mit einem Anhang: Briefwechsel des Königs Ludwig von Bayern mit Lord Stanhope." *Zeitschrift für bayerische Landesgeschichte* 6 (1933), pp. 415–84.

Tradowsky, Peter. *Kaspar Hauser oder das Ringen um den Geist: Ein Beitrag zum Verständnis des 19. und 20. Jahrhunderts.* Dornach: Philosophisch-Anthroposophischer Verlag Goetheanum, 1980.

The True Story of Kaspar Hauser from Official Documents by the Duchess of Cleveland (Catherine Lucy Wilhelmina Powlett, 1819–1901). London/New York: Macmillan & Co., 1893.

Tucher, Freiherr von. "Kaspar Hauser—Kein Betrüger." *Beilage zur Allgemeinen Zeitung* 40 (Feb. 9, 1872), pp. 597ff.

Wagler, Ludwig. *Die Enträtselung der oberrheinischen Flaschenpost von 1816: Ein kritischer Beitrag zur Kaspar Hauser-Frage.* Nuremberg: J.L. Schrag, 1926.

————. *Die Bilanz einer hundertjährigen Hauserforschung.* Nuremberg: J.L. Schrag, 1928.

————. *Ein Danaergeschenk Eduard Engels an die Kaspar-Hauser Literatur.* Ansbach: C. Brügel & Sohn, 1931.

Wassermann, Jakob. *Caspar Hauser oder die Trägheit des Herzens. Roman.* 1st ed. 1908. 10th ed., mit einem Nachwort von Golo Mann, 1992. Munich: Deutscher Taschenbuch Verlag, 1992.

————. "Erfahrungen mit der Veröffentlichung meines Kaspar Hauser-Romans." In *Mein Weg als Deutscher und Jude* (1921). Reprinted in Jakob Wassermann: *Deutscher und Jude. Reden und Schriften 1904–1933,* pp. 89–94. Edited by Dierk Rodewald. Heidelberg: Deutsche Akademie für Sprache und Dichtung, 1984:

————. "Akten zur Verteidigung Caspar Hausers." In J. Wassermann, *Lebensdienst,* pp. 113–48. Leipzig/Zurich, 1928.

————. "Der Kriminalist Feuerbach." In *Lebensdienst,* pp. 30–36. Leipzig/Zurich, 1928.

————. *Caspar Hauser: The Inertia of the Heart.* Translated by Michael Hulse. New York: Penguin Books, 1992.

Weckmann, Berthold. *Kaspar Hauser: Die Geschichte und ihre Geschichten.* Würzburg: Königshausen & Neumann, 1993.

Weech, Friedrich von. "Johann Heinrich David von Hennenhofer." *Badische Biographien,* pp. 360ff. Karlsruhe, 1881.

Wolf, Erik. "Feuerbach," in *Grosse Rechtsdenker der deutschen Geistesgeschichte,* pp. 536–83. Tübingen: J.C.B. Mohr, 1951.

Zimmermann, Johann Michael. *Kaspar Hauser in physiologischen, psychologischen und pathogenisch-pathologischen Untersuchungen beurtheilt von Johann Michael Zimmermann.* Nuremberg: Johann Adam Steinschen Buchhandlung, 1834.

INDEX